שולחן שבת

THE SABBATH TABLE

A MESSIANIC JEWISH RESOURCE

Vine of David

Published by Vine of David
United States / Israel

שולחן שבת

The Sabbath Table

Prayers, Blessings, and Songs for the Sabbath

Hebrew / English Edition

VINE OF DAVID

Design: Vine of David, Israel
Translation: Vine of David, United States

Comments and questions may be sent to: feedback@vineofdavid.org

---

Vine of David is a publishing arm of the ministry of First Fruits of Zion dedicated to providing liturgical resources for the Messianic Jewish movement and to resurrecting the voices of Messianic pioneers and luminaries. If you would like to assist in the publication of more resources like this, you can sponsor the translation, publication, and distribution of these important works. Please visit www.vineofdavid.org for needs and opportunities.

First Edition
First Printing: April 2014, China

ISBN: 978-1-892124-71-5 : Hebrew/English Edition
ISBN: 978-1-892124-72-2 : English/Transliterated Hebrew Edition

Also available: The Sabbath Table: Blessings and Songs
(Audio and video learning resources)

US Distribution Center: PO Box 649, Marshfield, Missouri 65706-0649 USA
Phone (417) 468-2741, www.vineofdavid.org

Contents

Publisher's Preface

This is a Messianic Jewish prayer book. Vine of David is a Messianic Jewish organization. That means that we practice Judaism as followers of Yeshua (Jesus) of Nazareth.

Messianic Jews hold firmly to their unique calling and identity as Jews and fully belong to the Jewish community. By virtue of both devotion to Yeshua and commitment to authentic Jewish life, Messianic Jews serve as a natural bridge that links believers among the nations with the descendants of Abraham, Isaac, and Jacob.

To those who view Jesus as a rebel against Judaism, Messianic Judaism sounds like a paradox. To us it makes perfect sense, since Yeshua was a faithful Jew who taught the very heart of Torah. Furthermore, he prophetically foresaw and wept over the destruction of the Temple and the dispersion that still endures today. While his teachings are often misunderstood, they provide the keys to bringing the ultimate redemption from exile.

This book represents a key component of faithful Jewish living. The Sabbath is a sign between God and Israel, and the dining table is the hub of Jewish worship. This book of Sabbath table blessings provides Messianic Jews, as well as those among the nations who are drawn to Israel's light, with expressions of praise and prayer deeply rooted in Jewish soil.

Vine of David seeks to reveal Yeshua as the light to the nations and as the hope and glory of his people Israel. We pray that this resource will be used toward accomplishing that mission and that it will bring honor to the holy Sabbath and to our Father in heaven to whom be the glory forever. Amen.

Turn again, O God of hosts! Look down from heaven, and see; have regard for this vine, the stock that your right hand planted, and for the son whom you made strong for yourself. (Tehillim 80:14–15)

Layout and Features

The Sabbath Table is available in two distinct editions both containing the same parallel prayers and songs ❶. Both the Hebrew/English and English/Transliterated Hebrew editions contain the same commentary, as well as short instructional cues and notes on every page that will help readers enjoy the wonderful blessings of the Sabbath prayers ❺.

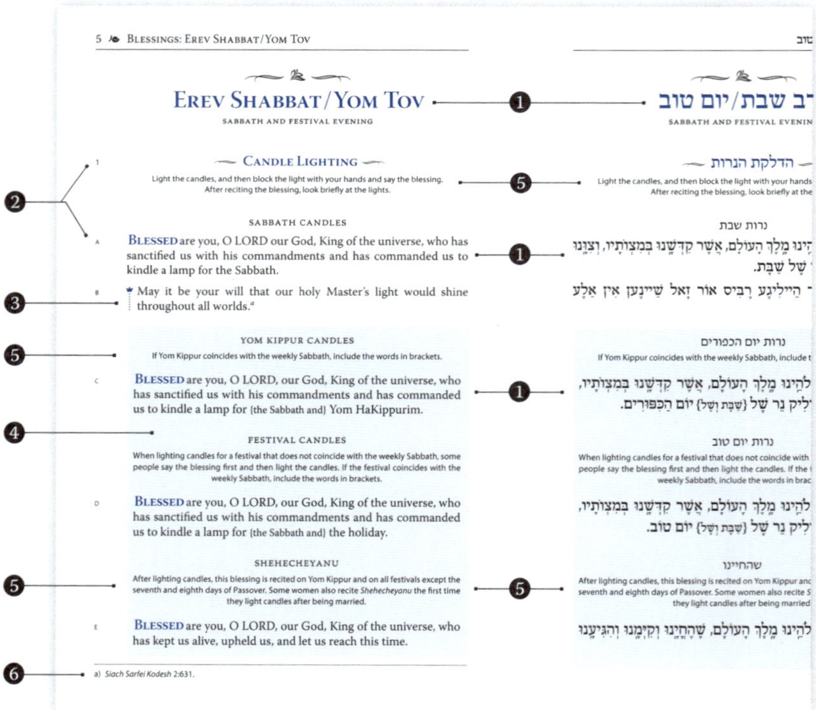
5 ❧ Blessings: Erev Shabbat/Yom Tov

Erev Shabbat/Yom Tov ❶

Sabbath and Festival Evening

❷ 1 Candle Lighting

Light the candles, and then block the light with your hands and say the blessing. After reciting the blessing, look briefly at the lights. ❺

Sabbath Candles

A **Blessed** are you, O LORD our God, King of the universe, who has sanctified us with his commandments and has commanded us to kindle a lamp for the Sabbath. ❶

❸ B May it be your will that our holy Master's light would shine throughout all worlds.[a]

❺ Yom Kippur Candles

If Yom Kippur coincides with the weekly Sabbath, include the words in brackets.

C **Blessed** are you, O LORD, our God, King of the universe, who has sanctified us with his commandments and has commanded us to kindle a lamp for {the Sabbath and} Yom HaKippurim. ❶

❹ Festival Candles

When lighting candles for a festival that does not coincide with the weekly Sabbath, some people say the blessing first and then light the candles. If the festival coincides with the weekly Sabbath, include the words in brackets.

D **Blessed** are you, O LORD, our God, King of the universe, who has sanctified us with his commandments and has commanded us to kindle a lamp for {the Sabbath and} the holiday.

Shehecheyanu

❺ After lighting candles, this blessing is recited on Yom Kippur and on all festivals except the seventh and eighth days of Passover. Some women also recite *Shehecheyanu* the first time they light candles after being married. ❺

E **Blessed** are you, O LORD, our God, King of the universe, who has kept us alive, upheld us, and let us reach this time.

❻ a) *Siach Sarfei Kodesh* 2:631.

Heading and Paragraph Numbering System ❷

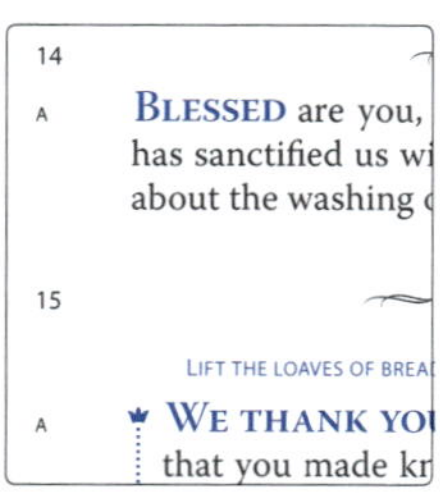
14

A **Blessed** are you,

has sanctified us wi

about the washing

15

Lift the loaves of brea

A **We thank yo**

that you made kn

Numbers and letters in the margins are used as references for the prayers. The major prayer sections are marked with numbers; each paragraph or subsection is marked with a letter. Using this system, the person who is leading prayers can direct others to a specific prayer or section. It is also used as reference for the commentary.

Messianic Insertions / Messianic Gentile Alternatives ❸

nended for Messianic Gentiles
E יְיָ צְבָאוֹת, אֱלֹהֵי יִ
בָּרָאתָ אֶת הָעוֹלָם בִּדְ
וְשַׁבָּת הִבְדַּלְתָּ לְזִכָּרוֹ
שָׁבַתָּ מִמְּלַאכְתְּךָ כְּדֵי

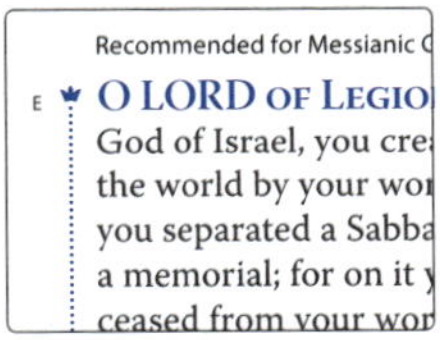

Recommended for Messianic G
E O LORD of Legio
God of Israel, you cre
the world by your wo
you separated a Sabba
a memorial; for on it y
ceased from your wor

We have used a crown with a dotted line to highlight prayers that are not found in a conventional prayer book. In some cases, these are additional prayers for all disciples of Yeshua, and they supplement the traditional readings. Other times as indicated, they are special alternatives provided for Messianic Gentiles in cases where the traditional prayer relates closely to Jewish identity. In both cases, the reader is advised to feel at liberty to utilize these blessings as desired.

Shaded Boxes ❹

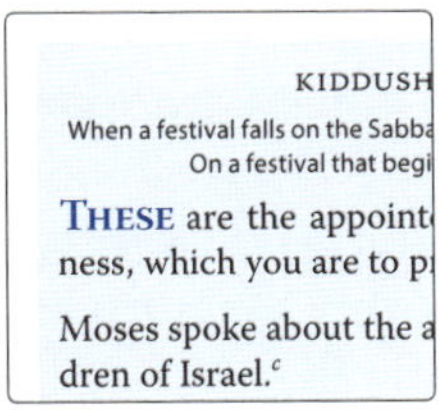

KIDDUSH
When a festival falls on the Sabba
On a festival that begi
These are the appoint
ness, which you are to p
Moses spoke about the a
dren of Israel.[c]

Shading on certain portions of this book indicates that one should recite the shaded section on certain special occasions but at other times may skip them. On special occasions, it is a good idea to review the text beforehand to determine which shaded portions to recite.

Footnotes ❻

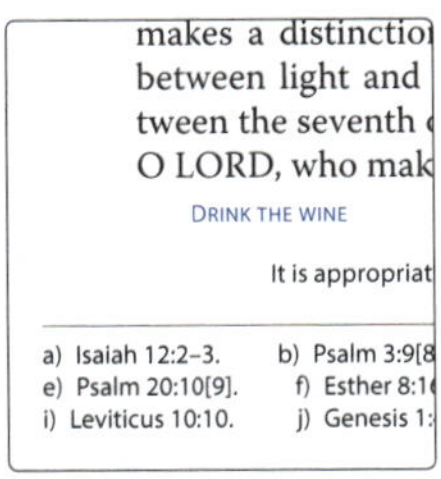

makes a distinctio
between light and
tween the seventh
O LORD, who mak
Drink the Wine
It is appropriat
a) Isaiah 12:2–3. b) Psalm 3:9[8
e) Psalm 20:10[9]. f) Esther 8:1
i) Leviticus 10:10. j) Genesis 1:

Footnotes appear to show the reader when language was borrowed directly from a passage of Scripture or from another source. The abbreviation “cf.” (Latin *confer*, “compare”) indicates references that bear similarity in language or to a word or phrase in the text but in which the language is not directly borrowed from the original.

Commentary and Instructions

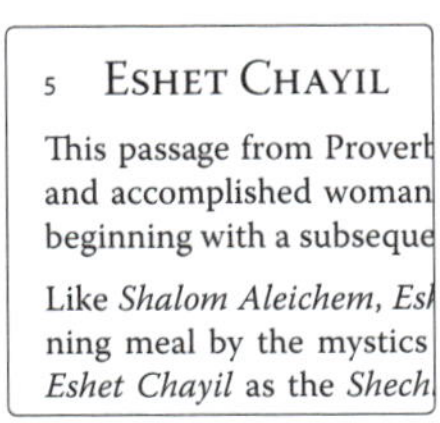

5 Eshet Chayil
This passage from Provert
and accomplished woman
beginning with a subseque
Like *Shalom Aleichem*, *Es*
ning meal by the mystics
Eshet Chayil as the *Shech*

Commentary on many of the prayers, blessings, and songs can be found toward the end of the book. Use the prayer number to find the corresponding commentary. In addition to commentary, the reader will also find useful instructional notes for how to prepare for and conduct special times and events.

The Name of God

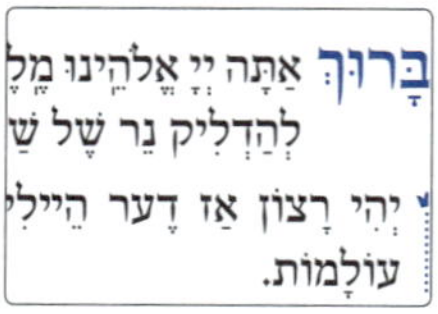

The personal name of God is indicated in this book using the abbreviation יְיָ. The abbreviation is used out of respect for God's name, because it is likely that this book will endure rough handling and spills. When reciting the blessings in this book at the appropriate occasions, one may pronounce this name as "Adonai." When rehearsing or merely talking about the blessings, it is customary to employ the more informal name "HaShem."

Symbols for Leaders/Groups

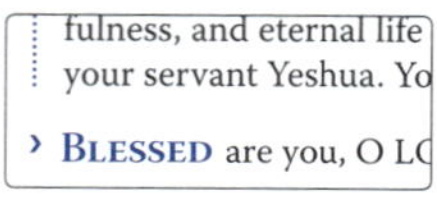

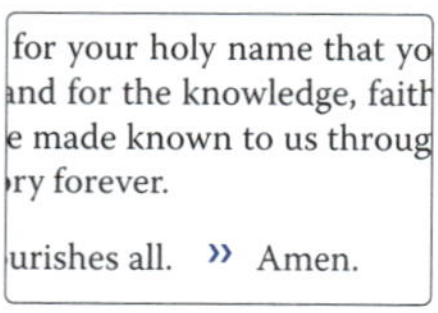

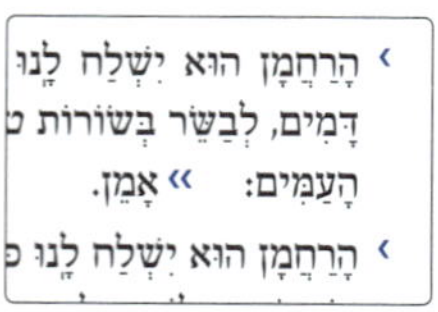

When a group of people recites the *Birkat HaMazon* (Grace after Meals) together, one person is designated to lead the group. Sometimes the whole prayer is recited out loud together; however, a more common way is that the leader starts off each section with a few words, then everyone prays quietly through to the end of the section. The leader then repeats the last line or two of that section out loud, which helps keep people together. The portion that the leader recites aloud is marked with this symbol: ›. Afterwards, the group often responds with "Amen" as indicated by this symbol: ».

Introduction

More than a Day of Rest

Even more than it is a day of rest, the Sabbath is a day of holiness. If the purpose of the Sabbath were just to give us one day a week to relax, it wouldn't matter what day of the week the Sabbath was. But resting on the Sabbath serves the specific purpose of setting it apart as holy, as the Torah says: "Protect the Sabbath to sanctify it" (Deuteronomy 5:12). The elevated sanctity of the Sabbath benefits us far more than a simple day off from work ever could.

And yet, sanctifying the Sabbath involves more than putting our lives on pause for twenty-four hours. The Torah also says, "Remember the Sabbath to sanctify it" (Exodus 20:8). The Hebrew word for "remember" is *zachor* (זָכוֹר), which also means "mention." Thus the Sabbath is sanctified by verbally taking note of it by the blessings, prayers, and songs on our lips.

While synagogue prayers are an important element of the Sabbath, the heart of Sabbath keeping is found in what takes place in the home around the dinner table with family and friends.

A Beautiful Tradition

How do we pass on our love for the Sabbath to the next generation? How can we help them to be enthralled with the Sabbath rather than to consider it a burden and an imposition?

Accomplishing this is one role that traditions play in our Sabbath observance. Children thrive on tradition because it provides a sense of stability and a frame of reference for all the things that are constantly changing in life.

Judaism teaches a principle known as *hiddur mitzvah* (הִדּוּר מִצְוָה), which means "beautifying the commandment." On this principle, one should not seek to observe a commandment only at a minimal level but in the most beautiful way possible.

There are multiple reasons for this. One is that it shows respect and honor to God when we do our best. But it has important benefits for us as well. By associating beauty with holiness, it endears us to those holy things.

It is possible to create meaningful and sentimental experiences anywhere, but a beautiful room produces a profound emotional impact. We set the table with our finest dishes, we serve visually appealing and delicious food, and we raise our voices in song as flames flicker on silver candlesticks. Memories are created that will last a lifetime.

This demonstrates why it is so essential for us to embellish the Sabbath with ceremonies and formalities, to learn the proper melodies, and to chant them with gusto. By doing so each week, we set ourselves and our children on a steady rhythm of life.

The goal of this book is to guide families in crafting their own meaningful Sabbath table traditions that will unite them with Jewish history and endear them to the Sabbath experience.

A Foretaste of the World to Come

If the Sabbath is important to the Jewish community as a whole, how much more so should it be to Messianic Judaism! The Sabbath is a foretaste of the future Messianic Kingdom. As the *Birkat HaMazon* (the blessing recited after eating) puts it, the Messianic Era is a "day of complete Sabbath and rest for eternal life."

Yeshua came proclaiming the nearness of this Messianic Kingdom, and those of us who follow him are citizens of that kingdom, even as we wait for it to be fully revealed. This means that we should feel quite at home in the Sabbath.

The Sabbath overflows with inherent messianic revelation. This book is designed to strengthen our attachment to Yeshua the Messiah and to his kingdom in a proper Jewish context. The commentary draws attention to the intrinsic messianic qualities of the Sabbath, while Messiah-focused songs and prayers of the ancient believers supplement the text.

All Flesh Shall Come

In that future Messianic Kingdom, Jews and Gentiles alike will honor the Sabbath: "From new moon to new moon, and from Sabbath to Sabbath, all flesh shall come to worship before me, declares the LORD" (Isaiah 66:23 ESV).

The Jewish people have been entrusted with the Sabbath. The Sabbath reflects a unique aspect of the covenant relationship between God and Israel. Nonetheless, the Sabbath also has a strong universal messianic facet, and thus it is appropriate for all followers of Yeshua to partake of its delights and to honor it with blessings, songs, and prayers.

However, the traditional Jewish prayers were written with a Jewish speaker in mind, and they rightly and naturally articulate Israel's special covenant status. When a Gentile expresses this status in a first-person voice, there is danger of eroding one's awareness of the distinction between Jewish and Gentile identities.

The Sabbath Table addresses this issue by offering alternative prayers that affirm both Jewish and Gentile identities and each one's distinct relationship to the Sabbath. These new blessings for non-Jewish participants were not composed of entirely new material; they have been culled from the most ancient strata of the prayers of early believers. Not only are these prayers affirming, beautiful, and ancient, they also represent a radical rebound from centuries of replacement theology.

Using this Prayer Book

This book incorporates prayers and concepts from a variety of sources, including passages from the Bible as well as historical Jewish and Christian tradition. Our use of and reference to extra-biblical works do not by any means imply that they should be regarded as canonical Scripture themselves. Nonetheless, these Jewish and Christian texts are deeply rooted in Scripture, and we respect them as a valuable heritage passed down from earlier generations.

We have endeavored to make this prayer book as user-friendly as possible. The resource accomplishes this with extensive commentary, instructions, visual cues, graphics, and other tools to help believers pray with understanding so that they may fully identify with the meaning and intent of each prayer.

This prayer book is offered in two editions; both present Hebrew and English on facing pages:

- The standard edition is best for people who can read Hebrew letters like this: שָׁלוֹם עֲלֵיכֶם.
- The transliterated edition is ideal for people who prefer to read Hebrew using the English alphabet like this: *shalom aleichem.*

תפילות וברכות

PRAYERS AND BLESSINGS

זמירות

ZEMIROT

Individuals may recite this prayer.

הֲרֵינִי מְקַשֵּׁר עַצְמִי

בָּאָדוֹן, יֵשׁוּעַ הַמָּשִׁיחַ
הַצַּדִּיק, שֶׁהוּא לֶחֶם הַחַיִּים
וְהָאוֹר הָאֲמִתִּי, מַמְצִיא תְּשׁוּעַת
עוֹלָמִים לְכָל שֹׁמְעָיו.

כְּמוֹ שָׂרִיג שֶׁעוֹמֵד בְּגֶפֶן,

כֵּן אֲנִי אֶעֱמוֹד בּוֹ, כַּאֲשֶׁר גַּם
הוּא עוֹמֵד בָּאָב וְהָאָב בּוֹ,
כְּדֵי שֶׁיַּעַמְדוּ בָּנוּ.

חֵן הָאָדוֹן יֵשׁוּעַ
הַמָּשִׁיחַ וְאַהֲבַת הָאֱלֹהִים וְחֶבְרַת
רוּחַ הַקֹּדֶשׁ יִרְבּוּ לָנוּ:

Individuals may recite this prayer.

I HEREBY JOIN MYSELF

to the Master, Yeshua the Messiah,
the righteous one, who is the bread of life
and the true light, the source of eternal
salvation for all those who hear him.

Like a branch that remains in a vine,
so may I remain in him, just as he also
remains in the Father and the Father in him,
in order that they may remain in us.

May the grace of the
Master, Yeshua the Messiah,
the love of God, and the fellowship
of the Holy Spirit abound to us.

ערב שבת/יום טוב

SABBATH AND FESTIVAL EVENING

1 הדלקת הנרות

Light the candles, and then block the light with your hands and say the blessing. After reciting the blessing, look briefly at the lights.

נרות שבת

A בָּרוּךְ אַתָּה יְיָ אֱלֹהֵינוּ מֶלֶךְ הָעוֹלָם, אֲשֶׁר קִדְּשָׁנוּ בְּמִצְוֹתָיו, וְצִוָּנוּ לְהַדְלִיק נֵר שֶׁל שַׁבָּת.

B יְהִי רָצוֹן אַז דֶער הֵיילִיגֶע רֶבִּיס אוֹר זָאל שַׁיינֶען אִין אַלֶע עוֹלָמוֹת.

נרות יום הכפורים

If Yom Kippur coincides with the weekly Sabbath, include the words in brackets.

C בָּרוּךְ אַתָּה יְיָ אֱלֹהֵינוּ מֶלֶךְ הָעוֹלָם, אֲשֶׁר קִדְּשָׁנוּ בְּמִצְוֹתָיו, וְצִוָּנוּ לְהַדְלִיק נֵר שֶׁל {שַׁבָּת וְשֶׁל} יוֹם הַכִּפּוּרִים.

נרות יום טוב

When lighting candles for a festival that does not coincide with the weekly Sabbath, some people say the blessing first and then light the candles. If the festival coincides with the weekly Sabbath, include the words in brackets.

D בָּרוּךְ אַתָּה יְיָ אֱלֹהֵינוּ מֶלֶךְ הָעוֹלָם, אֲשֶׁר קִדְּשָׁנוּ בְּמִצְוֹתָיו, וְצִוָּנוּ לְהַדְלִיק נֵר שֶׁל {שַׁבָּת וְשֶׁל} יוֹם טוֹב.

שהחיינו

After lighting candles, this blessing is recited on Yom Kippur and on all festivals except the seventh and eighth days of Passover. Some women also recite *Shehecheyanu* the first time they light candles after being married.

E בָּרוּךְ אַתָּה יְיָ אֱלֹהֵינוּ מֶלֶךְ הָעוֹלָם, שֶׁהֶחֱיָנוּ וְקִיְּמָנוּ וְהִגִּיעָנוּ לִזְמַן הַזֶּה.

Erev Shabbat/Yom Tov

SABBATH AND FESTIVAL EVENING

1 Candle Lighting

Light the candles, and then block the light with your hands and say the blessing. After reciting the blessing, look briefly at the lights.

SABBATH CANDLES

A **Blessed** are you, O LORD our God, King of the universe, who has sanctified us with his commandments and has commanded us to kindle a lamp for the Sabbath.

B May it be your will that our holy Master's light would shine throughout all worlds.[a]

YOM KIPPUR CANDLES

If Yom Kippur coincides with the weekly Sabbath, include the words in brackets.

C **Blessed** are you, O LORD, our God, King of the universe, who has sanctified us with his commandments and has commanded us to kindle a lamp for {the Sabbath and} Yom HaKippurim.

FESTIVAL CANDLES

When lighting candles for a festival that does not coincide with the weekly Sabbath, some people say the blessing first and then light the candles. If the festival coincides with the weekly Sabbath, include the words in brackets.

D **Blessed** are you, O LORD, our God, King of the universe, who has sanctified us with his commandments and has commanded us to kindle a lamp for {the Sabbath and} the holiday.

SHEHECHEYANU

After lighting candles, this blessing is recited on Yom Kippur and on all festivals except the seventh and eighth days of Passover. Some women also recite *Shehecheyanu* the first time they light candles after being married.

E **Blessed** are you, O LORD, our God, King of the universe, who has kept us alive, upheld us, and let us reach this time.

---

a) *Siach Sarfei Kodesh* 2:631.

תפילה לשלום המשפחה

The time of lighting candles is considered an appropriate and auspicious time for the woman of the house to offer requests to God privately on behalf of herself and her family. This can be a completely spontaneous and personal prayer, or it can be inspired by this traditional supplication. In the bracketed text, recite any parts that apply.

F **יְהִי רָצוֹן מִלְּפָנֶיךָ,** יְיָ אֱלֹהַי וֵאלֹהֵי אֲבוֹתַי, שֶׁתְּחוֹנֵן אוֹתִי {וְאֶת אִישִׁי, וְאֶת בָּנַי, וְאֶת בְּנוֹתַי, וְאֶת אָבִי, וְאֶת אִמִּי} וְאֶת כָּל קְרוֹבַי, וְתִתֶּן לָנוּ וּלְכָל יִשְׂרָאֵל חַיִּים טוֹבִים וַאֲרוּכִים, וְתִזְכְּרֵנוּ בְּזִכְרוֹן טוֹבָה וּבְרָכָה, וְתִפְקְדֵנוּ בִּפְקֻדַּת יְשׁוּעָה וְרַחֲמִים, וּתְבָרְכֵנוּ בְּרָכוֹת גְּדוֹלוֹת, וְתַשְׁלִים בָּתֵּינוּ, וְתַשְׁכֵּן שְׁכִינָתְךָ בֵּינֵינוּ, וְזַכֵּנִי לְגַדֵּל בָּנִים וּבְנֵי בָנִים חֲכָמִים וּנְבוֹנִים אוֹהֲבֵי יְיָ, יִרְאֵי אֱלֹהִים אַנְשֵׁי אֱמֶת זֶרַע קֹדֶשׁ, בַּייָ דְּבֵקִים, וּמְאִירִים אֶת הָעוֹלָם בַּתּוֹרָה וּבְמַעֲשִׂים טוֹבִים וּבְכָל מְלֶאכֶת עֲבוֹדַת הַבּוֹרֵא. אָנָּא, שְׁמַע אֶת תְּחִנָּתִי בִּזְכוּת שָׂרָה וְרִבְקָה רָחֵל וְלֵאָה אִמּוֹתֵינוּ, וְהָאֵר נֵרֵנוּ שֶׁלֹּא יִכְבֶּה לְעוֹלָם וָעֶד, וְהָאֵר פָּנֶיךָ וְנִוָּשֵׁעָה, אָמֵן.

2
ברכת הילדים

After returning home from the synagogue after reciting the *Ma'ariv* (evening prayers) for the Sabbath, it is customary for the father of the family to pronounce blessings on his children. He should lay both hands firmly on the child's head when saying the blessing.

For a boy

A יְשִׂמְךָ אֱלֹהִים כְּאֶפְרַיִם וְכִמְנַשֶּׁה.

For a girl

B יְשִׂמֵךְ אֱלֹהִים כְּשָׂרָה רִבְקָה רָחֵל וְלֵאָה.

Continue, for boys and girls

C יְבָרֶכְךָ יְיָ וְיִשְׁמְרֶךָ.

D יָאֵר יְיָ פָּנָיו אֵלֶיךָ וִיחֻנֶּךָּ.

E יִשָּׂא יְיָ פָּנָיו אֵלֶיךָ, וְיָשֵׂם לְךָ שָׁלוֹם.

Some add

F וְנָחָה עָלָיו רוּחַ יְיָ,
רוּחַ חָכְמָה וּבִינָה, רוּחַ עֵצָה וּגְבוּרָה,
רוּחַ דַּעַת וְיִרְאַת יְיָ.

PRAYER FOR FAMILY

The time of lighting candles is considered an appropriate and auspicious time for the woman of the house to offer requests to God privately on behalf of herself and her family. This can be a completely spontaneous and personal prayer, or it can be inspired by this traditional supplication. In the bracketed text, recite any parts that apply.

F **May it be your will,** O LORD, my God and God of my fathers, that you be gracious to me {my husband, my sons, my daughters, my father, my mother,} and all my extended family. Give to us and to all Israel a good, long life. Remember us by bringing goodness and blessing. Take note of us by bringing salvation and compassion. Bless us with great blessings and make our homes complete. Let your Dwelling Presence abide in our midst. Permit me the honor of raising wise children and grandchildren who love the LORD, who fear God, who are people of truth, holy offspring,[a] who cling to the LORD and illuminate the world with Torah and good deeds and through all their labor in service of the Creator. Please hear my request at this time in the merit of our mothers Sarah, Rebekah, Rachel, and Leah, and make our lamps burn so brightly that they will never be extinguished. Make your face shine, and we will be saved.[b] Amen.

2 Blessing the Children

After returning home from the synagogue after reciting the *Ma'ariv* (evening prayers) for the Sabbath, it is customary for the father of the family to pronounce blessings on his children. He should lay both hands firmly on the child's head when saying the blessing.

For a boy

A May God make you like Ephraim and Manasseh.[c]

For a girl

B May God make you like Sarah, Rebekah, Rachel, and Leah.

Continue, for boys and girls

C May the LORD bless you and protect you.

D May the LORD make his face shine toward you
and be gracious to you.

E May the LORD lift his face toward you
and establish peace for you.[d]

Some add

F Let the Spirit of the LORD rest on him:
a spirit of wisdom and discernment, a spirit of counsel and power,
a spirit of knowledge and fear of the LORD.[e]

a) Isaiah 6:13. b) Psalm 80:20[19]. c) Genesis 48:20. d) Numbers 6:24–26. e) Isaiah 11:2.

3 ## שלום עליכם

Some communities have the custom of reciting each verse three times.

A שָׁלוֹם עֲלֵיכֶם, מַלְאֲכֵי הַשָּׁרֵת, מַלְאֲכֵי עֶלְיוֹן,
מִמֶּלֶךְ מַלְכֵי הַמְּלָכִים, הַקָּדוֹשׁ בָּרוּךְ הוּא.

B בּוֹאֲכֶם לְשָׁלוֹם, מַלְאֲכֵי הַשָּׁלוֹם, מַלְאֲכֵי עֶלְיוֹן,
מִמֶּלֶךְ מַלְכֵי הַמְּלָכִים, הַקָּדוֹשׁ בָּרוּךְ הוּא.

C בָּרְכוּנִי לְשָׁלוֹם, מַלְאֲכֵי הַשָּׁלוֹם, מַלְאֲכֵי עֶלְיוֹן,
מִמֶּלֶךְ מַלְכֵי הַמְּלָכִים, הַקָּדוֹשׁ בָּרוּךְ הוּא.

D צֵאתְכֶם לְשָׁלוֹם, מַלְאֲכֵי הַשָּׁלוֹם, מַלְאֲכֵי עֶלְיוֹן,
מִמֶּלֶךְ מַלְכֵי הַמְּלָכִים, הַקָּדוֹשׁ בָּרוּךְ הוּא.

SOME ADD THESE VERSES

E כִּי מַלְאָכָיו יְצַוֶּה לָּךְ,
לִשְׁמָרְךָ בְּכָל דְּרָכֶיךָ.

F יְיָ יִשְׁמָר צֵאתְךָ וּבוֹאֶךָ
מֵעַתָּה וְעַד עוֹלָם

4 ## תפילת האב / רבון כל העולמים

Some communities omit this prayer out of concern for offering supplications on the Sabbath.

A רִבּוֹן כָּל הָעוֹלָמִים, אֲדוֹן כָּל הַנְּשָׁמוֹת, אֲדוֹן הַשָּׁלוֹם.

א מֶלֶךְ אַבִּיר,
ב מֶלֶךְ בָּרוּךְ,
ג מֶלֶךְ גָּדוֹל,
ד מֶלֶךְ דּוֹבֵר שָׁלוֹם,
ה מֶלֶךְ הָדוּר,
ו מֶלֶךְ וָתִיק,
ז מֶלֶךְ זָךְ,
ח מֶלֶךְ חֵי הָעוֹלָמִים,
ט מֶלֶךְ טוֹב וּמֵטִיב,
י מֶלֶךְ יָחִיד וּמְיֻחָד,

3 SHALOM ALEICHEM

Some communities have the custom of reciting each verse three times.

A **PEACE UPON YOU,** O ministering angels, angels of the Highest,
From the King of kings of kings, the blessed Holy One.

B **COME IN PEACE,** O angels of peace, angels of the Highest,
From the King of kings of kings, the blessed Holy One.

C **BLESS US WITH PEACE,** O angels of peace, angels of the Highest,
From the King of kings of kings, the blessed Holy One.

D **DEPART IN PEACE,** O angels of peace, angels of the Highest,
From the King of kings of kings, the blessed Holy One.

SOME ADD THESE VERSES

E He will command his angels regarding you
to protect your every path.[a]

F The LORD will protect you as you leave and as you come,
now and forever.[b]

4 A FATHER'S PRAYER / RIBBON KOL HAOLAMIM

Some communities omit this prayer out of concern for offering supplications on the Sabbath.

A **LORD OF ALL WORLDS,** Master of all souls, Master of peace,

א King who is mighty,
ב King who is blessed,
ג King who is great,
ד King who speaks peace,
ה King who is adorned,
ו King who is ancient,
ז King who is pure,
ח King who gives life to all worlds,
ט King who is good and beneficent,
י King who is unique and special,

a) Psalm 91:11. b) Psalm 121:8.

כ מֶֽלֶךְ כַּבִּיר,

ל מֶֽלֶךְ לוֹבֵשׁ רַחֲמִים,

מ מֶֽלֶךְ מַלְכֵי הַמְּלָכִים,

נ מֶֽלֶךְ נִשְׂגָּב,

ס מֶֽלֶךְ סוֹמֵךְ נוֹפְלִים,

ע מֶֽלֶךְ עֹשֶׂה מַעֲשֵׂה בְרֵאשִׁית,

פ מֶֽלֶךְ פּוֹדֶה וּמַצִּיל,

צ מֶֽלֶךְ צַח וְאָדוֹם,

ק מֶֽלֶךְ קָדוֹשׁ,

ר מֶֽלֶךְ רָם וְנִשָּׂא,

ש מֶֽלֶךְ שׁוֹמֵעַ תְּפִלָּה,

ת מֶֽלֶךְ תָּמִים דַּרְכּוֹ.

B **מוֹדֶה אֲנִי לְפָנֶֽיךָ** יְיָ אֱלֹהַי וֵאלֹהֵי אֲבוֹתַי, עַל כָּל הַחֶֽסֶד אֲשֶׁר עָשִֽׂיתָ עִמָּדִי וַאֲשֶׁר אַתָּה עָתִיד לַעֲשׂוֹת עִמִּי וְעִם כָּל בְּנֵי בֵיתִי וְעִם כָּל בְּרִיּוֹתֶֽיךָ בְּנֵי בְרִיתִי. וּבְרוּכִים הֵם מַלְאָכֶֽיךָ הַקְּדוֹשִׁים וְהַטְּהוֹרִים שֶׁעוֹשִׂים רְצוֹנֶֽךָ. אֲדוֹן הַשָּׁלוֹם מֶֽלֶךְ שֶׁהַשָּׁלוֹם שֶׁלּוֹ, בָּרְכֵֽנִי בַשָּׁלוֹם, וְתִפְקוֹד אוֹתִי וְאֶת כָּל בְּנֵי בֵיתִי וְכָל עַמְּךָ בֵּית יִשְׂרָאֵל לְחַיִּים טוֹבִים וּלְשָׁלוֹם.

C **מֶֽלֶךְ עֶלְיוֹן** עַל כָּל צְבָא מָרוֹם, יוֹצְרֵֽנוּ יוֹצֵר בְּרֵאשִׁית, אֲחַלֶּה פָנֶֽיךָ הַמְּאִירִים שֶׁתְּזַכֶּה אוֹתִי וְאֶת כָּל בְּנֵי בֵיתִי לִמְצֹא חֵן וְשֵֽׂכֶל טוֹב בְּעֵינֶֽיךָ וּבְעֵינֵי כָּל בְּנֵי אָדָם וְחַוָּה וּבְעֵינֵי כָּל רוֹאֵֽינוּ לַעֲבוֹדָתֶֽךָ. וְזַכֵּֽנוּ לְקַבֵּל שַׁבָּתוֹת מִתּוֹךְ רוֹב שִׂמְחָה וּמִתּוֹךְ עֹֽשֶׁר וְכָבוֹד וּמִתּוֹךְ מִעוּט עֲוֹנוֹת. וְהָסֵר מִמֶּֽנִּי וּמִכָּל בְּנֵי בֵיתִי וּמִכָּל עַמְּךָ בֵּית יִשְׂרָאֵל כָּל מִינֵי חֳלִי וְכָל מִינֵי מַדְוֶה וְכָל מִינֵי דַלּוּת וַעֲנִיּוּת וְאֶבְיוֹנוּת. וְתֵן בָּֽנוּ יֵֽצֶר טוֹב לְעָבְדְּךָ בֶּאֱמֶת וּבְיִרְאָה וּבְאַהֲבָה וּבְשִׂמְחָה. וְנִהְיֶה מְכֻבָּדִים בְּעֵינֶֽיךָ וּבְעֵינֵי כָּל רוֹאֵֽינוּ. כִּי אַתָּה הוּא מֶֽלֶךְ הַכָּבוֹד כִּי לְךָ נָאֶה כִּי לְךָ יָאֶה.

D **אָנָּא מֶֽלֶךְ מַלְכֵי הַמְּלָכִים** צַוֵּה לְמַלְאָכֶֽיךָ מַלְאֲכֵי הַשָּׁרֵת מְשָׁרְתֵי עֶלְיוֹן שֶׁיִּפְקְדֽוּנִי בְּרַחֲמִים וִיבָרְכֽוּנִי בְּבוֹאָם לְבֵיתִי בְּיוֹם

כ King who is magnificent,

ל King clothed in compassion,

מ King of kings of kings,

נ King who is sublime,

ס King who supports the fallen,

ע King who performs the work of creation,

פ King who ransoms and rescues,

צ King who is radiant and ruddy,

ק King who is holy,

ר King who is high and exalted,

ש King who hears prayer,

ת King who is perfect in his way—

B **I THANK YOU,** O LORD, my God and God of my fathers, for all the kindness that you have shown to me and that you will continue to show me and my entire family and all creatures, my covenant co-members. Your holy and pure angels who do your will are blessed. O Master of peace, King to whom peace itself belongs, bless me with peace and take note of me and all my family members and your entire nation, the house of Israel, for good life and for peace.

C **SUPREME KING** over the supernal legions, our Maker who formed creation, I implore your brilliant face that you permit me and all my family members the honor of finding favor and good consideration in your sight and in the sight of all children of Adam and Eve and in the sight of all who see us, in order to serve you. Permit us the honor to welcome Sabbaths amidst abounding joy, amidst wealth and honor, amidst the absence of iniquity. Take away from me, my family members, and your entire nation, the house of Israel, all manner of ailments, all kinds of disease, and any form of poverty, deprivation, or destitution. Allow our good inclination to serve you with sincerity, fear, love, and joy. May we be honored in your sight and in the sight of all who see us, for you are the King of glory, and glory is befitting and appropriate for you.

D **PLEASE, O KING OF KINGS OF KINGS,** command your angels, the ministering angels who serve the Highest, so that they will deal compassionately with me and bless me when they come to my home

קָדְשֵׁנוּ. כִּי הִדְלַקְתִּי נֵרוֹתַי וְהִצַּעְתִּי מִטָּתִי וְהֶחֱלַפְתִּי שִׂמְלוֹתַי לִכְבוֹד יוֹם הַשַּׁבָּת. וּבָאתִי לְבֵיתְךָ לְהַפִּיל תְּחִנָּתִי לְפָנֶיךָ שֶׁתַּעֲבִיר אַנְחָתִי. וָאָעִיד אֲשֶׁר בָּרָאתָ בְשִׁשָּׁה יָמִים כָּל הַיְצוּר וָאֶשְׁנֶה. וַאֲשַׁלֵּשׁ עוֹד לְהָעִיד עַל כּוֹסִי בְּתוֹךְ שִׂמְחָתִי. כַּאֲשֶׁר צִוִּיתַנִי לְזָכְרוֹ וּלְהִתְעַנֵּג בְּיֶתֶר נִשְׁמָתִי אֲשֶׁר נָתַתָּ בִּי. בּוֹ אֶשְׁבּוֹת כַּאֲשֶׁר צִוִּיתַנִי לְשָׁרְתֶךָ וְכֵן אַגִּיד גְּדֻלָּתְךָ בְּרִנָּה. וְשִׁוִּיתִי יְיָ לִקְרָאתִי שֶׁתְּרַחֲמֵנִי עוֹד בְּגָלוּתִי לְגָאֳלֵנִי וּלְעוֹרֵר לִבִּי לְאַהֲבָתֶךָ. וְאָז אֶשְׁמוֹר פִּקּוּדֶיךָ וְחֻקֶּיךָ בְּלִי עֶצֶב וְאֶתְפַּלֵּל כַּדָּת כָּרָאוּי וּכְנָכוֹן.

E מַלְאֲכֵי הַשָּׁלוֹם בּוֹאֲכֶם לְשָׁלוֹם. בָּרְכוּנִי לְשָׁלוֹם וְאִמְרוּ בָּרוּךְ לְשֻׁלְחָנִי הֶעָרוּךְ, וְצֵאתְכֶם לְשָׁלוֹם מֵעַתָּה וְעַד עוֹלָם. אָמֵן סֶלָה.

5 אשת חיל

A אֵשֶׁת חַיִל מִי יִמְצָא,
וְרָחֹק מִפְּנִינִים מִכְרָהּ.

B בָּטַח בָּהּ לֵב בַּעְלָהּ,
וְשָׁלָל לֹא יֶחְסָר.

C גְּמָלַתְהוּ טוֹב וְלֹא רָע,
כֹּל יְמֵי חַיֶּיהָ.

D דָּרְשָׁה צֶמֶר וּפִשְׁתִּים,
וַתַּעַשׂ בְּחֵפֶץ כַּפֶּיהָ.

E הָיְתָה כָּאֳנִיּוֹת סוֹחֵר,
מִמֶּרְחָק תָּבִיא לַחְמָהּ.

F וַתָּקָם בְּעוֹד לַיְלָה,
וַתִּתֵּן טֶרֶף לְבֵיתָהּ וְחֹק לְנַעֲרֹתֶיהָ.

G זָמְמָה שָׂדֶה וַתִּקָּחֵהוּ,
מִפְּרִי כַפֶּיהָ נָטְעָה כָּרֶם.

H חָגְרָה בְעוֹז מָתְנֶיהָ,
וַתְּאַמֵּץ זְרוֹעֹתֶיהָ.

on our holy day. For I have lit my candles, I have made my bed, and I have changed my clothes in honor of the Sabbath day. I have now come home to cast my supplication before you that you would remove my sorrow. I have testified that you created everything that exists in six days, and then I repeated it. I will yet testify a third time over my cup amidst rejoicing, just as you commanded me to remember it and to take delight with the extra measure of my soul that you placed within me. I will rest on it just as you have commanded me, in order to minister to you, and I will tell of your greatness with joyful singing. I have placed the LORD before me that you may show compassion to me even while I am in exile, to redeem me and to arouse my heart to love you. Then I will keep your orders and your statutes without pain, and I will pray in the fitting and proper way.

E **Angels of peace,** come for peace, bless me for peace, call my set table "blessed," and depart for peace, at this time and forever. Amen, selah.

5

Eshet Chayil

A א Who can find a capable woman?
Her value is far greater than pearls.

B ב Her husband's heart trusts her,
and he never lacks benefit.

C ג She shows him kindness and not harm
all the days of her life.

D ד Searching for wool and linen,
she works with willing hands.

E ה Like a fleet of merchant ships,
she brings food from far away.

F ו Arising while it is still nighttime,
she gives food to her household, and her maids their share.

G ז Considering a field, she buys it
and plants a vineyard with the fruit of her hands.

H ח Girding herself with might,
she strengthens her arms.

טָעֲמָה כִּי טוֹב סַחְרָהּ, I
לֹא יִכְבֶּה בַלַּיְלָה נֵרָהּ.

יָדֶיהָ שִׁלְּחָה בַכִּישׁוֹר, J
וְכַפֶּיהָ תָּמְכוּ פָלֶךְ.

כַּפָּהּ פָּרְשָׂה לֶעָנִי, K
וְיָדֶיהָ שִׁלְּחָה לָאֶבְיוֹן.

לֹא תִירָא לְבֵיתָהּ מִשָּׁלֶג, L
כִּי כָל בֵּיתָהּ לָבֻשׁ שָׁנִים.

מַרְבַדִּים עָשְׂתָה לָּהּ, M
שֵׁשׁ וְאַרְגָּמָן לְבוּשָׁהּ.

נוֹדָע בַּשְּׁעָרִים בַּעְלָהּ, N
בְּשִׁבְתּוֹ עִם זִקְנֵי אָרֶץ.

סָדִין עָשְׂתָה וַתִּמְכֹּר, O
וַחֲגוֹר נָתְנָה לַכְּנַעֲנִי.

עֹז וְהָדָר לְבוּשָׁהּ, P
וַתִּשְׂחַק לְיוֹם אַחֲרוֹן.

פִּיהָ פָּתְחָה בְחָכְמָה, Q
וְתוֹרַת חֶסֶד עַל לְשׁוֹנָהּ.

צוֹפִיָּה הֲלִיכוֹת בֵּיתָהּ, R
וְלֶחֶם עַצְלוּת לֹא תֹאכֵל.

קָמוּ בָנֶיהָ וַיְאַשְּׁרוּהָ, S
בַּעְלָהּ וַיְהַלְלָהּ.

רַבּוֹת בָּנוֹת עָשׂוּ חָיִל, T
וְאַתְּ עָלִית עַל כֻּלָּנָה.

שֶׁקֶר הַחֵן וְהֶבֶל הַיֹּפִי, U
אִשָּׁה יִרְאַת יְיָ הִיא תִתְהַלָּל.

תְּנוּ לָהּ מִפְּרִי יָדֶיהָ, V
וִיהַלְלוּהָ בַשְּׁעָרִים מַעֲשֶׂיהָ.

I ט As she discerns that her business is good,
her lamp does not go out at night.

J י Extending her hand to the distaff,
her palms support the spinning rod.

K כ Spreading her palm to the poor,
she extends her hand to the destitute.

L ל She does not fear for her household when snow comes,
since her whole household is clothed with crimson.

M מ She has made her own bedspreads,
and she is clothed in linen and purple.

N נ Her husband is renowned at the gates,
sitting among the elders of the land.

O ס She makes a cloak and sells it,
offering a sash to the merchant.

P ע Arrayed in strength and splendor,
she cheerfully awaits the final day.

Q פ Wise words go forth from her mouth,
and her tongue teaches devotion.

R צ Overseeing the activities of her house,
she does not eat the bread of idleness.

S ק Her children arise and gladden her;
her husband also, who praises her:

T ר "Many women have their accomplishments,
but you have risen above them all!"

U ש Grace deceives, and beauty vanishes;
a woman who fears the LORD should be praised.

V ת Let her have the fruit of her hands,
and may her own works commend her in the gates.

6

קידוש לשבת

When a festival begins on a Friday evening, begin with *Kiddush* for Festivals, prayer 7, page 18. At each of the Sabbath meals, it is customary to have two loaves of challah present. Leave the challah cover on the bread during *Kiddush*.

QUIETLY | HOLD THE CUP OF WINE

וַיְהִי עֶרֶב וַיְהִי בֹקֶר—

ALOUD

A **יוֹם הַשִּׁשִּׁי.** וַיְכֻלּוּ הַשָּׁמַיִם וְהָאָרֶץ וְכָל צְבָאָם. וַיְכַל אֱלֹהִים בַּיּוֹם הַשְּׁבִיעִי מְלַאכְתּוֹ אֲשֶׁר עָשָׂה, וַיִּשְׁבֹּת בַּיּוֹם הַשְּׁבִיעִי מִכָּל מְלַאכְתּוֹ אֲשֶׁר עָשָׂה. וַיְבָרֶךְ אֱלֹהִים אֶת יוֹם הַשְּׁבִיעִי וַיְקַדֵּשׁ אֹתוֹ, כִּי בוֹ שָׁבַת מִכָּל מְלַאכְתּוֹ, אֲשֶׁר בָּרָא אֱלֹהִים לַעֲשׂוֹת.

סַבְרִי—

B **נוֹדֶה לְךָ** אָבִינוּ, עַל הַגֶּפֶן הַקְּדוֹשָׁה לְדָוִד עַבְדֶּךָ שֶׁהוֹדַעְתָּנוּ עַל יְדֵי יֵשׁוּעַ עַבְדֶּךָ. לְךָ הַכָּבוֹד לְעוֹלָמִים.

C **בָּרוּךְ** אַתָּה יְיָ אֱלֹהֵינוּ מֶלֶךְ הָעוֹלָם, בּוֹרֵא פְּרִי הַגָּפֶן.

D **בָּרוּךְ** אַתָּה יְיָ אֱלֹהֵינוּ מֶלֶךְ הָעוֹלָם, אֲשֶׁר קִדְּשָׁנוּ בְּמִצְוֹתָיו וְרָצָה בָנוּ, וְשַׁבַּת קָדְשׁוֹ בְּאַהֲבָה וּבְרָצוֹן הִנְחִילָנוּ, זִכָּרוֹן לְמַעֲשֵׂה בְרֵאשִׁית. כִּי הוּא יוֹם תְּחִלָּה לְמִקְרָאֵי קֹדֶשׁ, זֵכֶר לִיצִיאַת מִצְרָיִם. כִּי בָנוּ בָחַרְתָּ וְאוֹתָנוּ קִדַּשְׁתָּ מִכָּל הָעַמִּים, וְשַׁבַּת קָדְשְׁךָ בְּאַהֲבָה וּבְרָצוֹן הִנְחַלְתָּנוּ. בָּרוּךְ אַתָּה יְיָ, מְקַדֵּשׁ הַשַּׁבָּת.

Recommended for Messianic Gentiles

E **יְיָ צְבָאוֹת,** אֱלֹהֵי יִשְׂרָאֵל, בָּרָאתָ אֶת הָעוֹלָם בִּדְבָרֶךָ, וְשַׁבָּת הִבְדַּלְתָּ לְזִכָּרוֹן, כִּי בוֹ שָׁבַתָּ מִמְּלַאכְתְּךָ כְּדֵי לַהֲגוֹת בְּדִבְרֵי תוֹרָתֶךָ. כִּי הַשַּׁבָּת הִיא מְנוּחָה מִן הַבְּרִיאָה, הַשְׁלָמַת עוֹלָם, דְּרִישַׁת דִּבְרֵי תוֹרָה, שֶׁבַח לֵאלֹהִים לְהוֹדוֹת עַל מָה שֶׁנָּתַן לִבְנֵי אָדָם. בָּרוּךְ אַתָּה יְיָ, מְקַדֵּשׁ הַשַּׁבָּת.

DRINK THE WINE

6 Kiddush for Shabbat

When a festival begins on a Friday evening, begin with *Kiddush* for Festivals, prayer 7, page 19. At each of the Sabbath meals, it is customary to have two loaves of challah present. Leave the challah cover on the bread during *Kiddush*.

Quietly | Hold the cup of wine

And there was evening, and there was morning—

Aloud

A **The sixth day.** Heaven and earth were completed and their entire legion. On the seventh day, God finished his work that he had done, and on the seventh day he ceased from all his work that he had done. God blessed the seventh day and sanctified it because on it he ceased from all his work that God created to make.[a]

With your permission—

B **We thank you,** our Father, for the holy vine of your servant David that you made known to us through your servant Yeshua. Yours is the glory forever.[b]

C **Blessed** are you, O LORD, our God, King of the universe, who creates the fruit of the vine.

D **Blessed** are you, O LORD, our God, King of the universe, who has sanctified us with his commandments and has shown us favor, and has lovingly and willingly let us inherit his holy Sabbath, a memorial of the work of creation. For it is the beginning day of the holy convocations, a remembrance of the exodus from Egypt. For you chose us and sanctified us from all of the peoples and lovingly and willingly let us inherit your holy Sabbath. Blessed are you, O LORD, who sanctifies the Sabbath.

Recommended for Messianic Gentiles

E **O LORD of Legions,** God of Israel, you created the world by your word, and you separated a Sabbath as a memorial; for on it you ceased from your work in order to meditate on the words of your Torah. For the Sabbath is a rest from creation, a completion of the world, a seeking of words of Torah, an expression of praise to God, to thank him for what he has given to mankind.[c] Blessed are you, O LORD, who sanctifies the Sabbath.

Drink the wine

a) Genesis 1:31–2:3. b) *Didache* 9:2. c) *Apostolic Constitutions* 7:36.

7 ## קידוש ליום טוב

When a festival begins on a Friday evening, begin here.

QUIETLY | HOLD THE CUP OF WINE

וַיְהִי עֶרֶב וַיְהִי בֹקֶר—

ALOUD

A **יוֹם הַשִּׁשִּׁי.** וַיְכֻלּוּ הַשָּׁמַיִם וְהָאָרֶץ וְכָל צְבָאָם. וַיְכַל אֱלֹהִים בַּיּוֹם הַשְּׁבִיעִי מְלַאכְתּוֹ אֲשֶׁר עָשָׂה, וַיִּשְׁבֹּת בַּיּוֹם הַשְּׁבִיעִי מִכָּל מְלַאכְתּוֹ אֲשֶׁר עָשָׂה. וַיְבָרֶךְ אֱלֹהִים אֶת יוֹם הַשְּׁבִיעִי וַיְקַדֵּשׁ אֹתוֹ, כִּי בוֹ שָׁבַת מִכָּל מְלַאכְתּוֹ, אֲשֶׁר בָּרָא אֱלֹהִים לַעֲשׂוֹת.

When a festival begins on a weekday or Saturday evening, begin here.

סַבְרִי—

B **נוֹדֶה לְךָ** אָבִינוּ, עַל הַגֶּפֶן הַקְּדוֹשָׁה לְדָוִד עַבְדֶּךָ שֶׁהוֹדַעְתָּנוּ עַל יְדֵי יֵשׁוּעַ עַבְדֶּךָ. לְךָ הַכָּבוֹד לְעוֹלָמִים.

C **בָּרוּךְ** אַתָּה יְיָ אֱלֹהֵינוּ מֶלֶךְ הָעוֹלָם, בּוֹרֵא פְּרִי הַגָּפֶן.

D **בָּרוּךְ** אַתָּה יְיָ אֱלֹהֵינוּ מֶלֶךְ הָעוֹלָם, אֲשֶׁר בָּחַר בָּנוּ מִכָּל עָם וְרוֹמְמָנוּ מִכָּל לָשׁוֹן, וְקִדְּשָׁנוּ בְּמִצְוֹתָיו. וַתִּתֶּן לָנוּ יְיָ אֱלֹהֵינוּ בְּאַהֲבָה {שַׁבָּתוֹת לִמְנוּחָה וּ} מוֹעֲדִים לְשִׂמְחָה, חַגִּים וּזְמַנִּים לְשָׂשׂוֹן, אֶת יוֹם {הַשַּׁבָּת הַזֶּה וְאֶת יוֹם}

Recommended for Messianic Gentiles

E **יְיָ צְבָאוֹת,** אֱלֹהֵי יִשְׂרָאֵל, בָּרָאתָ אֶת הָעוֹלָם בִּדְבָרֶךָ, {וְשַׁבָּת הִבְדַּלְתָּ לְזִכָּרוֹן}. וּמוֹעֲדִים קָבַעְתָּ לְשִׂמְחַת נַפְשׁוֹתֵינוּ, חַגִּים וּזְמַנִּים לְשָׂשׂוֹן, לְמַעַן נָבוֹא לִזְכּוֹר אֶת הַחָכְמָה אֲשֶׁר בָּרָאתָ. הֵם צֵל הַדְּבָרִים הָעֲתִידִים לָבֹא, וְגוּפָם הוּא בַּמָּשִׁיחַ. קָבַעְתָּ אֶת יוֹם {הַשַּׁבָּת הַזֶּה וְאֶת יוֹם}

7

Kiddush for Festivals

When a festival begins on a Friday evening, begin here.

Quietly | Hold the cup of wine

And there was evening, and there was morning—

Aloud

A **The sixth day.** Heaven and earth were completed and their entire legion. On the seventh day, God finished his work that he had done, and on the seventh day he ceased from all his work that he had done. God blessed the seventh day and sanctified it because on it he ceased from all his work that God created to make.

When a festival begins on a weekday or Saturday evening, begin here.

With your permission—

B **We thank you,** our Father, for the holy vine of your servant David that you made known to us through your servant Yeshua. Yours is the glory forever.

C **Blessed** are you, O LORD, our God, King of the universe, who creates the fruit of the vine.

D **Blessed** are you, O LORD, our God, King of the universe, who chose us out of every nation, elevated us above every language, and sanctified us with his commandments. You lovingly gave us, O LORD, our God, {Sabbaths for rest,} appointed times for gladness, festivals and seasons for rejoicing. You gave us {this Sabbath day and} this day of

Recommended for Messianic Gentiles

E **LORD of Legions,** God of Israel, you created the world by your word {and you separated a Sabbath as a memorial}. You also appointed set times for the gladness of our souls, festivals and seasons for rejoicing, so that we may come to remember the wisdom that you created. They are a shadow of things to come, and their essence is of Messiah.[a] You established {this Sabbath day and} this day of

a) Colossians 2:17.

On Passover

חַג הַמַּצּוֹת הַזֶּה, זְמַן חֵרוּתֵֽנוּ

חַג הַמַּצּוֹת הַזֶּה, זְמַן הַחֵרוּת

On Shavu'ot

חַג הַשָּׁבֻעוֹת הַזֶּה, זְמַן מַתַּן תּוֹרָתֵֽנוּ

חַג הַשָּׁבֻעוֹת הַזֶּה, זְמַן מַתַּן הַתּוֹרָה

On Sukkot

חַג הַסֻּכּוֹת הַזֶּה, זְמַן שִׂמְחָתֵֽנוּ

חַג הַסֻּכּוֹת הַזֶּה, זְמַן הַשִּׂמְחָה

On Shmini Atzeret and Simchat Torah

הַשְּׁמִינִי חַג הָעֲצֶֽרֶת הַזֶּה, זְמַן שִׂמְחָתֵֽנוּ

הַשְּׁמִינִי חַג הָעֲצֶֽרֶת הַזֶּה, זְמַן הַשִּׂמְחָה

{בְּאַהֲבָה} מִקְרָא קֹֽדֶשׁ, זֵֽכֶר לִיצִיאַת מִצְרָֽיִם. כִּי בָֽנוּ בָחַֽרְתָּ, וְאוֹתָֽנוּ קִדַּֽשְׁתָּ מִכָּל הָעַמִּים {וְשַׁבָּת} וּמוֹעֲדֵי קָדְשֶֽׁךָ {בְּאַהֲבָה וּבְרָצוֹן} בְּשִׂמְחָה וּבְשָׂשׂוֹן הִנְחַלְתָּֽנוּ. בָּרוּךְ אַתָּה יְיָ מְקַדֵּשׁ {הַשַּׁבָּת וְ} יִשְׂרָאֵל וְהַזְּמַנִּים.

כִּי יִזְכְּרוּ וְיָשֻֽׁבוּ אֶל יְיָ כָּל אַפְסֵי אָֽרֶץ, וְיִשְׁתַּחֲווּ לְפָנֶֽיךָ כָּל מִשְׁפְּחוֹת גּוֹיִם. כִּי לַייָ הַמְּלוּכָה וּמֹשֵׁל בַּגּוֹיִם. בָּרוּךְ אַתָּה יְיָ מְקַדֵּשׁ {הַשַּׁבָּת וְ} יִשְׂרָאֵל וְהַזְּמַנִּים.

יום טוב שחל במוצאי שבת

Begin with the *Kiddush* for Festivals and then continue here.

Gaze into the light of the holiday candles (see prayer D, page 4). (A special *Havdalah* candle and spices are not needed.)

F **בָּרוּךְ** אַתָּה יְיָ אֱלֹהֵֽינוּ מֶֽלֶךְ הָעוֹלָם, בּוֹרֵא מְאוֹרֵי הָאֵשׁ.

G **בָּרוּךְ** אַתָּה יְיָ אֱלֹהֵֽינוּ מֶֽלֶךְ הָעוֹלָם, הַמַּבְדִּיל בֵּין קֹֽדֶשׁ לְחוֹל, בֵּין אוֹר לְחֹֽשֶׁךְ, בֵּין יִשְׂרָאֵל לָעַמִּים, בֵּין יוֹם הַשְּׁבִיעִי, לְשֵֽׁשֶׁת יְמֵי הַמַּעֲשֶׂה. בֵּין קְדֻשַּׁת שַׁבָּת לִקְדֻשַּׁת יוֹם טוֹב הִבְדַּֽלְתָּ, וְאֶת יוֹם הַשְּׁבִיעִי מִשֵּֽׁשֶׁת יְמֵי הַמַּעֲשֶׂה קִדַּֽשְׁתָּ, הִבְדַּֽלְתָּ וְקִדַּֽשְׁתָּ אֶת עַמְּךָ יִשְׂרָאֵל בִּקְדֻשָּׁתֶֽךָ. בָּרוּךְ אַתָּה יְיָ הַמַּבְדִּיל בֵּין קֹֽדֶשׁ לְקֹֽדֶשׁ.

the Festival of Matzot, the season of our freedom,	On Passover	the Festival of Matzot, the season of freedom,
the Festival of Shavu'ot, the season of the giving of our Torah,	On Shavu'ot	the Festival of Shavu'ot, the season of the giving of the Torah,
the Festival of Sukkot, the season of our joy,	On Sukkot	the Festival of Sukkot, the season of joy,
the Festival of Shmini Atzeret, the season of our joy,	On Shmini Atzeret and Simchat Torah	the Festival of Shmini Atzeret, the season of joy,

{lovingly,} a holy convocation, as a remembrance of the exodus from Egypt. For you chose us and sanctified us from all of the nations, and you lovingly let us inherit {the Sabbath and} your holy appointed times. Blessed are you, O LORD, who sanctifies {the Sabbath,} Israel and the seasons.

for all the ends of the earth shall remember and turn to the LORD, and all the families of the nations shall bow before you, because the kingship is the LORD's, and he rules over the nations.[a] Blessed are you, O LORD, who sanctifies {the Sabbath,} Israel and the seasons.

FESTIVAL THAT BEGINS ON SATURDAY EVENING

Begin with the *Kiddush* for Festivals and then continue here.

Gaze into the light of the holiday candles (see prayer D, page 5).

(A special *Havdalah* candle and spices are not needed.)

F **Blessed** are you, O LORD, our God, King of the universe, who creates the firelight.

G **Blessed** are you, O LORD, our God, King of the universe, who makes a distinction between what is holy and what is common,[b] between light and darkness,[c] between Israel and the nations,[d] between the seventh day and the six days of creation. You made a distinction between the holiness of the Sabbath and the holiness of a festival; you sanctified the seventh day beyond the six days of creation. You distinguished and sanctified your nation Israel with your holiness. Blessed are you, O LORD, who makes a distinction between one type of holiness and another.

a) Psalm 22:28–29[27–28]. b) Leviticus 10:10. c) Genesis 1:4, 18. d) Leviticus 20:24, 26.

לישב בסוכה

Jewish readers include this line if you recite *Kiddush* inside the *sukkah* on Sukkot.

H **בָּרוּךְ** אַתָּה יְיָ אֱלֹהֵינוּ מֶלֶךְ הָעוֹלָם, אֲשֶׁר קִדְּשָׁנוּ בְּמִצְוֹתָיו וְצִוָּנוּ לֵישֵׁב בַּסֻּכָּה.

שהחיינו

Recite *Shehecheyanu* on all festivals except the seventh and eighth day of Passover.

I **בָּרוּךְ** אַתָּה יְיָ אֱלֹהֵינוּ מֶלֶךְ הָעוֹלָם, שֶׁהֶחֱיָנוּ וְקִיְּמָנוּ וְהִגִּיעָנוּ לַזְּמַן הַזֶּה.

DRINK THE WINE

8 נטילת ידיים

A **בָּרוּךְ** אַתָּה יְיָ אֱלֹהֵינוּ מֶלֶךְ הָעוֹלָם אֲשֶׁר קִדְּשָׁנוּ בְּמִצְוֹתָיו, וְצִוָּנוּ עַל נְטִילַת יָדָיִם.

9 המוציא

LIFT THE LOAVES OF BREAD

A **נוֹדֶה לְךָ** אָבִינוּ, עַל הַחַיִּים וְעַל הַדַּעַת שֶׁהוֹדַעְתָּנוּ עַל יְדֵי יֵשׁוּעַ עַבְדֶּךָ. לְךָ הַכָּבוֹד לְעוֹלָמִים.

B כְּמוֹ שֶׁהַפַּת הַזֹּאת הָיְתָה נְפוֹצָה עַל הֶהָרִים וְנִקְבְּצָה יַחַד, כֵּן תִּקָּבֵץ קְהִילָּתְךָ מֵאַפְסֵי אֶרֶץ אֶל מַלְכוּתֶךָ. כִּי לְךָ הַכָּבוֹד וְהַגְּבוּרָה עַל יְדֵי יֵשׁוּעַ לְעוֹלָמִים.

C **בָּרוּךְ** אַתָּה יְיָ אֱלֹהֵינוּ מֶלֶךְ הָעוֹלָם, הַמּוֹצִיא לֶחֶם מִן הָאָרֶץ.

SHARE AND EAT THE BREAD

For the *Birkat HaMazon*, go to prayer 50, page 94.

DWELLING IN A SUKKAH

Jewish readers include this line if you recite *Kiddush* inside the *sukkah* on Sukkot.

H **Blessed** are you, O LORD, our God, King of the universe, who has sanctified us with his commandments and commanded us to dwell in the *sukkah*.

SHEHECHEYANU

Recite *Shehecheyanu* on all festivals except the seventh and eighth day of Passover.

I **Blessed** are you, O LORD, our God, King of the universe, who has kept us alive, upheld us, and let us reach this time.

Drink the wine

8 Hand Washing

A **Blessed** are you, O LORD, our God, King of the universe, who has sanctified us with his commandments and has commanded us about the washing of hands.

9 Blessing for Bread

Lift the loaves of bread

A **We thank you**, our Father, for the life and for the knowledge that you made known to us through your servant Yeshua. Yours is the glory forever.

B Just as this piece of bread was scattered over the mountains and gathered together, so may your assembly be gathered from the ends of the earth into your kingdom. For yours is the glory and the power through Yeshua forever.[a]

C **Blessed** are you, O LORD, our God, King of the universe, who brings bread out of the earth.

Share and eat the bread

For the *Birkat HaMazon* (Grace after Meals), go to prayer 50, page 95.

a) *Didache* 9:3–4.

יום שבת/יום טוב

SABBATH AND FESTIVAL DAY

Some have the custom of reciting Psalm 23 before *Kiddusha Rabba*, prayer 17, page 32. Customs vary as to where to begin *Kiddusha Rabba*. See below.

10 קידושא רבא

HOLD THE CUP OF WINE

A עַל כֵּן נִשְׁאֲרָה עוֹד מְנוּחַת שַׁבָּת לְעַם אֱלֹהִים. כִּי הַבָּא אֶל מְנוּחָתוֹ גַּם הוּא שָׁבַת מִמְּלַאכְתּוֹ כַּאֲשֶׁר הָאֱלֹהִים מִשֶּׁלּוֹ. לָכֵן נִשְׁקְדָה נָּא לָבוֹא אֶל הַמְּנוּחָה הַהִיא.

B אִם תָּשִׁיב מִשַּׁבָּת רַגְלֶךָ עֲשׂוֹת חֲפָצֶךָ בְּיוֹם קָדְשִׁי וְקָרָאתָ לַשַּׁבָּת עֹנֶג לִקְדוֹשׁ יְיָ מְכֻבָּד וְכִבַּדְתּוֹ מֵעֲשׂוֹת דְּרָכֶיךָ מִמְּצוֹא חֶפְצְךָ וְדַבֵּר דָּבָר, אָז תִּתְעַנַּג עַל יְיָ וְהִרְכַּבְתִּיךָ עַל בָּמֳתֵי אָרֶץ וְהַאֲכַלְתִּיךָ נַחֲלַת יַעֲקֹב אָבִיךָ כִּי פִּי יְיָ דִּבֵּר.

Most congregations begin *Kiddusha Rabba* here.

C וְשָׁמְרוּ בְנֵי יִשְׂרָאֵל אֶת הַשַּׁבָּת לַעֲשׂוֹת אֶת הַשַּׁבָּת לְדֹרֹתָם בְּרִית עוֹלָם. בֵּינִי וּבֵין בְּנֵי יִשְׂרָאֵל אוֹת הִיא לְעֹלָם כִּי שֵׁשֶׁת יָמִים עָשָׂה יְיָ אֶת הַשָּׁמַיִם וְאֶת הָאָרֶץ וּבַיּוֹם הַשְּׁבִיעִי שָׁבַת וַיִּנָּפַשׁ.

D זָכוֹר אֶת יוֹם הַשַּׁבָּת לְקַדְּשׁוֹ. שֵׁשֶׁת יָמִים תַּעֲבֹד וְעָשִׂיתָ כָּל מְלַאכְתֶּךָ. וְיוֹם הַשְּׁבִיעִי שַׁבָּת לַייָ אֱלֹהֶיךָ, לֹא תַעֲשֶׂה כָל מְלָאכָה אַתָּה וּבִנְךָ וּבִתֶּךָ עַבְדְּךָ וַאֲמָתְךָ וּבְהֶמְתֶּךָ וְגֵרְךָ אֲשֶׁר בִּשְׁעָרֶיךָ. כִּי שֵׁשֶׁת יָמִים עָשָׂה יְיָ אֶת הַשָּׁמַיִם וְאֶת הָאָרֶץ אֶת הַיָּם וְאֶת כָּל אֲשֶׁר בָּם וַיָּנַח בַּיּוֹם הַשְּׁבִיעִי.

Recommended for Messianic Gentiles

E וּבְנֵי הַנֵּכָר הַנִּלְוִים עַל יְיָ לְשָׁרְתוֹ וּלְאַהֲבָה אֶת שֵׁם יְיָ לִהְיוֹת לוֹ לַעֲבָדִים, כָּל שֹׁמֵר שַׁבָּת מֵחַלְּלוֹ וּמַחֲזִיקִים בִּבְרִיתִי. וַהֲבִיאוֹתִים אֶל הַר קָדְשִׁי וְשִׂמַּחְתִּים בְּבֵית תְּפִלָּתִי, עוֹלֹתֵיהֶם וְזִבְחֵיהֶם לְרָצוֹן עַל מִזְבְּחִי, כִּי בֵיתִי בֵּית תְּפִלָּה יִקָּרֵא לְכָל הָעַמִּים:

Yom Shabbat/Yom Tov

SABBATH AND FESTIVAL DAY

Some have the custom of reciting Psalm 23 before *Kiddusha Rabba*, prayer 17, page 33. Customs vary as to where to begin *Kiddusha Rabba*. See below.

10 ## Kiddusha Rabba

Hold the cup of wine

A **Therefore,** a Sabbath rest still remains for the people of God. For one who has entered his rest has ceased from his work, just as God did with his. Thus, let us be careful to enter that rest.[a]

B **If you hold back** your feet on account of the Sabbath from doing whatever you please on my holy day, if you call the Sabbath a delight and call the holy one of the LORD honored, if you honor it by not making your own way, seeking whatever you please, or speaking inappropriately, then you will delight in the LORD, and I will let you ride upon the heights of the earth, and I will feed you with the inheritance of your father Jacob, for the mouth of the LORD has spoken.[b]

Most congregations begin *Kiddusha Rabba* here.

C **The children of Israel shall observe** the Sabbath, making the Sabbath an eternal covenant throughout their generations. Between me and the children of Israel it is a sign that in six days the LORD created heaven and earth, and on the seventh day he ceased and was refreshed.[c]

D **Remember the Sabbath day** to sanctify it. Six days you may labor and do all of your work, but the seventh day is the Sabbath for the LORD your God. You may not do any work—you, your son, your daughter, your male or female servant, your livestock, or the sojourner who is in your gates. For in six days the LORD made heaven, earth, the sea, and all that is in them, and he rested on the seventh day.

Recommended for Messianic Gentiles

E **Foreigners** who are joined to the LORD, to serve him and to love the name of the LORD, to be his servants, everyone who keeps from desecrating the Sabbath, and those who hold tightly to my covenant—I will bring them to my holy mountain, and I will make them glad in my house of prayer; their burnt offerings and sacrifices will be favorable on my altar, for my House will be called a house of prayer for all nations.[d]

a) Hebrews 4:9–11. b) Isaiah 58:13–14. c) Exodus 31:16–17. d) Isaiah 56:6–7

Some congregations begin *Kiddusha Rabba* here.

F עַל כֵּן בֵּרַךְ יְיָ אֶת יוֹם הַשַּׁבָּת וַיְקַדְּשֵׁהוּ.

קידושא רבא ליום טוב

When a festival falls on the Sabbath, begin with *Kiddusha Rabba* and then continue here.
On a festival that begins on any other day of the week, begin here.

G **אֵלֶּה** מוֹעֲדֵי יְיָ מִקְרָאֵי קֹדֶשׁ אֲשֶׁר תִּקְרְאוּ אֹתָם בְּמוֹעֲדָם.

H וַיְדַבֵּר מֹשֶׁה אֶת מֹעֲדֵי יְיָ אֶל בְּנֵי יִשְׂרָאֵל.

ON ROSH HASHANAH, ADD

I תִּקְעוּ בַחֹדֶשׁ שׁוֹפָר, בַּכֵּסֶה לְיוֹם חַגֵּנוּ. כִּי חֹק לְיִשְׂרָאֵל הוּא,
מִשְׁפָּט לֵאלֹהֵי יַעֲקֹב.

סַבְרִי—

J **נוֹדֶה לְּךָ** אָבִינוּ, עַל הַגֶּפֶן הַקְּדוֹשָׁה לְדָוִד עַבְדֶּךָ שֶׁהוֹדַעְתָּנוּ עַל יְדֵי יֵשׁוּעַ עַבְדֶּךָ. לְךָ הַכָּבוֹד לְעוֹלָמִים.

K **בָּרוּךְ** אַתָּה יְיָ אֱלֹהֵינוּ מֶלֶךְ הָעוֹלָם, בּוֹרֵא פְּרִי הַגָּפֶן.

לישב בסוכה

Jewish readers include this line if you recite *Kiddusha Rabba* inside the *sukkah* on Sukkot.

L **בָּרוּךְ** אַתָּה יְיָ אֱלֹהֵינוּ מֶלֶךְ הָעוֹלָם, אֲשֶׁר קִדְּשָׁנוּ בְּמִצְוֹתָיו וְצִוָּנוּ לֵישֵׁב בַּסֻּכָּה.

DRINK THE WINE

11 נטילת ידיים

A **בָּרוּךְ** אַתָּה יְיָ אֱלֹהֵינוּ מֶלֶךְ הָעוֹלָם אֲשֶׁר קִדְּשָׁנוּ בְּמִצְוֹתָיו, וְצִוָּנוּ עַל נְטִילַת יָדָיִם.

Some congregations begin *Kiddusha Rabba* here.

F Therefore, the LORD blessed the Sabbath day and sanctified it.[a]

KIDDUSHA RABBA FOR FESTIVALS

When a festival falls on the Sabbath, begin with *Kiddusha Rabba* and then continue here. On a festival that begins on any other day of the week, begin here.

G **These** are the appointed times of the LORD, callings of holiness, which you are to proclaim at their appointed time.[b]

H Moses spoke about the appointed times of the LORD to the children of Israel.[c]

On Rosh HaShanah, add

I Blast the shofar at the new month, at the proper time of our festival. For it is a statute for Israel, a judgment for the God of Jacob.[d]

With your permission—

J **We thank you,** our Father, for the holy vine of your servant David that you made known to us through your servant Yeshua. Yours is the glory forever.[e]

K **Blessed** are you, O LORD, our God, King of the universe, who creates the fruit of the vine.

DWELLING IN A SUKKAH

Jewish readers include this line if you recite *Kiddusha Rabba* inside the *sukkah* on Sukkot.

L **Blessed** are you, O LORD, our God, King of the universe, who has sanctified us with his commandments and commanded us to dwell in the *sukkah*.

Drink the wine

11 Hand Washing

A **Blessed** are you, O LORD, our God, King of the universe, who has sanctified us with his commandments and has commanded us about the washing of hands.

a) Exodus 20:8–11. b) Leviticus 23:4. c) Leviticus 23:44. d) Psalm 81:4–5[3–4].
e) *Didache* 9:2.

12

המוציא

LIFT THE LOAVES OF BREAD

A נוֹדֶה לְךָ אָבִינוּ, עַל הַחַיִּים וְעַל הַדַּעַת שֶׁהוֹדַעְתָּנוּ עַל יְדֵי יֵשׁוּעַ עַבְדֶּךָ. לְךָ הַכָּבוֹד לְעוֹלָמִים.

B כְּמוֹ שֶׁהַפַּת הַזֹּאת הָיְתָה נְפוֹצָה עַל הֶהָרִים וְנִקְבְּצָה יַחַד, כֵּן תִּקָּבֵץ קְהִילָּתְךָ מֵאַפְסֵי אָרֶץ אֶל מַלְכוּתֶךָ. כִּי לְךָ הַכָּבוֹד וְהַגְּבוּרָה עַל יְדֵי יֵשׁוּעַ לְעוֹלָמִים.

C בָּרוּךְ אַתָּה יְיָ אֱלֹהֵינוּ מֶלֶךְ הָעוֹלָם, הַמּוֹצִיא לֶחֶם מִן הָאָרֶץ.

SHARE AND EAT THE BREAD

For the *Birkat HaMazon*, go to prayer 50, page 94.

12

BLESSING FOR BREAD

LIFT THE LOAVES OF BREAD

A **WE THANK YOU,** our Father, for the life and for the knowledge that you made known to us through your servant Yeshua. Yours is the glory forever.

B Just as this piece of bread was scattered over the mountains and gathered together, so may your assembly be gathered from the ends of the earth into your kingdom. For yours is the glory and the power through Yeshua forever.[a]

C **BLESSED** are you, O LORD, our God, King of the universe, who brings bread out of the earth.

SHARE AND EAT THE BREAD

For the *Birkat HaMazon* (Grace after Meals), go to prayer 50, page 95.

a) *Didache* 9:3–4.

סעודה שלישית

THIRD MEAL

13 אכלוהו היום

Most congregations omit this reading.

A וַיֹּאמֶר מֹשֶׁה אִכְלֻהוּ הַיּוֹם כִּי שַׁבָּת הַיּוֹם לַייָ, הַיּוֹם לֹא תִמְצָאֻהוּ בַּשָּׂדֶה. שֵׁשֶׁת יָמִים תִּלְקְטֻהוּ, וּבַיּוֹם הַשְּׁבִיעִי שַׁבָּת לֹא יִהְיֶה בּוֹ. וַיְהִי בַּיּוֹם הַשְּׁבִיעִי, יָצְאוּ מִן הָעָם לִלְקֹט וְלֹא מָצָאוּ.

B וַיֹּאמֶר יְיָ אֶל מֹשֶׁה, עַד אָנָה מֵאַנְתֶּם לִשְׁמֹר מִצְוֹתַי וְתוֹרֹתָי. רְאוּ כִּי יְיָ נָתַן לָכֶם הַשַּׁבָּת, עַל כֵּן הוּא נֹתֵן לָכֶם בַּיּוֹם הַשִּׁשִּׁי לֶחֶם יוֹמָיִם, שְׁבוּ אִישׁ תַּחְתָּיו, אַל יֵצֵא אִישׁ מִמְּקֹמוֹ בַּיּוֹם הַשְּׁבִיעִי. וַיִּשְׁבְּתוּ הָעָם בַּיּוֹם הַשְּׁבִעִי.

14 נטילת ידיים

A **בָּרוּךְ** אַתָּה יְיָ אֱלֹהֵינוּ מֶלֶךְ הָעוֹלָם אֲשֶׁר קִדְּשָׁנוּ בְּמִצְוֹתָיו, וְצִוָּנוּ עַל נְטִילַת יָדָיִם.

15 המוציא

LIFT THE LOAVES OF BREAD

A **נוֹדֶה לְךָ** אָבִינוּ, עַל הַחַיִּים וְעַל הַדַּעַת שֶׁהוֹדַעְתָּנוּ עַל יְדֵי יֵשׁוּעַ עַבְדֶּךָ. לְךָ הַכָּבוֹד לְעוֹלָמִים.

B כְּמוֹ שֶׁהַפַּת הַזֹּאת הָיְתָה נְפוּצָה עַל הֶהָרִים וְנִקְבְּצָה יַחַד, כֵּן תִּקָּבֵץ קְהִילָּתְךָ מֵאַפְסֵי אֶרֶץ אֶל מַלְכוּתֶךָ. כִּי לְךָ הַכָּבוֹד וְהַגְּבוּרָה עַל יְדֵי יֵשׁוּעַ לְעוֹלָמִים.

C **בָּרוּךְ** אַתָּה יְיָ אֱלֹהֵינוּ מֶלֶךְ הָעוֹלָם, הַמּוֹצִיא לֶחֶם מִן הָאָרֶץ.

SHARE AND EAT THE BREAD

SE'UDAH SHLISHIT

THIRD MEAL

13

EAT IT TODAY

Most congregations omit this reading.

A Moses said, "Eat it today, for today is the Sabbath to the LORD. Today you will not find it in the field. For six days you may gather it, but the seventh day is the Sabbath; it will not be there." On the seventh day, some of the people went out to gather, but they did not find any.

B The LORD said to Moses, "How long will you refuse to keep my commandments and teachings? Look, the LORD has given you the Sabbath. Accordingly on the sixth day he gives you bread for two days. Let everyone remain settled. No one shall go out from his place on the seventh day." So the people rested on the seventh day.[a]

14

HAND WASHING

A **BLESSED** are you, O LORD, our God, King of the universe, who has sanctified us with his commandments and has commanded us about the washing of hands.

15

BLESSING FOR BREAD

LIFT THE LOAVES OF BREAD

A **WE THANK YOU,** our Father, for the life and for the knowledge that you made known to us through your servant Yeshua. Yours is the glory forever.

B Just as this piece of bread was scattered over the mountains and gathered together, so may your assembly be gathered from the ends of the earth into your kingdom. For yours is the glory and the power through Yeshua forever.[b]

C **BLESSED** are you, O LORD, our God, King of the universe, who brings bread out of the earth.

SHARE AND EAT THE BREAD

a) Exodus 16:25–30. b) *Didache* 9:3–4.

16 ## בורא פרי הגפן

IF ONE IS DRINKING WINE

סַבְרִי—

A נוֹדֶה לְךָ אָבִינוּ, עַל הַגֶּפֶן הַקְּדוֹשָׁה לְדָוִד עַבְדֶּךָ שֶׁהוֹדַעְתָּנוּ עַל יְדֵי יֵשׁוּעַ עַבְדֶּךָ. לְךָ הַכָּבוֹד לְעוֹלָמִים.

B בָּרוּךְ אַתָּה יְיָ אֱלֹהֵינוּ מֶלֶךְ הָעוֹלָם, בּוֹרֵא פְּרִי הַגָּפֶן.

DRINK THE WINE

17 ## תהילים כג

A מִזְמוֹר לְדָוִד

B יְיָ רֹעִי
לֹא אֶחְסָר:

C בִּנְאוֹת דֶּשֶׁא יַרְבִּיצֵנִי
עַל מֵי מְנֻחוֹת יְנַהֲלֵנִי:

D נַפְשִׁי יְשׁוֹבֵב
יַנְחֵנִי בְמַעְגְּלֵי צֶדֶק
לְמַעַן שְׁמוֹ:

E גַּם כִּי אֵלֵךְ בְּגֵיא צַלְמָוֶת
לֹא אִירָא רָע כִּי אַתָּה עִמָּדִי
שִׁבְטְךָ וּמִשְׁעַנְתֶּךָ הֵמָּה יְנַחֲמֻנִי:

F תַּעֲרֹךְ לְפָנַי שֻׁלְחָן
נֶגֶד צֹרְרָי

G דִּשַּׁנְתָּ בַשֶּׁמֶן רֹאשִׁי
כּוֹסִי רְוָיָה:

H אַךְ טוֹב וָחֶסֶד יִרְדְּפוּנִי
כָּל יְמֵי חַיָּי

I וְשַׁבְתִּי בְּבֵית יְיָ
לְאֹרֶךְ יָמִים:

For the *Birkat HaMazon*, go to prayer 50, page 94.

16 ## Blessing for Wine

IF ONE IS DRINKING WINE

With your permission—

A **WE THANK YOU**, our Father, for the holy vine of your servant David that you made known to us through your servant Yeshua. Yours is the glory forever.[a]

B **BLESSED** are you, O LORD, our God, King of the universe, who creates the fruit of the vine.

DRINK THE WINE

17 ## Psalm 23

A A hymn of David.

B The LORD is my shepherd;
I will not lack.

C He lays me down in grassy meadows;
he leads me to calm water.

D He restores my soul.
He guides me on paths of righteousness
for his name's sake.

E Though I walk in a death-dark valley,
I will not fear evil, because you are with me.
Your rod and your staff comfort me.

F You set a table before me
opposite my tormentors;

G You have moistened my head with oil;
my cup overflows.

H May only goodness and devotion pursue me
all the days of my life,

I And I will dwell in the House of the LORD
for as long as I live.

For the *Birkat HaMazon* (Grace after Meals), go to prayer 50, page 95.

a) *Didache* 9:2.

הבדלה

CONCLUSION OF THE SABBATH

The *Havdalah* ceremony is performed at the end of the Sabbath and festivals. When a festival begins on Saturday night, *Havdalah* is included in the *Kiddush for Festivals*, prayer 7, page 18

תפילות לפני הבדלה

Some people pray *Got Fun Avrohom* and/or *Anna Eloheinu* before *Havdalah*. Most begin with *Hinneh El Yeshu'ati*, prayer 20, page 36.

18 גאט פון אברהם

A גָאט פוּן אַבְרָהָם אוּן פוּן יִצְחָק אוּן פוּן יַעֲקֹב, בֶּעהִיט דַיין לֵיבּ פָאלְק יִשְׂרָאֵל פוּן אַלֶעם בֵּייזֶען אִין דַיינֶעם לוֹיבּ, אַז דֶער לִיבֶּער שַׁבָּת קֹדֶשׁ גֵייט אַוֶועק, אַז דִי וָואךְ אוּן דֶער חֹדֶשׁ אוּן דֶער יָאר, זָאל אוּנְז צוּא קוּמֶען צוּ אֱמוּנָה שְׁלֵמָה, צוּ אֱמוּנַת חֲכָמִים, צוּ אַהֲבַת חֲבֵרִים, צוּ דְבֵקוּת הַבּוֹרֵא בָּרוּךְ הוּא, מַאֲמִין צוּ זַיין בִּשְׁלֹשׁ עֶשְׂרֵה עִקָּרִים שֶׁלָּךְ, וּבִגְאוּלָה קְרוֹבָה בִּמְהֵרָה בְיָמֵינוּ, וּבִתְחִיַּת הַמֵּתִים, וּבִנְבוּאַת מֹשֶׁה רַבֵּנוּ עָלָיו הַשָּׁלוֹם.

B רִבּוֹנוֹ שֶׁל עוֹלָם דוּ בִּיזְט דָאךְ הַנּוֹתֵן לַיָּעֵף כֹּחַ, גִיבּ דַיינֶע לִיבֶּע אִידִישֶׁע קִינְדֶערְלִיךְ אוֹיךְ כֹּחַ דִיךְ צוּ לוֹיבֶּען אוּן נָאר דִיךְ צוּ דִינֶען אוּן קֵיין אַנְדֶערְן חָלִילָה נִישְׁט, אוּן אַז דִי וָואךְ אוּן דֶער חֹדֶשׁ אוּן דֶער יָאר זָאל אוּנְז קוּמֶען צוּ גֶעזוּנְד אוּן צוּ מַזָּל אוּן צוּ בְּרָכָה וְהַצְלָחָה אוּן צוּ חֶסֶד אוּן צוּ בָּנֵי חַיֵּי אֲרִיכֵי וּמְזוֹנֵי רְוִיחֵי וְסִיַּעְתָּא דִשְׁמַיָּא לָנוּ וּלְכָל יִשְׂרָאֵל וְנֹאמַר אָמֵן.

19 אנא אלהינו

A אָנָּא אֱלֹהֵינוּ וֵאלֹהֵי אֲבוֹתֵינוּ. שִׂים תּוֹחַלְתֵּנוּ שָׁלוֹם. שִׂים תִּקְוָתֵנוּ שָׁלוֹם. שִׂים פַּחְדֵּנוּ שָׁלוֹם. שִׂים דַּרְכֵּנוּ שָׁלוֹם. שִׂים פִּתְרוֹן כָּל חֲלוֹמוֹתֵינוּ שָׁלוֹם. הַשְׁמִיעֵנוּ שָׁלוֹם מִפִּי שַׂר הַשָּׁלוֹם. מִשְׁמֶרֶת הַשָּׁלוֹם תְּהֵא פְּרוּסָה מֵאִתְּךָ עָלֵינוּ וְעַל עַמְּךָ בֵּית יִשְׂרָאֵל לְקַיֵּם קְרָא דִכְתִיב, יְיָ עֹז לְעַמּוֹ יִתֵּן יְיָ יְבָרֵךְ אֶת עַמּוֹ בַשָּׁלוֹם. אַתָּה יְיָ לֹא תִכְלָא רַחֲמֶיךָ מִמֶּנּוּ חַסְדְּךָ וַאֲמִתְּךָ תָּמִיד יִצְּרוּנוּ. לְךָ דֻמִיָּה תְהִלָּה.

HAVDALAH

CONCLUSION OF THE SABBATH

The *Havdalah* ceremony is performed at the end of the Sabbath and festivals. When a festival begins on Saturday night, *Havdalah* is included in the *Kiddush for Festivals*, prayer 7, page 19.

PRAYERS BEFORE HAVDALAH

Some people pray *Got Fun Avrohom* and/or *Anna Eloheinu* before *Havdalah*. Most begin with *Hinneh El Yeshu'ati*, prayer 20, page 37.

18 GOT FUN AVROHOM

A God of Abraham, Isaac, and Jacob, for your praise, protect your beloved people Israel from all harm. As the beloved, holy Sabbath is passing, let the coming week and month and year bring us to complete faith, to faith in the sages, to love for our fellow, to closeness to the blessed Creator, to belief in your thirteen principles, and in the redemption soon, quickly, and in our days, and in the resurrection of the dead, and in the prophecy of our teacher Moses, peace be upon him.

B Master of the world, you are the one who gives strength to the weary. Give to your beloved children of Israel strength as well, that we may give thanks to you and serve you alone and no other. Let the coming week and month and year bring us to health, fortune, blessing, success, kindness, children, long life, ample food, and heavenly help, for us and for all Israel. Amen.

19 ANNA ELOHEINU

A Please, our God and God of our fathers, make peace our expectation. Make peace our hope. Make peace our awe. Make peace our way. Make peace the interpretation of all of our dreams. Proclaim to us peace from the mouth of the Prince of Peace. Let the preservation of peace be spread over us by you, and over all your people, the house of Israel, to fulfill the verse that says, "The LORD gives strength to his people; the LORD will bless his people with peace."[a] O LORD, you will not withhold your compassionate acts from us, and your kindness and truth will watch over us always. To you, silence is praise.[b]

a) Psalm 29:11. b) Psalm 65:2[1].

20

הנה אל ישועתי

LIFT THE CUP OF WINE

A הִנֵּה אֵל יְשׁוּעָתִי אֶבְטַח וְלֹא אֶפְחָד, כִּי עָזִּי וְזִמְרָת יָהּ יְיָ וַיְהִי לִי לִישׁוּעָה. וּשְׁאַבְתֶּם מַיִם בְּשָׂשׂוֹן מִמַּעַיְנֵי הַיְשׁוּעָה. לַייָ הַיְשׁוּעָה, עַל עַמְּךָ בִרְכָתֶךָ, סֶּלָה. יְיָ צְבָאוֹת עִמָּנוּ מִשְׂגָּב לָנוּ אֱלֹהֵי יַעֲקֹב סֶלָה. יְיָ צְבָאוֹת אַשְׁרֵי אָדָם בֹּטֵחַ בָּךְ. יְיָ הוֹשִׁיעָה הַמֶּלֶךְ יַעֲנֵנוּ בְיוֹם קָרְאֵנוּ. לַיְּהוּדִים הָיְתָה אוֹרָה וְשִׂמְחָה וְשָׂשֹׂן וִיקָר, כֵּן תִּהְיֶה לָּנוּ. כּוֹס יְשׁוּעוֹת אֶשָּׂא, וּבְשֵׁם יְיָ אֶקְרָא.

סַבְרִי—

B נוֹדֶה לְךָ אָבִינוּ, עַל הַגֶּפֶן הַקְּדוֹשָׁה לְדָוִד עַבְדֶּךָ שֶׁהוֹדַעְתָּנוּ עַל יְדֵי יֵשׁוּעַ עַבְדֶּךָ. לְךָ הַכָּבוֹד לְעוֹלָמִים.

C בָּרוּךְ אַתָּה יְיָ אֱלֹהֵינוּ מֶלֶךְ הָעוֹלָם, בּוֹרֵא פְּרִי הַגָּפֶן.

At the end of a festival, omit the blessings for the spices and firelight.
At the end of Yom Kippur, just omit the blessing for the spices.

LIFT THE SPICES

D בָּרוּךְ אַתָּה יְיָ אֱלֹהֵינוּ מֶלֶךְ הָעוֹלָם, בּוֹרֵא מִינֵי בְשָׂמִים.

EXTEND HANDS TO THE LIGHT

E בָּרוּךְ אַתָּה יְיָ אֱלֹהֵינוּ מֶלֶךְ הָעוֹלָם, בּוֹרֵא מְאוֹרֵי הָאֵשׁ.

LIFT THE CUP OF WINE

F בָּרוּךְ אַתָּה יְיָ אֱלֹהֵינוּ מֶלֶךְ הָעוֹלָם, הַמַּבְדִּיל בֵּין קֹדֶשׁ לְחוֹל, בֵּין אוֹר לְחֹשֶׁךְ, בֵּין יִשְׂרָאֵל לָעַמִּים, בֵּין יוֹם הַשְּׁבִיעִי לְשֵׁשֶׁת יְמֵי הַמַּעֲשֶׂה. בָּרוּךְ אַתָּה יְיָ, הַמַּבְדִּיל בֵּין קֹדֶשׁ לְחוֹל.

DRINK THE WINE

It is appropriate to recite the after-blessing for wine, prayer 59, page 118.

20 HINNEH EL YESHU'ATI

LIFT THE CUP OF WINE

A **BEHOLD, GOD IS MY SALVATION;** I will trust and not be afraid. For God, the LORD, is my strength and my song, and he has been my salvation. You will joyfully draw water from the wells of salvation.[a] Salvation belongs to the LORD; your blessing is upon your people, selah.[b] The LORD of Legions is with us; the God of Jacob is a stronghold for us, selah.[c] O LORD of Legions, contentment awaits any man who trusts in you.[d] O LORD, save! May the King answer us on the day we call.[e] For the Jews there was light and gladness, joy and honor.[f] So may it be for us! I will lift the cup of salvations, and I will call on the name of the LORD.[g]

With your permission—

B **WE THANK YOU**, our Father, for the holy vine of your servant David that you made known to us through your servant Yeshua. Yours is the glory forever.[h]

C **BLESSED** are you, O LORD, our God, King of the universe, who creates the fruit of the vine.

At the end of a festival, omit the blessings for the spices and firelight.
At the end of Yom Kippur, just omit the blessing for the spices.

LIFT THE SPICES

D **BLESSED** are you, O LORD, our God, King of the universe, who creates different kinds of spices.

EXTEND HANDS TO THE LIGHT

E **BLESSED** are you, O LORD, our God, King of the universe, who creates the firelight.

LIFT THE CUP OF WINE

F **BLESSED** are you, O LORD, our God, King of the universe, who makes a distinction between what is holy and what is common,[i] between light and darkness,[j] between Israel and the nations,[k] between the seventh day and the six days of creation. Blessed are you, O LORD, who makes a distinction between holy and common.

DRINK THE WINE

It is appropriate to recite the after-blessing for wine, prayer 59, page 119

a) Isaiah 12:2–3. b) Psalm 3:9[8]. c) Psalm 46:8, 12 [7, 11]. d) Psalm 84:13[12].
e) Psalm 20:10[9]. f) Esther 8:16. g) Psalm 116:13. h) *Didache* 9:2.
i) Leviticus 10:10. j) Genesis 1:4, 18. k) Leviticus 20:24, 26.

מלוה מלכה

ESCORTING THE SABBATH QUEEN

רבון העולמים 21

Opinions vary as to whether this prayer should be recited before *Havdalah*, after *Havdalah*, or after all of the evening's prayers and songs. On Saturday night, include the word שֵׁשֶׁת in brackets. Omit שֵׁשֶׁת after a festival that concludes during the week.

A רִבּוֹן הָעוֹלָמִים, אַב הָרַחֲמִים וְהַסְּלִיחוֹת, בְּסִמָּן טוֹב וּבְמַזָּל טוֹב הָחֵל עָלֵינוּ אֶת {שֵׁשֶׁת} יְמֵי הַמַּעֲשֶׂה הַבָּאִים לִקְרָאתֵנוּ לְשָׁלוֹם, חֲשׂוּכִים מִכָּל חֵטְא וָפֶשַׁע וּמְנֻקִּים מִכָּל עָוֹן וְאַשְׁמָה וָרֶשַׁע, וּמְדֻבָּקִים בְּתַלְמוּד תּוֹרָה וּבְמַעֲשִׂים טוֹבִים, וְחָנֵּנוּ דֵּעָה בִּינָה וְהַשְׂכֵּל מֵאִתְּךָ, וְתַשְׁמִיעֵנוּ בָּהֶם שָׂשׂוֹן וְשִׂמְחָה וְלֹא תַעֲלֶה קִנְאָתֵנוּ עַל לֵב אָדָם וְלֹא קִנְאַת אָדָם תַּעֲלֶה עַל לִבֵּנוּ.

B מַלְכֵּנוּ אֱלֹהֵינוּ, הָאָב הָרַחֲמָן, שִׂים בְּרָכָה וּרְוָחָה וְהַצְלָחָה בְּכָל מַעֲשֵׂה יָדֵינוּ. וְכָל הַיּוֹעֵץ עַל עַמְּךָ בֵּית יִשְׂרָאֵל עֵצָה טוֹבָה וּמַחֲשָׁבָה טוֹבָה אַמְּצוֹ, בָּרְכוֹ גַּדְּלוֹ וְקַיְּמוֹ. קַיֵּם עֲצָתוֹ כַּדָּבָר שֶׁנֶּאֱמַר, יִתֶּן לְךָ כִלְבָבֶךָ וְכָל עֲצָתְךָ יְמַלֵּא. וְנֶאֱמַר וְתִגְזַר אֹמֶר וְיָקָם לָךְ וְעַל דְּרָכֶיךָ נָגַהּ אוֹר.

C וְכָל הַיּוֹעֵץ עָלֵינוּ וְעַל כָּל עַמְּךָ בֵּית יִשְׂרָאֵל עֵצָה שֶׁאֵינָהּ טוֹבָה וּמַחֲשָׁבָה שֶׁאֵינָהּ טוֹבָה תּוּפַר עֲצָתוֹ, כַּדָּבָר שֶׁנֶּאֱמַר, יְיָ הֵפִיר עֲצַת גּוֹיִם הֵנִיא מַחְשְׁבוֹת עַמִּים. וְנֶאֱמַר עֻצוּ עֵצָה וְתֻפָר דַּבְּרוּ דָבָר וְלֹא יָקוּם כִּי עִמָּנוּ אֵל.

D וּפְתַח לָנוּ יְיָ אֱלֹהֵינוּ אַב הָרַחֲמִים אֲדוֹן הַסְּלִיחוֹת בָּזֶה הַשָּׁבוּעַ וּבְכָל שָׁבוּעַ,

א שַׁעֲרֵי אוֹרָה,

א שַׁעֲרֵי אֹרֶךְ יָמִים וְשָׁנִים,

א שַׁעֲרֵי אֲרִיכַת אַפַּיִם,

ב שַׁעֲרֵי בְרָכָה,

ב שַׁעֲרֵי בִינָה,

MELAVEH MALKAH

ESCORTING THE SABBATH QUEEN

21 RIBBON HAOLAMIM

Opinions vary as to whether this prayer should be recited before *Havdalah*, after *Havdalah*, or after all of the evening's prayers and songs. On Saturday night, include the word "six" in brackets. Omit "six" after a festival that concludes during the week.

A **MASTER OF THE WORLDS**, compassionate and forgiving Father, begin these {six} days of labor that are coming peacefully to greet us with a good sign and good fortune. May we be devoid of any sin or transgression, cleansed from any iniquity, guilt, or wickedness, and cleaving to Torah study and good deeds. Grace us with knowledge, discernment, and understanding from you, and proclaim to us at this time gladness and joy. Let us not be jealous of other people, nor let others be jealous of us.

B Our King, our God, compassionate Father, place blessing, relief, and success on all of the works of our hands. If anyone has good intentions and plans regarding your people, the house of Israel, reinforce him, bless him, strengthen him, and uphold him. Uphold his intentions, as the verse states, "May he grant you your heart's desires, and may all your intentions be fulfilled."[a] As it is said, "If you pronounce a decree, it will be upheld for you, and all your ways will be as bright as the dawn."[b]

C If anyone has intentions or plans regarding your people Israel that are not good, overturn his plan. As the verse states, "The LORD has overturned the intentions of the nations and thwarted the plans of the peoples."[c] And it is said, "Make your plans, but they will be overturned. Speak your words, but they will not endure, for God is with us."[d]

D LORD our God, compassionate Father, master of forgiveness, open for us this week and every week

א the gates of light,
א the gates of long life,
א the gates of longsuffering,
ב the gates of blessing,
ב the gates of discernment,

a) Psalm 20:5[4]. b) Job 22:28. c) Psalm 33:10. d) Isaiah 8:10.

ג שַׁעֲרֵי גִילָה,
ג שַׁעֲרֵי גְדֻלָּה,
ג שַׁעֲרֵי גְאֻלָּה,
ג שַׁעֲרֵי גְבוּרָה,
ד שַׁעֲרֵי דִיצָה,
ד שַׁעֲרֵי דֵעָה,
ה שַׁעֲרֵי הוֹד,
ה שַׁעֲרֵי הָדָר,
ה שַׁעֲרֵי הַצְלָחָה,
ה שַׁעֲרֵי הַרְוָחָה,
ו שַׁעֲרֵי וַעַד טוֹב,
ו שַׁעֲרֵי וָתִיקוּת,
ז שַׁעֲרֵי זְרִיזוּת,
ז שַׁעֲרֵי זִמְרָה,
ז שַׁעֲרֵי זְכִיּוֹת,
ז שַׁעֲרֵי זִיו,
ז שַׁעֲרֵי זֹהַר תּוֹרָה,
ז שַׁעֲרֵי זֹהַר חָכְמָה,
ז שַׁעֲרֵי זֹהַר בִּינָה,
ז שַׁעֲרֵי זֹהַר דַּעַת,
ח שַׁעֲרֵי חֶדְוָה,
ח שַׁעֲרֵי חֶמְלָה,
ח שַׁעֲרֵי חֵן וָחֶסֶד,
ח שַׁעֲרֵי חַיִּים טוֹבִים,
ח שַׁעֲרֵי חָכְמָה,
ט שַׁעֲרֵי טוֹבָה,
ט שַׁעֲרֵי טֹהַר,
י שַׁעֲרֵי יְשׁוּעָה,
י שַׁעֲרֵי יֹשֶׁר,
כ שַׁעֲרֵי כַפָּרָה,
כ שַׁעֲרֵי כַלְכָּלָה,
כ שַׁעֲרֵי כָבוֹד,
ל שַׁעֲרֵי לִמּוּד,
מ שַׁעֲרֵי מָזוֹן,
מ שַׁעֲרֵי מְנוּחוֹת,
מ שַׁעֲרֵי מְחִילוֹת,
מ שַׁעֲרֵי מַדָּע,
נ שַׁעֲרֵי נֶחָמָה,

ג the gates of celebration,
ג the gates of greatness,
ג the gates of redemption,
ג the gates of power,
ד the gates of excitement,
ד the gates of knowledge,
ה the gates of beauty,
ה the gates of splendor,
ה the gates of success,
ה the gates of relief,
ו the gates of good counsel,
ו the gates of piety,
ז the gates of enthusiasm,
ז the gates of song,
ז the gates of virtues,
ז the gates of radiance,
ז the gates of brilliant Torah,
ז the gates of brilliant wisdom,
ז the gates of brilliant discernment,
ז the gates of brilliant knowledge,
ח the gates of festivity,
ח the gates of mercy,
ח the gates of grace and kindness,
ח the gates of good life,
ח the gates of wisdom,
ט the gates of goodness,
ט the gates of purity,
י the gates of salvation,
י the gates of uprightness,
כ the gates of atonement,
כ the gates of sustenance,
כ the gates of glory,
ל the gates of learning,
מ the gates of nourishment,
מ the gates of rest,
מ the gates of pardon,
מ the gates of information,
נ the gates of consolation,

נ שַׁעֲרֵי נְקִיּוּת,
ס שַׁעֲרֵי סְלִיחָה,
ס שַׁעֲרֵי סִיַּעְתָּא דִשְׁמַיָּא,
ע שַׁעֲרֵי עֶזְרָה,
פ שַׁעֲרֵי פְדוּת,
פ שַׁעֲרֵי פַּרְנָסָה טוֹבָה,
צ שַׁעֲרֵי צְדָקָה,
צ שַׁעֲרֵי צָהֳלָה,
ק שַׁעֲרֵי קְדֻשָּׁה,
ק שַׁעֲרֵי קוֹמְמִיּוּת,
ר שַׁעֲרֵי רַחֲמִים,
ר שַׁעֲרֵי רָצוֹן,
ר שַׁעֲרֵי רְפוּאָה שְׁלֵמָה,
ש שַׁעֲרֵי שָׁלוֹם,
ש שַׁעֲרֵי שִׂמְחָה,
ש שַׁעֲרֵי שְׁמוּעוֹת טוֹבוֹת,
ש שַׁעֲרֵי שַׁלְוָה,
ת שַׁעֲרֵי תוֹרָה,
ת שַׁעֲרֵי תְפִלָּה,
ת שַׁעֲרֵי תְשׁוּבָה,
ת שַׁעֲרֵי תְשׁוּעָה.

E כְּדִכְתִיב, וּתְשׁוּעַת צַדִּיקִים מֵיְיָ מָעוּזָּם בְּעֵת צָרָה. וַיַּעְזְרֵם יְיָ וַיְפַלְּטֵם יְפַלְּטֵם מֵרְשָׁעִים וְיוֹשִׁיעֵם, כִּי חָסוּ בוֹ. וְנֶאֱמַר, חָשַׂף יְיָ אֶת זְרוֹעַ קָדְשׁוֹ לְעֵינֵי כָּל הַגּוֹיִם, וְרָאוּ כָּל אַפְסֵי אָרֶץ אֵת יְשׁוּעַת אֱלֹהֵינוּ. וְנֶאֱמַר, קוֹל צֹפַיִךְ נָשְׂאוּ קוֹל יַחְדָּו יְרַנֵּנוּ, כִּי עַיִן בְּעַיִן יִרְאוּ בְּשׁוּב יְיָ צִיּוֹן.

F וְקַיֵּם לָנוּ יְיָ אֱלֹהֵינוּ מִקְרָא שֶׁכָּתוּב מַה נָּאווּ עַל הֶהָרִים רַגְלֵי מְבַשֵּׂר מַשְׁמִיעַ שָׁלוֹם מְבַשֵּׂר טוֹב מַשְׁמִיעַ יְשׁוּעָה, אֹמֵר לְצִיּוֹן מָלַךְ אֱלֹהָיִךְ. רִאשׁוֹן לְצִיּוֹן הִנֵּה הִנָּם, וְלִירוּשָׁלַיִם מְבַשֵּׂר אֶתֵּן. אָמֵן סֶלָה.

נ the gates of innocence,
ס the gates of forgiveness,
ע the gates of heavenly assistance,
ע the gates of help,
פ the gates of ransom,
פ the gates of good livelihood,
צ the gates of righteousness,
צ the gates of merriment,
ק the gates of holiness,
ק the gates of independence,
ר the gates of compassion,
ר the gates of favor,
ר the gates of complete healing,
ש the gates of peace,
ש the gates of joy,
ש the gates of good reports,
ש the gates of tranquility,
ת the gates of Torah,
ת the gates of prayer,
ת the gates of repentance,
ת the gates of victory.

E As it is written, "The victory of the righteous is from the LORD, who strengthens them in their time of trouble. He will help them, and he will rescue them. He will rescue them from the wicked and save them, because they take refuge in him."[a] And it is said, "The LORD has bared his holy arm in the sight of all the nations, and all those scattered on the earth will see the salvation of our God."[b] And it is said, "The voice of your watchmen—they have raised their voices together. They will sing because they will have seen with their own eyes when the LORD returns to Zion."[c]

F Uphold for us the passage where it is written, "How lovely on the mountains are the feet of the messenger, proclaiming peace, announcing good news, proclaiming salvation, saying to Zion, 'Your God has reigned!'"[d] "The first to Zion: 'Look, here they are!' And I will give a messenger to Jerusalem."[e] Amen, selah.

a) Psalm 37:39–40. b) Isaiah 52:10. c) Isaiah 52:8. d) Isaiah 52:7. e) Isaiah 41:27.

22 סעודתא דדוד

דָּא הִיא סְעוּדָתָא דְדָוִד מַלְכָּא מְשִׁיחָא.

A אַשְׁרֵי הָאֹכֵל לֶחֶם בְּמַלְכוּת הָאֱלֹהִים. בֹּאוּ כִּי הַכֹּל מוּכָן.
נִשְׂמְחָה וְנָגִילָה וְנִתְּנָה לוֹ הַכָּבוֹד כִּי בָאָה חֲתוּנַּת הַשֶּׂה וְאִשְׁתּוֹ
הִתְקַדָּשָׁה. אַשְׁרֵי הַקְּרוּאִים אֶל מִשְׁתֵּה חֲתוּנַּת הַשֶּׂה. רַבִּים יָבֹאוּ
מִמִּזְרָח וּמִמַּעֲרָב וְיָסֵבּוּ עִם אַבְרָהָם וְיִצְחָק וְיַעֲקֹב בְּמַלְכוּת
הַשָּׁמָיִם.

B כַּאֲשֶׁר הֵסֵב עִמָּהֶם וַיִּקַּח אֶת הַלֶּחֶם, וַיְבָרֶךְ וַיִּבְצַע וַיִּתֵּן לָהֶם.
וַתִּפָּקַחְנָה עֵינֵיהֶם וַיַּכִּירֻהוּ, וְהוּא חָמַק עָבַר מֵעֵינֵיהֶם. וַיֹּאמְרוּ
אִישׁ אֶל רֵעֵהוּ, הֲלֹא בֹעֵר הָיָה לְבָבֵנוּ בְּקִרְבֵּנוּ בְּדַבְּרוֹ אֵלֵינוּ
בַּדֶּרֶךְ וַיְּפַתֵּר לָנוּ אֵת הַכְּתוּבִים. וַיָּקוּמוּ בַּשָּׁעָה הַהִיא וַיָּשׁוּבוּ
יְרוּשָׁלַיִם, וַיִּמְצְאוּ אֶת עַשְׁתֵּי הֶעָשָׂר וְאֵת אֲשֶׁר אִתָּם, וְהֵם
נִקְהָלִים יָחַד. וְאֹמְרִים אָכֵן קָם הָאָדוֹן מִן הַמֵּתִים, וְנִרְאָה אֶל
שִׁמְעוֹן. וַיְסַפְּרוּ גַּם הֵם אֵת אֲשֶׁר קָרָם בַּדֶּרֶךְ, וְאֵת אֲשֶׁר הִכִּירֻהוּ
בִּבְצִיעַת הַלָּחֶם.

C דָּוִד מֶלֶךְ יִשְׂרָאֵל חַי וְקַיָּם.

D סִימָן טוֹב וּמַזָּל טוֹב יְהֵא לָנוּ וּלְכָל יִשְׂרָאֵל, אָמֵן.

23 תהילים כג

A מִזְמוֹר לְדָוִד

B יְיָ רֹעִי
לֹא אֶחְסָר:

C בִּנְאוֹת דֶּשֶׁא יַרְבִּיצֵנִי
עַל מֵי מְנֻחוֹת יְנַהֲלֵנִי:

D נַפְשִׁי יְשׁוֹבֵב
יַנְחֵנִי בְמַעְגְּלֵי צֶדֶק
לְמַעַן שְׁמוֹ:

E גַּם כִּי אֵלֵךְ בְּגֵיא צַלְמָוֶת
לֹא אִירָא רָע כִּי אַתָּה עִמָּדִי
שִׁבְטְךָ וּמִשְׁעַנְתֶּךָ הֵמָּה יְנַחֲמֻנִי:

22

The Meal of David

This is the meal of David, the anointed king.

A CONTENTMENT awaits the one who eats bread in the kingdom of God![a] Come, for everything is ready.[b] Let us rejoice and celebrate and give him glory, for the wedding feast of the Lamb has come, and his wife has prepared herself! Contentment awaits those who are invited to the wedding feast of the Lamb! [c] Many will come from the east and from the west and recline with Abraham, Isaac, and Jacob in the kingdom of Heaven.[d]

B When he reclined with them, he took the bread, made a blessing, broke it, and gave it to them. Then their eyes were opened and they recognized him, but he turned aside and passed from their eyes! They said to one another, "Were our hearts not burning within us as he spoke to us on the road and interpreted the Scriptures?" They arose that hour and returned to Jerusalem and found the eleven and those who were with them. They were assembled together, saying, "Surely the Master has risen from the dead and appeared to Shim'on!" They also told what had happened to them on the road and that they recognized him in the breaking of the bread.[e]

C David, king of Israel, lives and endures.

D May there be a good sign and good fortune for us and for all Israel. Amen.

23

Psalm 23

A A hymn of David.

B The LORD is my shepherd;
I will not lack.

C He lays me down in grassy meadows;
he leads me to calm water.

D He restores my soul.
He guides me on paths of righteousness
for his name's sake.

E Though I walk in a death-dark valley,
I will not fear evil, because you are with me.
Your rod and your staff comfort me.

a) Luke 14:15. b) Luke 14:17. c) Revelation 19:7, 9. d) Matthew 8:11. e) Luke 24:30–35.

F תַּעֲרֹךְ לְפָנַי שֻׁלְחָן
נֶגֶד צֹרְרָי

G דִּשַּׁנְתָּ בַשֶּׁמֶן רֹאשִׁי
כּוֹסִי רְוָיָה:

H אַךְ טוֹב וָחֶסֶד יִרְדְּפוּנִי
כָּל יְמֵי חַיָּי

I וְשַׁבְתִּי בְּבֵית יְיָ
לְאֹרֶךְ יָמִים:

24 נטילת ידיים

IF ONE IS EATING BREAD

A **בָּרוּךְ** אַתָּה יְיָ אֱלֹהֵינוּ מֶלֶךְ הָעוֹלָם אֲשֶׁר קִדְּשָׁנוּ בְּמִצְוֹתָיו, וְצִוָּנוּ עַל נְטִילַת יָדָיִם.

25 המוציא

LIFT THE LOAVES OF BREAD

A **נוֹדֶה לְךָ** אָבִינוּ, עַל הַחַיִּים וְעַל הַדַּעַת שֶׁהוֹדַעְתָּנוּ עַל יְדֵי יֵשׁוּעַ עַבְדֶּךָ. לְךָ הַכָּבוֹד לְעוֹלָמִים.

B כְּמוֹ שֶׁהַפַּת הַזֹּאת הָיְתָה נְפוֹצָה עַל הֶהָרִים וְנִקְבְּצָה יַחַד, כֵּן תִּקָּבֵץ קְהִילָּתְךָ מֵאַפְסֵי אָרֶץ אֶל מַלְכוּתֶךָ. כִּי לְךָ הַכָּבוֹד וְהַגְּבוּרָה עַל יְדֵי יֵשׁוּעַ לְעוֹלָמִים.

C **בָּרוּךְ** אַתָּה יְיָ אֱלֹהֵינוּ מֶלֶךְ הָעוֹלָם, הַמּוֹצִיא לֶחֶם מִן הָאָרֶץ.

SHARE AND EAT THE BREAD

26 בורא פרי הגפן

IF ONE IS DRINKING WINE

סַבְרִי—

A **נוֹדֶה לְךָ** אָבִינוּ, עַל הַגֶּפֶן הַקְּדוֹשָׁה לְדָוִד עַבְדֶּךָ שֶׁהוֹדַעְתָּנוּ עַל יְדֵי יֵשׁוּעַ עַבְדֶּךָ. לְךָ הַכָּבוֹד לְעוֹלָמִים.

B **בָּרוּךְ** אַתָּה יְיָ אֱלֹהֵינוּ מֶלֶךְ הָעוֹלָם, בּוֹרֵא פְּרִי הַגָּפֶן.

DRINK THE WINE

For the *Birkat HaMazon*, go to prayer 50, page 94.

F You set a table before me
opposite my tormentors;

G You have moistened my head with oil;
my cup overflows.

H May only goodness and devotion pursue me
all the days of my life,

I And I will dwell in the House of the LORD
for as long as I live.

24 HAND WASHING

IF ONE IS EATING BREAD

A **BLESSED** are you, O LORD, our God, King of the universe, who has sanctified us with his commandments and has commanded us about the washing of hands.

25 BLESSING FOR BREAD

LIFT THE LOAVES OF BREAD

A **WE THANK YOU,** our Father, for the life and for the knowledge that you made known to us through your servant Yeshua. Yours is the glory forever.

B Just as this piece of bread was scattered over the mountains and gathered together, so may your assembly be gathered from the ends of the earth into your kingdom. For yours is the glory and the power through Yeshua forever.[a]

C **BLESSED** are you, O LORD, our God, King of the universe, who brings bread out of the earth.

SHARE AND EAT THE BREAD

26 BLESSING FOR WINE

IF ONE IS DRINKING WINE

With your permission—

A **WE THANK YOU,** our Father, for the holy vine of your servant David that you made known to us through your servant Yeshua. Yours is the glory forever.[b]

B **BLESSED** are you, O LORD, our God, King of the universe, who creates the fruit of the vine.

DRINK THE WINE

For the *Birkat HaMazon* (Grace after Meals), go to prayer 50, page 95.

a) *Didache* 9:3–4. b) *Didache* 9:2.

זמירות לערב שבת

SONGS FOR FRIDAY EVENING

27

חפצה נפשי

MY SOUL DESIRES

A
חָפְצָה נַפְשִׁי לִטְעוֹם אֶת נֹעַם שַׁבָּת,
יָבוֹא בְשָׂרִי אֶל מְנוּחָתוֹ.

B
יִהְיֶה מִדֵּי שַׁבָּת בְּשַׁבַּתּוֹ
כָּל בָּשָׂר בְּשַׁבָּת יָבוֹא לְעִיר קָדְשׁוֹ.
יָבִיא אוֹתָם הָאֵל לְהַר הָאֲרִיאֵל
אֶת כָּל הַמַּחֲזִיקִים בְּאוֹת בְּרִיתוֹ.

C
שָׁבְתוּ בַּשַּׁבָּת כְּפִי הַמִּצְוָה.
מֻתָּר בַּשַּׁבָּת לַעֲשׂוֹת טוֹבָה.
כִּי קֹדֶשׁ הִיא לָכֶם מְסוּרָה בְּיֶדְכֶם,
וְלֹא אַתֶּם מְסוּרִים בְּיָדָהּ.

D
וְשָׁמְרוּ אֶת הַשַּׁבָּת לְדוֹרוֹתָם,
לַעֲשׂוֹת אֶת הַשַּׁבָּת בְּרִית עוֹלָם.
כִּי עֲבָדִים הָיִינוּ וְאֶת יַד יְיָ רָאִינוּ,
וְהוֹצִיאָנוּ אֱלֹהֵי מִשָּׁם.

E
עוֹד נִשְׁאָרָה שַׁבָּת לְעַם הָאֱלֹהִים,
יוֹם שֶׁכֻּלּוֹ שַׁבָּת לְחַיֵּי הָעוֹלָמִים.
מֵעֵין עוֹלָם הַבָּא יוֹם שַׁבָּת מְנוּחָה,
צֵל הִיא לִדְבָרִים שֶׁהֵם עֲדַיִן בָּאִים.

Zemirot for Erev Shabbat

SONGS FOR FRIDAY EVENING

27 Chafetzah Nafshi

MY SOUL DESIRES

A My soul desires to taste the sweet pleasantness of the Sabbath;
My flesh will enter his rest.

B It will be from Sabbath to Sabbath
All flesh on the Sabbath will come to his holy city.
God will bring to Mount Ariel
All who cling to the sign of his covenant.

C They ceased on the Sabbath according to the commandment.
It is permitted on the Sabbath to do good.
For "it is holy to you"—it is committed into your hand,
But you are not committed to its hand.

D They shall keep the Sabbath for their generations,
Making the Sabbath an eternal covenant;
For we were slaves, but we saw the LORD's hand,
And my God took us out from there.

E There still remains a Sabbath for the people of God,
A day that is entirely Sabbath for eternal life.
Sabbath rest is a taste of the world to come;
It is a shadow of things that are yet coming.

28

הדר לבושה

CLOTHED IN BEAUTY

A אָכֵן בְּרוּכָה מִתְּחִילַּת הַבְּרִיאָה,
בְּפִי חֲתָנָהּ מְקוּדֶּשֶׁת בְּשִׂמְחָה,
הָדָר לְבוּשָׁהּ מְתוּקֶּנֶת לְבַעְלָהּ,
הַשַּׁבָּת לִבְנֵי אָדָם נִתְּנָה.

B הָדָר לְבוּשָׁהּ מְתוּקֶּנֶת לְבַעְלָהּ,
הַשַּׁבָּת לִבְנֵי אָדָם נִתְּנָה.

C הַר סִינַי וְעָמְדָה סְגוּלָּתֶךָ,
הוֹרִיד סַפִּירִים נֶאֱמַן בֵּיתֶךָ.
בָּהֶם כָּתוּב "אַתָּה וּבִנְךָ וּבִתֶּךָ".
הַשַּׁבָּת לִבְנֵי אָדָם נִתְּנָה.

D רוֹפְאֵנוּ עָלָה לְסֵפֶר הַנְּבִיאִים.
מָשַׁח יְיָ אֹתִי לְבַשֵּׂר עֲנָוִים.
הַיּוֹם הַדְּבָרִים הָאֵלֶּה נִתְמַלְּאִים.
הַשַּׁבָּת לִבְנֵי אָדָם נִתְּנָה.

E נִשְׂבַּע מִטּוּבוֹ בְּשָׁלֹשׁ סְעוּדוֹת.
נְהַלֵּל אֵת מַלְכֵּנוּ בְּשִׁיר וּבְרָכוֹת.
לַשֻּׁלְחָן בַּמַּלְכוּת עֵינֵינוּ צוֹפוֹת.
הַשַּׁבָּת לִבְנֵי אָדָם נִתְּנָה.

28

Hadar Levushah

CLOTHED IN BEAUTY

A Surely it is blessed from the beginning of creation,
Sanctified (betrothed) with joy by the mouth of her groom.
Clothed in beauty, prepared for her husband,
The Sabbath is given to man.

B Clothed in beauty, prepared for her husband,
The Sabbath is given to man.

C At Mount Sinai stood your treasure;
The faithful of the house brought down sapphires.
Upon them was written, "You, your son, and your daughter."
The Sabbath is given to man.

D Our healer ascended to the scroll of the prophets,
The LORD has anointed me to bring good news to the poor.
Today these words are fulfilled.
The Sabbath is given to man.

E Let us be satisfied from his goodness with three meals.
Let us praise our King with song and blessings,
Our eyes anticipating the table in the kingdom.
The Sabbath is given to man.

29

מה ידידות מנוחתך

HOW BELOVED IS YOUR REST

A מַה יְּדִידוּת מְנוּחָתֵךְ, אַתְּ שַׁבָּת הַמַּלְכָּה.
בְּכֵן נָרוּץ לִקְרָאתֵךְ, בּוֹאִי כַלָּה נְסוּכָה.
לְבוּשׁ בִּגְדֵי חֲמוּדוֹת, לְהַדְלִיק נֵר בִּבְרָכָה.
וַתֵּכֶל כָּל הָעֲבוֹדוֹת, לֹא תַעֲשׂוּ מְלָאכָה.

B לְהִתְעַנֵּג בְּתַעֲנוּגִים, בַּרְבּוּרִים וּשְׂלָיו וְדָגִים.

C מֵעֶרֶב מַזְמִינִים, כָּל מִינֵי מַטְעַמִּים.
מִבְּעוֹד יוֹם מוּכָנִים, תַּרְנְגוֹלִים מְפֻטָּמִים.
וְלַעֲרוֹךְ כַּמָּה מִינִים, שְׁתוֹת יֵינוֹת מְבֻשָּׂמִים.
וְתַפְנוּקֵי מַעֲדַנִּים, בְּכָל שָׁלֹשׁ פְּעָמִים.

D נַחֲלַת יַעֲקֹב יִירָשׁ, בְּלִי מְצָרִים נַחֲלָה.
וִיכַבְּדוּהוּ עָשִׁיר וָרָשׁ, וְתִזְכּוּ לִגְאֻלָּה.
יוֹם שַׁבָּת אִם תִּשְׁמֹרוּ, וִהְיִיתֶם לִי סְגֻלָּה.
שֵׁשֶׁת יָמִים תַּעֲבֹדוּ, וּבַשְּׁבִיעִי נָגִילָה.

E חֲפָצֶיךָ אֲסוּרִים, וְגַם לַחֲשׁוֹב חֶשְׁבּוֹנוֹת.
הִרְהוּרִים מֻתָּרִים, וּלְשַׁדֵּךְ הַבָּנוֹת.
וְתִינוֹק לְלַמְּדוֹ סֵפֶר, לַמְנַצֵּחַ בִּנְגִינוֹת.
וְלַהֲגוֹת בְּאִמְרֵי שֶׁפֶר, בְּכָל פִּנּוֹת וּמַחֲנוֹת.

F הִלּוּכָךְ תְּהֵא בְנַחַת, עֹנֶג קְרָא לַשַּׁבָּת.
וְהַשֵּׁנָה מְשֻׁבַּחַת, כְּדַת נֶפֶשׁ מְשִׁיבַת.
בְּכֵן נַפְשִׁי לְךָ עָרְגָה, וְלָנוּחַ בְּחִבַּת.
כַּשּׁוֹשַׁנִּים סוּגָה, בּוֹ יָנוּחוּ בֵּן וּבַת.

G מֵעֵין עוֹלָם הַבָּא, יוֹם שַׁבָּת מְנוּחָה.
כָּל הַמִּתְעַנְּגִים בָּהּ, יִזְכּוּ לְרוֹב שִׂמְחָה.
מֵחֶבְלֵי מָשִׁיחַ, יֻצָּלוּ לִרְוָחָה.
פְּדוּתֵנוּ תַצְמִיחַ, וְנָס יָגוֹן וַאֲנָחָה.

29

MAH YEDIDUT MENUCHATECH

HOW BELOVED IS YOUR REST

A How beloved is your rest, you Sabbath Queen.
Thus, we will run to greet you: "Come, O royal bride!"
Clothed in fancy garments, lighting a candle with a blessing,
And all the labors end: "You shall not do any work."

B To take pleasure in delights: fattened poultry, fowl, and fish.

C The prior day, we make all kinds of savory dishes;
While it is yet daytime, we prepare fattened chickens.
We set out a variety of food, drinking aromatic wines,
And indulging in delicacies, all three times.

D He will possess Jacob's inheritance, an inheritance without limits;
Rich and poor will honor it, and they will merit redemption.
If you keep the Sabbath day, you will be my treasure;
For six days, you may labor, but on the seventh, rejoice.

E Personal desires are forbidden, and reckoning accounts;
Contemplation is permitted, as well as arranging matches.
To teach a book to a child, to chant the Psalms,
And to engage in uplifting words, in any corner or camp.

F Walk with enjoyment; call the Sabbath a delight!
It is praiseworthy to sleep sufficiently to restore the soul.
So my soul thirsts for you, and to rest with love;
Fenced in like a flower garden, sons and daughters rest on it.

G The Sabbath day rest is a foretaste of the world to come;
All who delight in it will merit great joy.
They will be rescued to safety from the birth pangs of Messiah;
Our ransom will sprout forth, and sorrow and grief will flee.

30

מנוחה ושמחה

REST AND GLADNESS

A מְנוּחָה וְשִׂמְחָה, אוֹר לַיְּהוּדִים,
יוֹם שַׁבָּתוֹן, יוֹם מַחֲמַדִּים,
שׁוֹמְרָיו וְזוֹכְרָיו, הֵמָּה מְעִידִים,
כִּי לְשִׁשָּׁה כֹּל בְּרוּאִים וְעוֹמְדִים.

B שְׁמֵי שָׁמַיִם, אֶרֶץ וְיַמִּים,
כָּל צְבָא מָרוֹם גְּבוֹהִים וְרָמִים,
תַּנִּין וְאָדָם וְחַיַּת רְאֵמִים,
כִּי בְּיָהּ יְיָ צוּר עוֹלָמִים.

C הוּא אֲשֶׁר דִּבֶּר לְעַם סְגֻלָּתוֹ,
שָׁמוֹר לְקַדְּשׁוֹ מִבּוֹאוֹ וְעַד צֵאתוֹ,
שַׁבַּת קֹדֶשׁ, יוֹם חֶמְדָּתוֹ,
כִּי בוֹ שָׁבַת אֵל מִכָּל מְלַאכְתּוֹ.

D בְּמִצְוַת שַׁבָּת אֵל יַחֲלִיצָךְ,
קוּם קְרָא אֵלָיו, יָחִישׁ לְאַמְּצָךְ,
נִשְׁמַת כָּל חַי וְגַם נַעֲרִיצָךְ,
אֱכוֹל בְּשִׂמְחָה, כִּי כְבָר רָצָךְ.

E בְּמִשְׁנֶה לֶחֶם וְקִדּוּשׁ רַבָּה,
בְּרֹב מַטְעַמִּים וְרוּחַ נְדִיבָה,
יִזְכּוּ לְרַב טוּב הַמִּתְעַנְּגִים בָּהּ,
בְּבִיאַת גּוֹאֵל לְחַיֵּי הָעוֹלָם הַבָּא.

30

Menuchah Vesimchah

REST AND GLADNESS

A Rest and gladness, light for the Jews,
A day of ceasing, a day of delights.
Those who keep it and remember it testify
That in six days everything was created and remains.

B The highest heavens, land and seas,
Every legion above, high and lofty,
Sea giants, mankind, and the wild beasts
Testify that the LORD is the Creator of all.

C He who instructed his treasured people,
"Take care to sanctify it from beginning to end,"
The holy Sabbath is the day of his delight;
For God rested on it from all his creative activity.

D With the commandment of the Sabbath, God will fortify you.
Arise, call to him; he will hasten to strengthen you!
Singing "The breath of all living" as well as "We will esteem you,"
Eat joyfully, for he has already shown favor.

E With the double loaves and the Great Kiddush,
With an abundance of delicacies and a willing spirit,
The one who delights in it will merit abundant goodness
When the redeemer comes, for the life of the world to come.

31

יה אכסוף

LORD, I LONG

A

יָהּ אֶכְסֹף נֹעַם שַׁבָּת,
הַמַּתְאֶמֶת וּמִתְאַחֶדֶת בִּסְגֻלָּתֶךָ.
מְשֹׁךְ נֹעַם יִרְאָתְךָ,
לְעַם מְבַקְשֵׁי רְצוֹנֶךָ.
קַדְּשֵׁם בִּקְדֻשַּׁת הַשַּׁבָּת,
הַמִּתְאַחֶדֶת בְּתוֹרָתֶךָ.
פְּתַח לָהֶם נֹעַם וְרָצוֹן,
לִפְתּוֹחַ שַׁעֲרֵי רְצוֹנֶךָ.

B

יָהּ אֶכְסֹף נֹעַם שַׁבָּת,
הַמַּתְאֶמֶת וּמִתְאַחֶדֶת בִּסְגֻלָּתֶךָ.

C

הָיָה הֹוֶה, שְׁמוֹר שׁוֹמְרֵי
וּמְצַפִּים שַׁבַּת קָדְשֶׁךָ.
כְּאַיָּל תַּעֲרֹג עַל אֲפִיקֵי מָיִם,
כֵּן נַפְשָׁם תַּעֲרֹג
לְקַבֵּל נֹעַם שַׁבָּת
הַמִּתְאַחֶדֶת בְּשֵׁם קָדְשֶׁךָ.
הַצֵּל מְאַחֲרֵי לִפְרֹשׁ מִן הַשַּׁבָּת,
לְבִלְתִּי תִּהְיֶה סָגוּר מֵהֶם
שִׁשָּׁה יָמִים הַמְקַבְּלִים קְדֻשָּׁה.
מִשַּׁבַּת קָדְשֶׁךָ
וְטַהֵר לִבָּם בֶּאֱמֶת
וּבֶאֱמוּנָה לְעָבְדֶךָ.

D

וְיִהְיוּ רַחֲמֶיךָ מִתְגּוֹלְלִים
עַל עַם קָדְשֶׁךָ,
לְהַשְׁקוֹת צְמֵאֵי חַסְדֶּךָ.
מִנָּהָר הַיּוֹצֵא מֵעֵדֶן,
לְעַטֵּר אֶת יִשְׂרָאֵל בְּתִפְאֶרֶת,
הַמְפָאֲרִים אוֹתְךָ
עַל יְדֵי שַׁבַּת קָדְשֶׁךָ,
כָּל שִׁשָּׁה יָמִים לְהַנְחִילָם
נַחֲלַת יַעֲקֹב בְּחִירֶךָ.

31

Yah Echsof

LORD, I LONG

A LORD, I long for the sweetness of the Sabbath
That resembles and unifies with your treasure.
Draw the sweetness of your fear
To the nation that seeks your will.
Sanctify them with the holiness of the Sabbath
That unifies with your Torah.
Unlock for them sweetness and willingness
That they may open the gates of your favor.

B LORD, I long for the sweetness of the Sabbath
That resembles and unifies with your treasure.

C He Who Was and Is, protect those who protect
And anticipate your holy Sabbath.
As a deer longs for streams of water,
So their soul longs to receive the sweetness
Of the Sabbath, which unifies
With your holy name.
Rescue those who delay parting from the Sabbath
That it may not be closed off from them
During the six days that receive holiness
From your holy Sabbath.
And purify their heart with truth
And with faith to serve you.

D May your compassions flow like waves
Over your holy people,
To give drink to those who thirst for your devotion.
From the river that comes forth from Eden;
To crown Israel with majesty,
Those who glorify you
Through your holy Sabbath;
All six days, to let them inherit
The inheritance of Jacob, your chosen one.

E הַשַּׁבָּת נֹעַם הַנְּשָׁמוֹת,
וְהַשְּׁבִיעִי עֹנֶג הָרוּחוֹת
וְעֵדֶן הַנְּפָשׁוֹת,
לְהִתְעַדֵּן בְּאַהֲבָתְךָ וְיִרְאָתֶךָ.
שַׁבָּת קֹדֶשׁ נַפְשִׁי חוֹלַת אַהֲבָתֶךָ.
שַׁבָּת קֹדֶשׁ נַפְשׁוֹת יִשְׂרָאֵל
בְּצֵל כְּנָפֶיךָ יֶחֱסָיוּן,
יִרְוְיֻן מִדֶּשֶׁן בֵּיתֶךָ.

32

יה רבון עלם

LORD, MASTER OF THE WORLD

A יָהּ רִבּוֹן עָלַם וְעָלְמַיָּא,
אַנְתְּ הוּא מַלְכָּא מֶלֶךְ מַלְכַיָּא.
עוֹבַד גְּבוּרְתֵּךְ וְתִמְהַיָּא,
שְׁפַר קֳדָמָךְ לְהַחֲוָיָא.

B יָהּ רִבּוֹן עָלַם וְעָלְמַיָּא,
אַנְתְּ הוּא מַלְכָּא מֶלֶךְ מַלְכַיָּא.

C שְׁבָחִין אֲסַדֵּר צַפְרָא וְרַמְשָׁא,
לָךְ אֱלָהָא קַדִּישָׁא דִּי בְרָא כָּל נַפְשָׁא.
עִירִין קַדִּישִׁין וּבְנֵי אֱנָשָׁא,
חֵיוַת בָּרָא וְעוֹפֵי שְׁמַיָּא.

D רַבְרְבִין עוֹבְדֵיךְ וְתַקִּיפִין,
מָכִיךְ רָמַיָּא וְזָקִיף כְּפִיפִין.
לוּ יִחְיֶה גְבַר שְׁנִין אַלְפִין,
לָא יֵעוֹל גְּבוּרְתֵּךְ בְּחֻשְׁבְּנַיָּא.

E אֱלָהָא דִּי לֵהּ יְקַר וּרְבוּתָא,
פְּרוֹק יַת עָנָךְ מִפּוּם אַרְיְוָתָא.
וְאַפֵּיק יַת עַמֵּךְ מִגּוֹ גָלוּתָא,
עַמֵּךְ דִּי בְחַרְתְּ מִכָּל אֻמַּיָּא.

F לְמִקְדָּשֵׁךְ תּוּב וּלְקֹדֶשׁ קֻדְשִׁין,
אֲתַר דִּי בֵהּ יֶחֱדוּן רוּחִין וְנַפְשִׁין.
וִיזַמְּרוּן לָךְ שִׁירִין וְרַחֲשִׁין,
בִּירוּשְׁלֵם קַרְתָּא דְשׁוּפְרַיָּא.

E The Sabbath is the sweetness of our souls,
And the seventh day is the delight of our spirits
and the pleasure of our lives,
To take pleasure in your love and fear.
Holy Sabbath, my soul is lovesick for you.
Holy Sabbath, the lives of Israel
Take refuge in the shadow of your wings;
They drink deeply of the richness of your house.

32 Yah Ribbon Alam

LORD, MASTER OF THE WORLD

A LORD, master of every world,
You are the King, the King of kings.
Your works of power and wonder—
It is fitting to proclaim them before you.

B LORD, master of every world,
You are the King, the King of kings.

C I will arrange praises morning and evening
To you, holy God who created all life:
Holy angels, human beings,
Beasts of the field, and birds of the sky.

D Your works are very great and mighty;
You humble the proud and straighten the bent.
Even if a man lived a thousand years,
He could not possibly comprehend your power.

E God, to whom is all honor and greatness,
Rescue your flock from the mouth of lions,
And remove your people from the midst of exile,
The people that you chose out of all nations.

F Return to your Sanctuary and to the holy of holies,
The place in which our spirits and souls delight,
And we will sing songs and praises to you
In Jerusalem, the city of beauty.

33

צור משלו אכלנו

THE CREATOR WHOSE FOOD WE HAVE EATEN

A צוּר מִשֶּׁלּוֹ אָכַלְנוּ,
בָּרְכוּ אֱמוּנַי,
שָׂבַעְנוּ וְהוֹתַרְנוּ,
כִּדְבַר יְיָ.

B הַזָּן אֶת עוֹלָמוֹ,
רוֹעֵנוּ אָבִינוּ,
אָכַלְנוּ אֶת לַחְמוֹ,
וְיֵינוֹ שָׁתִינוּ.

C עַל כֵּן נוֹדֶה לִשְׁמוֹ,
וּנְהַלְלוֹ בְּפִינוּ,
אָמַרְנוּ וְעָנִינוּ,
אֵין קָדוֹשׁ כַּייָ.

D בְּשִׁיר וְקוֹל תּוֹדָה,
נְבָרֵךְ לֵאלֹהֵינוּ,
עַל אֶרֶץ חֶמְדָּה טוֹבָה,
שֶׁהִנְחִיל לַאֲבוֹתֵינוּ.

E מָזוֹן וְצֵדָה,
הִשְׂבִּיעַ לְנַפְשֵׁנוּ,
חַסְדּוֹ גָּבַר עָלֵינוּ,
וֶאֱמֶת יְיָ.

F רַחֵם בְּחַסְדֶּךָ,
עַל עַמְּךָ צוּרֵנוּ,
עַל צִיּוֹן מִשְׁכַּן כְּבוֹדֶךָ,
זְבוּל בֵּית תִּפְאַרְתֵּנוּ.

G בֶּן דָּוִד עַבְדֶּךָ,
יָבֹא וְיִגְאָלֵנוּ,
רוּחַ אַפֵּינוּ,
מְשִׁיחַ יְיָ.

33

Tzur Mishelo Achalnu

THE CREATOR WHOSE FOOD WE HAVE EATEN

A The Creator whose food we have eaten:
Bless him, faithful friends!
We are satisfied and have extra,
According to the LORD's word.

B The one who nourishes his world,
Our shepherd, our Father:
We ate his bread
And drank his wine.

C Therefore, let us give thanks to his name
And praise him with our mouths.
We have said and repeated:
There is none as holy as the LORD.

D Singing and voicing our thanks,
Let us bless our God
For the pleasant, good, and spacious land
That he gave as an inheritance to our fathers.

E With food and meat
He satisfied our souls;
He has asserted his devotion toward us,
And the LORD is true.

F Have compassion in your devoted kindness
On your people, our Creator,
On Zion, the dwelling place of your glory,
The domain of our majestic house.

G May the Son of David, your servant,
Come and redeem us,
The breath of our nostrils,
The Messiah of the LORD.

H יִבָּנֶה הַמִּקְדָּשׁ,
עִיר צִיּוֹן תְּמַלֵּא,
וְשָׁם נָשִׁיר שִׁיר חָדָשׁ,
וּבִרְנָנָה נַעֲלֶה.

I הָרַחֲמָן הַנִּקְדָּשׁ,
יִתְבָּרַךְ וְיִתְעַלֶּה,
עַל כּוֹס יַיִן מָלֵא,
כְּבִרְכַּת יְיָ.

34 יום זה לישראל
THIS DAY FOR ISRAEL

A יוֹם זֶה לְיִשְׂרָאֵל אוֹרָה וְשִׂמְחָה, שַׁבַּת מְנוּחָה.

B צִוִּיתָ פִּקּוּדִים בְּמַעֲמַד הַר סִינַי,
שַׁבָּת וּמוֹעֲדִים לִשְׁמוֹר בְּכָל שָׁנַי,
לַעֲרֹךְ לְפָנַי מַשְׂאֵת וַאֲרוּחָה,
שַׁבַּת מְנוּחָה.

C חֶמְדַּת הַלְּבָבוֹת לְאֻמָּה שְׁבוּרָה,
לִנְפָשׁוֹת נִכְאָבוֹת נְשָׁמָה יְתֵרָה,
לְנֶפֶשׁ מְצֵרָה תָּסִיר אֲנָחָה,
שַׁבַּת מְנוּחָה.

D קִדַּשְׁתָּ בֵּרַכְתָּ אוֹתוֹ מִכָּל יָמִים,
בְּשֵׁשֶׁת כִּלִּיתָ מְלֶאכֶת עוֹלָמִים,
בּוֹ מָצְאוּ עֲגוּמִים הַשְׁקֵט וּבִטְחָה,
שַׁבַּת מְנוּחָה.

E לְאִסּוּר מְלָאכָה צִוִּיתָנוּ נוֹרָא,
אֶזְכֶּה הוֹד מְלוּכָה אִם שַׁבָּת אֶשְׁמְרָה,
אַקְרִיב שַׁי לַמּוֹרָא, מִנְחָה מֶרְקָחָה,
שַׁבַּת מְנוּחָה.

F חַדֵּשׁ מִקְדָּשֵׁנוּ זָכְרָה נֶחֱרֶבֶת,
טוּבְךָ, מוֹשִׁיעֵנוּ, תְּנָה לַנֶּעֱצֶבֶת,
בְּשַׁבָּת יוֹשֶׁבֶת בְּזֶמֶר וּשְׁבָחָה,
שַׁבַּת מְנוּחָה.

H May the Temple be built;
Fill the city of Zion!
There we will sing a new song,
And ascend, cheering.

I May the sanctified, Compassionate One
Be blessed and exalted
Over a full cup of wine,
In accordance with the LORD's blessing.

34 YOM ZEH LEYISRA'EL

THIS DAY FOR ISRAEL

A This day for Israel is light and gladness, a Sabbath of rest.

B You commanded decrees at Mount Sinai,
Sabbath and festivals to keep as long as I live;
To spread before myself courses and festive meals,
A Sabbath of rest.

C It is cherished in the hearts of the broken nation;
For pained lives, an additional soul.
For a troubled life, it alleviates the sorrow,
A Sabbath of rest.

D You sanctified and blessed it more than other days.
In six days you finished the creation of the world.
On it, those who grieve find stillness and assurance,
A Sabbath of rest.

E You commanded us, prohibiting creative activity, Awesome One.
I will merit royal beauty if I keep the Sabbath.
I bring tribute to the Fearsome One, an aromatic offering,
A Sabbath of rest.

F Restore our Temple; remember the destroyed one.
Send your goodness, our Savior, to the grieved one,
Who spends the Sabbath singing and praising,
A Sabbath of rest.

35

לחם במלכות שמים

BREAD IN THE KINGDOM OF HEAVEN

A
אַשְׁרֵי מִי שֶׁיֹּאכַל לֶחֶם
בְּמַלְכוּת שָׁמַיִם.

B
אֵת אֲשֶׁר אוֹפֶה אָפִיתִי,
אֵת אֲשֶׁר אֲבַשֵּׁל בִּשַּׁלְתִּי,
וּבִזְכוּת זֶה טַעַם אֶטְעַם,
מִן הַמָּן הַגָּנוּז.

C
הַכּוֹס מָלֵא בְּיַיִן טוֹב אָדוֹם,
הֵרַמְתִּי בֵּרַכְתִּי וְקִדַּשְׁתִּי אֵת הַיּוֹם,
וּבִזְכוּת זֶה שָׁתֹה אֶשְׁתֶּה,
חָדָשׁ בְּמַלְכוּת אָבִי.

D
רַבִּים אוֹרְחִים הִזְמַנְתִּי לְהָסֵב,
רְחֹבוֹת וְחוּצוֹת מִזְרַח וּמַעֲרַב,
וּבִזְכוּת זֶה אָכֹל אֹכַל,
עִם אַבְרָהָם יִצְחַק וְיַעֲקֹב.

E
נְדַבְּרָה נָא דִבְרֵי תוֹרָה,
נִשְׁמַע בְּלֵב בּוֹעֵר חָכְמָה,
וּבִזְכוּת זֶה הַכֵּר נַכִּירוֹ,
בִּבְצִיעַת הַלֶּחֶם.

35

LECHEM BEMALCHUT SHAMAYIM

BREAD IN THE KINGDOM OF HEAVEN

A Blessed is he who will eat bread
in the kingdom of Heaven!

B I have baked what I will bake,
I have boiled what I will boil.
So may I merit to receive
Some of the hidden manna.

C My cup is full with good and pleasant wine;
I lift it and bless and sanctify the time.
So may I merit to drink it
New in my Father's kingdom.

D I went out inviting many guests,
To highways and byways, to the east and to the west.
So may I merit to recline
With Abraham, Isaac, and Jacob.

E Let us sit with Torah to learn
And hear the word with hearts that burn.
So may we merit to recognize him
In the breaking of the bread.

זמירות ליום שבת

SONGS FOR SATURDAY MORNING

36 ברוך אל עליון

BLESSED IS THE SUPREME GOD

A בָּרוּךְ אֵל עֶלְיוֹן אֲשֶׁר נָתַן מְנוּחָה,
לְנַפְשֵׁנוּ פִּדְיוֹן מִשֵּׁאת וַאֲנָחָה,
וְהוּא יִדְרוֹשׁ לְצִיּוֹן עִיר הַנִּדָּחָה,
עַד אָנָה תּוּגְיוֹן נֶפֶשׁ נֶאֱנָחָה.

B הַשּׁוֹמֵר שַׁבָּת הַבֵּן עִם הַבַּת,
לָאֵל יֵרָצוּ כְּמִנְחָה עַל מַחֲבַת.

C רוֹכֵב בָּעֲרָבוֹת מֶלֶךְ עוֹלָמִים,
אֶת עַמּוֹ לִשְׁבּוֹת אִזֵּן בַּנְּעִימִים,
בְּמַאֲכָלֵי עֲרֵבוֹת בְּמִינֵי מַטְעַמִּים,
בְּמַלְבּוּשֵׁי כָבוֹד זֶבַח מִשְׁפָּחָה.

D וְאַשְׁרֵי כָּל חוֹכֶה לְתַשְׁלוּמֵי כֵפֶל,
מֵאֵת כָּל סוֹכֶה שׁוֹכֵן בָּעֲרָפֶל,
נַחֲלָה לוֹ יִזְכֶּה בָּהָר וּבַשָּׁפֶל,
נַחֲלָה וּמְנוּחָה כַּשֶּׁמֶשׁ לוֹ זָרְחָה.

E כָּל שׁוֹמֵר שַׁבָּת כַּדָּת מֵחַלְּלוֹ,
הֵן הֶכְשַׁר חִבַּת קֹדֶשׁ גּוֹרָלוֹ,
וְאִם יֵצֵא חוֹבַת הַיּוֹם אַשְׁרֵי לוֹ,
אֶל אֵל אָדוֹן מְחוֹלְלוֹ מִנְחָה הִיא שְׁלוּחָה.

F חֶמְדַּת הַיָּמִים קְרָאוֹ אֵלִי צוּר,
וְאַשְׁרֵי לִתְמִימִים אִם יִהְיֶה נָצוּר,
כֶּתֶר הִלּוּמִים עַל רֹאשָׁם יָצוּר,
צוּר הָעוֹלָמִים רוּחוֹ בָּם נָחָה.

Zemirot for Yom Shabbat

SONGS FOR SATURDAY MORNING

36 Baruch El Elyon

BLESSED IS THE SUPREME GOD

A Blessed is the supreme God who gave rest,
Ransom for our souls from devastation and sorrow.
And he will search after Zion, the outcast city;
When will the sorrowful soul's grief end?

B When a person keeps the Sabbath, whether a woman or a man,
God is pleased with it like a grain offering in a pan.

C He who rides upon the heavens, the King of the ages,
He pleasantly announced for his people to cease.
With sweet foods, with a variety of delicacies,
With honorable raiment, a family's offering.

D Contentment awaits all who wait for the double payment,
From the one who sees all, dwelling in the thick darkness,
He will merit an inheritance on the mountain and lowlands,
An inheritance and resting place like the one for whom the sun shone.

E Whoever properly keeps the Sabbath from being profaned,
His lot is to be qualified for an affinity to holiness.
If he meets the day's duties, contentment awaits him,
It is an offering to God, the master who made him.

F My God, the Creator, called it the most cherished of days,
And contentment awaits the wholehearted if it is safeguarded.
He will fashion a suitable crown for their heads,
The Creator of all, his Spirit will rest upon them.

G זָכוֹר אֶת יוֹם הַשַּׁבָּת לְקַדְּשׁוֹ,
קַרְנוֹ כִּי גָבְהָה נֵזֶר עַל רֹאשׁוֹ,
עַל כֵּן יִתֵּן הָאָדָם לְנַפְשׁוֹ,
עֹנֶג וְגַם שִׂמְחָה בָּהֶם לְמָשְׁחָה.

H קֹדֶשׁ הִיא לָכֶם שַׁבָּת הַמַּלְכָּה,
אֶל תּוֹךְ בָּתֵּיכֶם לְהָנִיחַ בְּרָכָה,
בְּכָל מוֹשְׁבוֹתֵיכֶם לֹא תַעֲשׂוּ מְלָאכָה,
בְּנֵיכֶם וּבְנוֹתֵיכֶם עֶבֶד וְגַם שִׁפְחָה.

37 כי אשמרה שבת

IF I KEEP THE SABBATH

A כִּי אֶשְׁמְרָה שַׁבָּת אֵל יִשְׁמְרֵנִי,
אוֹת הִיא לְעוֹלְמֵי עַד בֵּינוֹ וּבֵינִי.

B אָסוּר מְצֹא חֵפֶץ לַעֲשׂוֹת דְּרָכִים,
גַּם מִלְּדַבֵּר בּוֹ דִּבְרֵי צְרָכִים,
דִּבְרֵי סְחוֹרָה אוֹ דִּבְרֵי מְלָכִים,
אֶהְגֶּה בְּתוֹרַת אֵל וּתְחַכְּמֵנִי.

C בּוֹ אֶמְצְאָה תָמִיד נֹוחַ לְנַפְשִׁי,
הִנֵּה לְדוֹר רִאשׁוֹן נָתַן קְדוֹשִׁי,
מוֹפֵת בְּתֵת לֶחֶם מִשְׁנֶה בַּשִּׁשִּׁי,
כָּכָה בְּכָל שִׁשִּׁי יַכְפִּיל מְזוֹנִי.

D רָשַׁם בְּדַת הָאֵל חֹק אֶל סְגָנָיו,
בּוֹ לַעֲרֹךְ לֶחֶם פָּנִים לְפָנָיו,
עַל כֵּן לְהִתְעַנּוֹת בּוֹ עַל פִּי נְבוֹנָיו,
אָסוּר לְבַד מִיּוֹם כִּפּוּר עֲוֹנִי.

E הַיּוֹם מְכֻבָּד הוּא יוֹם תַּעֲנוּגִים,
לֶחֶם וְיַיִן טוֹב בָּשָׂר וְדָגִים,
הַשְּׂמֵחִים בּוֹ הֵם שִׂמְחָה מַשִּׂיגִים,
כִּי יוֹם שְׂמָחוֹת הוּא וּתְשַׂמְּחֵנִי.

F מֵחֵל מְלָאכָה בּוֹ סוֹפוֹ לְהַכְרִית,
עַל כֵּן אֲכַבֵּס בּוֹ לִבִּי כְּבוֹרִית,
אֶתְפַּלְּלָה אֶל אֵל עַרְבִית וְשַׁחֲרִית,
מוּסָף וְגַם מִנְחָה הוּא יַעֲנֵנִי.

G Remember the Sabbath day, to sanctify it.
If one does so, his honor will be bestowed as a royal headpiece.
Therefore let each man provide for himself
Delight and joy with which to be anointed.

H The Sabbath queen is holy for you,
To let blessing rest in the midst of your homes.
Do not do creative activity in all your dwelling places,
Neither sons nor daughters, slaves or maidservants.

37 KI ESHMERAH SHABBAT

IF I KEEP THE SABBATH

A If I keep the Sabbath, God will keep me.
It is a sign forever between him and me.

B It is forbidden to do as you please or make your way,
Or even to speak about matters of necessity,
Matters of commerce, or political issues.
I will ponder God's Torah, and it will make me wise.

C On it may I always find comfort for my soul.
To the first generation, the Holy One gave a sign
By giving them double bread on the sixth day.
So too, on every sixth day, may he multiply my food.

D God wrote his instruction, a statute for his deputies,
To arrange the Bread of the Presence before him.
Therefore, fasting on the Sabbath (according to his wise ones),
Is forbidden, except on the Day of Atonement for my iniquity.

E This is an honored day, a day of delights:
Bread and good wine, meat and fish.
Those who rejoice on it truly apprehend joy,
For it is a day of joys, and it will make me joyful.

F Profaning it with forbidden activity leads to excision.
Therefore, I will cleanse my heart as if with soap.
I will pray to God *Ma'ariv* and *Shacharit*,
Musaf and *Minchah*; he will answer me.

38

יום שבתון

DAY OF CEASING

A יוֹם שַׁבָּתוֹן אֵין לִשְׁכֹּחַ,
זִכְרוֹ כְּרֵיחַ הַנִּיחֹוחַ,
יוֹנָה מָצְאָה בוֹ מָנוֹחַ,
וְשָׁם יָנוּחוּ יְגִיעֵי כֹחַ.

B יוֹנָה מָצְאָה בוֹ מָנוֹחַ,
וְשָׁם יָנוּחוּ יְגִיעֵי כֹחַ.

C הַיּוֹם נִכְבָּד לִבְנֵי אֱמוּנִים,
זְהִירִים לְשָׁמְרוֹ אָבוֹת וּבָנִים,
חָקוּק בִּשְׁנֵי לֻחוֹת אֲבָנִים,
מֵרֹב אוֹנִים וְאַמִּיץ כֹּחַ.

D וּבָאוּ כֻלָּם בִּבְרִית יַחַד,
נַעֲשֶׂה וְנִשְׁמַע אָמְרוּ כְּאֶחָד,
וּפָתְחוּ וְעָנוּ יְיָ אֶחָד,
בָּרוּךְ הַנּוֹתֵן לַיָּעֵף כֹּחַ.

E דִּבֶּר בְּקָדְשׁוֹ בְּהַר הַמֹּר,
יוֹם הַשְּׁבִיעִי זָכוֹר וְשָׁמוֹר,
וְכָל פִּקּוּדָיו יַחַד לִגְמֹר,
חַזֵּק מָתְנַיִם וְאַמֵּץ כֹּחַ.

F הָעָם אֲשֶׁר נָע כַּצֹּאן תָּעָה,
יִזְכּוֹר לְפָקְדוֹ בִּבְרִית וּשְׁבוּעָה,
לְבַל יַעֲבָר בָּם מִקְרֵי רָעָה,
כַּאֲשֶׁר נִשְׁבַּעְתָּ עַל מֵי נֹחַ.

38

Yom Shabbaton

DAY OF CEASING

A There is no forgetting the day of ceasing;
Its remembrance is like a pleasing aroma.
On it a dove found comfort,
And it is where those who are weary will rest.

B On it a dove found comfort,
And it is where those who are weary will rest.

C This day is honored by the faithful;
Both fathers and sons are careful to observe it.
It was engraved in the two stone tablets
By the Great in Power and Firm in Strength.

D They all entered a covenant together:
"We will do, and we will heed," they said as one.
They opened their mouths and responded, "The LORD is one!"
Blessed is he who gives strength to the weary.

E He spoke in his holiness on the Mount of Myrrh:
Remember and keep the seventh day
To complete all its precepts together.
Brace yourself, and gather your strength!

F The nation that traveled like a wandering flock
May he remember it in covenant and oath,
So that no evil incident should happen to them,
Just as you swore at the waters of Noah.

39

יום זה מכובד

THIS DAY IS HONORED

A יוֹם זֶה מְכֻבָּד מִכָּל יָמִים,
כִּי בוֹ שָׁבַת צוּר עוֹלָמִים.

B שֵׁשֶׁת יָמִים תַּעֲשֶׂה מְלַאכְתֶּךָ,
וְיוֹם הַשְּׁבִיעִי לֵאלֹהֶיךָ,
שַׁבָּת לֹא תַעֲשֶׂה בוֹ מְלָאכָה,
כִּי כֹל עָשָׂה שֵׁשֶׁת יָמִים.

C רִאשׁוֹן הוּא לְמִקְרָאֵי קֹדֶשׁ,
יוֹם שַׁבָּתוֹן יוֹם שַׁבַּת קֹדֶשׁ,
עַל כֵּן כָּל אִישׁ בְּיֵינוֹ יְקַדֵּשׁ,
עַל שְׁתֵּי לֶחֶם יִבְצְעוּ תְמִימִים.

D אֱכוֹל מַשְׁמַנִּים שְׁתֵה מַמְתַּקִּים,
כִּי אֵל יִתֵּן לְכֹל בּוֹ דְבֵקִים,
בֶּגֶד לִלְבּשׁ, לֶחֶם חֻקִּים,
בָּשָׂר וְדָגִים וְכָל מַטְעַמִּים.

E לֹא תֶחְסַר כֹּל בּוֹ וְאָכַלְתָּ,
וְשָׂבָעְתָּ וּבֵרַכְתָּ,
אֶת יְיָ אֱלֹהֶיךָ אֲשֶׁר אָהַבְתָּ,
כִּי בֵרַכְךָ מִכָּל הָעַמִּים.

F הַשָּׁמַיִם מְסַפְּרִים כְּבוֹדוֹ,
וְגַם הָאָרֶץ מָלְאָה חַסְדּוֹ,
רְאוּ כִּי כָל אֵלֶּה עָשְׂתָה יָדוֹ,
כִּי הוּא הַצּוּר, פָּעֳלוֹ תָמִים.

39

Yom Zeh Mechubbad

THIS DAY IS HONORED

A This day is honored above all others,
Because the Maker of all rested on it.

B You may do your work for six days,
But the seventh day is for your God.
On the Sabbath, do not do work,
Because he made all things in six days.

C It is first of the holy assemblies,
A day of ceasing, the holy Sabbath day.
Therefore let every man sanctify with wine,
And break two complete loaves of bread.

D Eat rich foods, drink sweet drinks,
Because God will give those who cling to him
Clothing to wear, their daily bread,
Meat, fish, and other delicacies.

E On it you will lack nothing, but you will eat
And be satisfied and bless
The LORD your God whom you love,
For he has blessed you more than all other peoples.

F The heavens declare his glory,
And the earth is also filled with his devotion.
See that his hand has made all these,
For he is the Maker, whose deeds are perfect.

40

ובשבת

ON THE SABBATH

A אָכְלוּ אֵת הַמָּן לְאַרְבָּעִים שָׁנָה,
הִמְטִיר דְּגַן שָׁמַיִם עַל הָאֲדָמָה,
בְּיוֹם שִׁשִּׁי לָקְטוּ בְּכֵפֶל הַמִּדָּה,
וּבַשַּׁבָּת שָׁבְתוּ כְּפִי הַמִּצְוָה.

B הוֹצִיאָם מִמִּצְרַיִם וְצִוָּה אֵת הָעָם,
וְעָשׂוּ לִי מִקְדָּשׁ וְשָׁכַנְתִּי בְּתוֹכָם,
אִמְצוּ זְרוֹעוֹתָם וְרָצָה בַּמְּלָאכָה,
וּבַשַּׁבָּת שָׁבְתוּ כְּפִי הַמִּצְוָה.

C רוֹעֵה הַצֹּאן הוּכָּה בְּיוֹם הֲכָנָתָם,
וַיָּנַח בְּלֵב הָאָרֶץ בְּחֶדֶר הַנִּסְתָּם,
וְגַם כִּי גֵיא צַלְמָוֶת יִזַּל לָהֶם דִּמְעָה,
וּבַשַּׁבָּת שָׁבְתוּ כְּפִי הַמִּצְוָה.

D נִרְאֶה בְּבוֹאוֹ שִׁילֹה אֶל מַלְכוּתוֹ,
צִיּוֹן תִּהְיֶה כִּסְאוֹ וְכָבוֹד מְנֻחָתוֹ,
כָּל בָּשָׂר יָבוֹא אֶל מְקוֹם הַמְּנוּחָה,
וּבַשַּׁבָּת שָׁבְתוּ כְּפִי הַמִּצְוָה.

40

Uvashabbat

ON THE SABBATH

A They ate the manna for forty years;
He rained down the grain of heaven on the land.
On the sixth day, they gathered in a double measure,
And on the Sabbath
they ceased according to the commandment.

B He took them from Egypt, and he commanded the people,
Make me a Sanctuary, and I will dwell among them.
They strengthened their arms, and he was pleased with the labor;
And on the Sabbath
they ceased according to the commandment.

C The shepherd of the flock was struck on the day of their preparation;
He rested in the heart of the earth in the sealed chamber.
And although the valley of death's shadow would flow tears for them,
On the Sabbath
they ceased according to the commandment.

D We will see when Shiloh comes into his kingdom
Zion will be his throne, and his resting place will be glorious.
All flesh will come to the resting place.
And on the Sabbath
they ceased according to the commandment.

זמירות לסעודה שלישית

SONGS FOR THE THIRD MEAL

ידיד נפש

41

BELOVED OF THE SOUL

A
יְדִיד נֶפֶשׁ אָב הָרַחֲמָן,
מְשֹׁךְ עַבְדְּךָ אֶל רְצוֹנֶךָ.
יָרוּץ עַבְדְּךָ כְּמוֹ אַיָּל,
יִשְׁתַּחֲוֶה אֶל מוּל הֲדָרֶךָ.
יֶעֱרַב לוֹ יְדִידוֹתֶיךָ,
מִנֹּפֶת צוּף וְכָל טָעַם.

B
הָדוּר, נָאֶה, זִיו הָעוֹלָם,
נַפְשִׁי חוֹלַת אַהֲבָתֶךָ.
אָנָּא אֵל נָא רְפָא נָא לָהּ,
בְּהַרְאוֹת לָהּ נֹעַם זִיוֶךָ.
אָז תִּתְחַזֵּק וְתִתְרַפֵּא,
וְהָיְתָה לָהּ שִׂמְחַת עוֹלָם.

C
וָתִיק, יֶהֱמוּ נָא רַחֲמֶיךָ,
וְחוּסָה נָּא עַל בֵּן אֲהוּבֶךָ.
כִּי זֶה כַּמָּה נִכְסֹף נִכְסַפְתִּי,
לִרְאוֹת מְהֵרָה בְּתִפְאֶרֶת עֻזֶּךָ.
אֵלֶּה חָמְדָה לִבִּי,
וְחוּסָה נָּא וְאַל תִּתְעַלָּם.

D
הִגָּלֶה נָא וּפְרֹשׂ חֲבִיבִי עָלַי,
אֶת סֻכַּת שְׁלוֹמֶךָ.
תָּאִיר אֶרֶץ מִכְּבוֹדֶךָ,
נָגִילָה וְנִשְׂמְחָה בָּךְ.
מַהֵר אֱהֹב כִּי בָא מוֹעֵד,
וְחָנֵּנוּ כִּימֵי עוֹלָם.

Zemirot for Se'udah Shlishit

SONGS FOR THE THIRD MEAL

41

Yedid Nefesh

BELOVED OF THE SOUL

A Beloved of the soul, compassionate Father,
draw your servant into your favor.
Your servant will run like a deer;
he will bow in worship before your beauty.
He will find your acts of love even sweeter
than the honey from a honeycomb or any flavor.

B Beautiful, lovely, brightness of the universe!
My soul is lovesick for you.
Please God, please heal my soul,
by showing it your pleasant brightness.
Then it will be strengthened and healed
and have eternal gladness.

C Ancient One, may your compassion be incited,
and please have pity upon your beloved son.
For so long I have yearned desperately for this,
to see your majestic strength.
My heart has cherished these things;
please have pity and do not remain concealed.

D Be revealed, my dear one,
and spread your shelter of peace over me.
May the earth be illuminated by your glory;
let us rejoice and be glad in you.
Hasten to show love, for the appointed time has come,
and be gracious to us as in days long ago.

זמירות למוצאי שבת

SONGS FOR SATURDAY NIGHT

42 אליהו הנביא

ELIJAH THE PROPHET

A אֵלִיָּהוּ הַנָּבִיא אֵלִיָּהוּ הַתִּשְׁבִּי אֵלִיָּהוּ הַגִּלְעָדִי,
בִּמְהֵרָה יָבוֹא אֵלֵינוּ עִם מָשִׁיחַ בֶּן דָּוִד.

B א אִישׁ אֲשֶׁר קִנֵּא לְשֵׁם הָאֵל,
ב אִישׁ בְּשַׂר שָׁלוֹם עַל יַד יְקוּתִיאֵל,
ג אִישׁ גַּשׁ וַיְכַפֵּר עַל בְּנֵי יִשְׂרָאֵל.

C ד אִישׁ דּוֹרוֹת שְׁנֵים עָשָׂר רָאוּ עֵינָיו,
ה אִישׁ הַנִּקְרָא בַּעַל שֵׂעָר בְּסִימָנָיו,
ו אִישׁ וְאֵזוֹר עוֹר אָזוּר בְּמָתְנָיו.

D ז אִישׁ זָעַף עַל עוֹבְדֵי חַמָּנִים,
ח אִישׁ חָשׁ וְנִשְׁבַּע מִהְיוֹת גִּשְׁמֵי מְעוֹנִים,
ט אִישׁ טַל וּמָטָר עָצַר שָׁלֹשׁ שָׁנִים.

E י אִישׁ יָצָא לִמְצוֹא לְנַפְשׁוֹ נַחַת,
כ אִישׁ כִּלְכְּלוּהוּ הָעֹרְבִים וְלֹא מֵת לַשַּׁחַת,
ל אִישׁ לְמַעֲנוֹ נִתְבָּרְכוּ כַּד וְצַפַּחַת.

F מ אִישׁ מוּסָרָיו הִקְשִׁיבוּ כְמֵהִים,
נ אִישׁ נַעֲנָה בָאֵשׁ מִשְּׁמֵי גְבוֹהִים,
ס אִישׁ סָחוּ אַחֲרָיו יְיָ הוּא הָאֱלֹהִים.

G ע אִישׁ עָתִיד לְהִשְׁתַּלֵּחַ מִשְּׁמֵי עֲרָבוֹת,
פ אִישׁ פָּקִיד עַל כָּל בְּשׂוֹרוֹת טוֹבוֹת,
צ אִישׁ צִיר נֶאֱמָן לְהָשִׁיב לֵב בָּנִים עַל אָבוֹת.

H ק אִישׁ קָרָא קַנֹּא קִנֵּאתִי לַייָ בְּתִפְאָרָה,
ר אִישׁ רָכַב עַל סוּסֵי אֵשׁ בִּסְעָרָה,
ש אִישׁ שֶׁלֹּא טָעַם טַעַם מִיתָה וּקְבוּרָה.

I ת אִישׁ תִּשְׁבִּי עַל שְׁמוֹ נִקְרָא,
תַּצְלִיחֵנוּ עַל יָדוֹ בַּתּוֹרָה,
תַּשְׁמִיעֵנוּ מִפִּיו בְּשׂוֹרָה טוֹבָה בִּמְהֵרָה,
בִּמְהֵרָה תּוֹצִיאֵנוּ מֵאֲפֵלָה לְאוֹרָה.

Zemirot for Motza'ei Shabbat

SONGS FOR SATURDAY EVENING

42 Eliyahu HaNavi

ELIJAH THE PROPHET

A Elijah the Prophet, Elijah the Tishbite, Elijah the Gileadite,
May he come to us soon with the Messiah, son of David.

B א The man who was zealous for the sake of God,
ב The man who was assured of peace by Yekutiel,
ג The man who came near and atoned for the children of Israel.

C ד The man whose eyes saw twelve generations,
ה The man who is called "hairy" because of his features,
ו The man wearing a leather belt around his waist.

D ז The man who was furious about sun worship,
ח The man who hastily swore against seasonal rain,
ט The man who withheld dew and rain for three years.

E י The man who departed to find comfort for his soul,
כ The man whom ravens fed and who did not die,
ל The man for whose sake pitchers and jars were blessed.

F מ The man whose rebuke was heeded by the yearning ones,
נ The man who was answered with fire from the highest heaven,
ס The man after whom they repeated, "The LORD is God!"

G ע The man who will ultimately be sent from the uppermost heavens,
פ The man who is entrusted with all good news,
צ The man who is faithful to return the hearts of children to fathers.

H ק The man who majestically cried, "I am fiercely zealous for the LORD,"
ר The man who rode upon horses of fire in the storm wind,
ש The man who did not taste the flavor of death and burial.

I ת The man who is called "Tishbite" by name.
Grant us success in the Torah through him.
Proclaim good news quickly from him.
Take us out from gloom to light.

J אִישׁ תִּשְׁבִּי תַּצִּלֵנוּ מִפִּי אֲרָיוֹת,
תְּבַשְּׂרֵנוּ בְּשׂוֹרוֹת טוֹבוֹת,
תְּשַׂמְּחֵנוּ בָּנִים עַל אָבוֹת בְּמוֹצָאֵי שַׁבָּתוֹת.

K כַּכָּתוּב הִנֵּה אָנֹכִי שֹׁלֵחַ לָכֶם אֵת אֵלִיָּה הַנָּבִיא,
לִפְנֵי בּוֹא יוֹם יְיָ הַגָּדוֹל וְהַנּוֹרָא,
וְהֵשִׁיב לֵב אָבוֹת עַל בָּנִים,
וְלֵב בָּנִים עַל אֲבוֹתָם.

L אַשְׁרֵי מִי שֶׁרָאָה פָנָיו בַּחֲלוֹם,
אַשְׁרֵי מִי שֶׁנָּתַן לוֹ שָׁלוֹם וְהֶחֱזִיר לוֹ שָׁלוֹם,
יְיָ יְבָרֵךְ אֶת עַמּוֹ בַשָּׁלוֹם.

43 המבדיל

HE WHO SEPARATES

A הַמַּבְדִּיל בֵּין קֹדֶשׁ לְחוֹל,
חַטֹּאתֵינוּ יִמְחוֹל,
זַרְעֵנוּ וְכַסְפֵּנוּ יַרְבֶּה כַּחוֹל,
וְכַכּוֹכָבִים בַּלָּיְלָה.

B יוֹם פָּנָה כְּצֵל תֹּמֶר,
אֶקְרָא לָאֵל עָלַי גּוֹמֵר,
יוֹם אֲשֶׁר אָמַר שׁוֹמֵר,
אָתָא בֹקֶר וְגַם לָיְלָה.

C צִדְקָתְךָ כְּהַר תָּבוֹר,
עֲלֵי פְשָׁעַי עָבֹר תַּעֲבוֹר,
כְּיוֹם אֶתְמוֹל כִּי יַעֲבוֹר,
וְאַשְׁמוּרָה בַלָּיְלָה.

D חָלְפָה עוֹנַת מִנְחָתִי,
מִי יִתֵּן מְנוּחָתִי,
יָגַעְתִּי בְאַנְחָתִי,
אַשְׂחֶה בְכָל לָיְלָה.

E קוֹלִי בַּל יֻנְטָל,
פְּתַח לִי שַׁעַר הַמְנֻטָּל,
שֶׁרֹּאשִׁי נִמְלָא טָל,
קְוֻצּוֹתַי רְסִיסֵי לָיְלָה.

J The man, the Tishbite—rescue us from the lions' mouths.
Proclaim to us good news.
Gladden both children and fathers after the Sabbath ends.

K As it is written, "Behold I send to you Elijah the prophet
Before the great and awesome day of the LORD comes.
He will return the hearts of fathers to children,
And the hearts of children to their fathers."

L Contentment awaits one who sees his face in a dream.
Contentment awaits one who exchanges greeting with him.
May the LORD bless his people with peace.

43 HaMavdil

HE WHO SEPARATES

A May he who separates between holy and common,
Also pardon our sins.
Make our offspring and wealth as numerous as sand,
And like the stars at night.

B The day stretched on like the palm tree's shade.
I ask that God fulfill for me
What the watchman said:
"Morning has come as well as night."

C Your righteousness is like Mount Tabor;
Surely you will let my sins pass away,
Just as yesterday has passed,
Or like a watch of the night.

D The time of the afternoon prayer has passed.
Who will grant me my rest?
I have grown weary with sighing,
I swim in sorrows each night.

E May my voice not be suppressed;
Open for me the supernal gate,
For my head is saturated with dew,
My curls with the dampness of the night.

F הֲעָתֵר נוֹרָא וְאָיוֹם,
אֲשַׁוֵּעַ תְּנָה פִדְיוֹם,
בְּנֶשֶׁף בְּעֶרֶב יוֹם,
בְּאִישׁוֹן לָיְלָה.

G קְרָאתִיךָ יָהּ הוֹשִׁיעֵנִי,
אֹרַח חַיִּים תּוֹדִיעֵנִי,
מִדַּלּוּת תְּבַצְּעֵנִי,
מִיּוֹם וְעַד לָיְלָה.

H טַהֵר טִנּוּף מַעֲשַׂי,
פֶּן יֹאמְרוּ מַכְעִיסַי,
אַיֵּה נָא אֱלוֹהַּ עוֹשָׂי,
נוֹתֵן זְמִירוֹת בַּלָּיְלָה.

I נַחְנוּ בְיָדְךָ כַּחֹמֶר,
סְלַח נָא עַל קַל וָחֹמֶר,
יוֹם לְיוֹם יַבִּיעַ אֹמֶר,
וְלַיְלָה לְלָיְלָה.

44 לנר ולבשמים

FOR THE CANDLE AND SPICES

A לַנֵּר וְלִבְשָׂמִים נַפְשִׁי מְיַחֲלָה,
אִם תִּתְּנוּ לִי כּוֹס יַיִן לְהַבְדָּלָה.

B סֹלּוּ דְּרָכִים לִי פַּנּוּ לְנָבוֹכָה,
פִּתְחוּ שְׁעָרִים לִי כָּל מַלְאֲכֵי מַעְלָה.

C עֵינַי אֲנִי אֶשָּׂא אֶל אֵל בְּלֵב כּוֹסֵף,
מַמְצִיא צְרָכַי לִי בַּיּוֹם וּבַלָּיְלָה.

D דֵּי מַחְסוֹר תֶּן לִי מֵאוֹצְרוֹת טוּבָךְ,
כִּי לַחֲסָדֶיךָ אֵין קֵץ וְאֵין תִּכְלָה.

E יִתְחַדְּשָׁה גִּילִי טַרְפִּי וְטוֹבָתִי,
תָּסִיר יְגוֹנוֹתַי מַכְאוֹב וּמַאְפֵלָה.

F הִנֵּה יְמֵי מַעְשֶׂה מִתְחַדְּשִׁים תָּמִיד,
יִתְחַדְּשָׁה בָּהֶם שָׁלוֹם וְטוֹב סֶלָה.

F Accept my entreaty, Fearsome One,
I will cry out; grant me ransom.
At dusk, at evening time,
In the blackness of the night.

G I have called to you: LORD, save me.
Let me know the path of life.
Lift me out of my poverty,
As day turns to night.

H Purify the filth of my deeds,
Lest those who upset me say,
"Where is the God who made me,
Who makes you sing at night?"

I We are like clay in your hand.
Please forgive the minor and severe.
Day speaks forth to day
And night to night.

44 LaNer Velivsamim

FOR THE CANDLE AND SPICES

A For the candle and spices my soul waits,
If you would give me a cup of wine for *Havdalah.*

B Build me a road, clear my confused way,
Open gates for me, all you angels above.

C With longing in my heart, I lift my eyes to God,
The one who meets my needs by night and by day.

D Grant me what I lack from your good treasuries,
For there is no end or stop to your kindness.

E May my joy and food and goodness renew,
Let my groans and sorrows and gloom depart.

F The days of labor always come back again;
May peace and goodness come with them.

קריאות נוספות

In addition to the traditional hymn-like *zemirot* in this book, there are many short popular Sabbath table songs that are just a few lines long. These are usually a small extract from one of the traditional songs, a passage from the Bible, or the Sabbath synagogue liturgy. Since there is an inexhaustible list of songs of this type, we have provided some of the more common sources.

45 תהילים צב

A מִזְמוֹר שִׁיר לְיוֹם הַשַּׁבָּת.

B טוֹב לְהֹדוֹת לַייָ,
וּלְזַמֵּר לְשִׁמְךָ עֶלְיוֹן.

C לְהַגִּיד בַּבֹּקֶר חַסְדֶּךָ,
וֶאֱמוּנָתְךָ בַּלֵּילוֹת.

D עֲלֵי עָשׂוֹר וַעֲלֵי נָבֶל,
עֲלֵי הִגָּיוֹן בְּכִנּוֹר.

E כִּי שִׂמַּחְתַּנִי יְיָ בְּפָעֳלֶךָ,
בְּמַעֲשֵׂי יָדֶיךָ אֲרַנֵּן.

F מַה גָּדְלוּ מַעֲשֶׂיךָ יְיָ,
מְאֹד עָמְקוּ מַחְשְׁבֹתֶיךָ.

G אִישׁ בַּעַר לֹא יֵדָע,
וּכְסִיל לֹא יָבִין אֶת זֹאת.

H בִּפְרֹחַ רְשָׁעִים כְּמוֹ עֵשֶׂב,
וַיָּצִיצוּ כָּל פֹּעֲלֵי אָוֶן,
לְהִשָּׁמְדָם עֲדֵי עַד.

I וְאַתָּה מָרוֹם לְעֹלָם יְיָ.

J כִּי הִנֵּה אֹיְבֶיךָ יְיָ,
כִּי הִנֵּה אֹיְבֶיךָ יֹאבֵדוּ,
יִתְפָּרְדוּ כָּל פֹּעֲלֵי אָוֶן.

K וַתָּרֶם כִּרְאֵים קַרְנִי,
בַּלֹּתִי בְּשֶׁמֶן רַעֲנָן.

Additional Readings

In addition to the traditional hymn-like *zemirot* in this book, there are many short popular Sabbath table songs that are just a few lines long. These are usually a small extract from one of the traditional songs, a passage from the Bible, or the Sabbath synagogue liturgy. Since there is an inexhaustible list of songs of this type, we have provided some of the more common sources.

45 Psalm 92

A A psalm. A song for the Sabbath day.

B It is good to give thanks to the LORD,
to make music to your name, Most High;

C To tell of your devotion in the morning
and your faithfulness at night,

D Upon the ten-string and upon the harp,
with a soft meditation upon the lyre.

E For you have made me glad, O LORD, by what you have done;
I will sing joyfully about your handiwork.

F How great your works are, O LORD;
how very deep are your thoughts!

G An ignorant man does not know,
and a fool does not discern this.

H When the wicked flourish like grass
and evildoers spring up,
it is to their permanent destruction.

I But you are supreme forever, O LORD!

J For behold your enemies, O LORD;
for behold, your enemies will perish,
and all evildoers will be removed.

K You uplift me like the horn of a wild ox;
I have been drenched in fresh oil.

L וַתַּבֵּט עֵינִי בְּשׁוּרָי,
בַּקָּמִים עָלַי מְרֵעִים, תִּשְׁמַעְנָה אָזְנָי.

M צַדִּיק כַּתָּמָר יִפְרָח,
כְּאֶרֶז בַּלְּבָנוֹן יִשְׂגֶּה.

N שְׁתוּלִים בְּבֵית יְיָ,
בְּחַצְרוֹת אֱלֹהֵינוּ יַפְרִיחוּ.

O עוֹד יְנוּבוּן בְּשֵׂיבָה,
דְּשֵׁנִים וְרַעֲנַנִּים יִהְיוּ.

P לְהַגִּיד כִּי יָשָׁר יְיָ,
צוּרִי וְלֹא עַוְלָתָה בּוֹ.

46 מתי יא : כח-ל

FROM THE DELITZSCH HEBREW GOSPELS

A פְּנוּ אֵלַי כָּל הָעֲמֵלִים וְהַטְּעוּנִים,
וַאֲנִי אֲנִיחַ לָכֶם.

B קַבְּלוּ עֲלֵיכֶם אֶת עֻלִּי וְלִמְדוּ מִמֶּנִּי,
כִּי עָנָו וּשְׁפַל רוּחַ אָנֹכִי,
וּמִצְאוּ מַרְגּוֹעַ לְנַפְשֹׁתֵיכֶם.

C כִּי עֻלִּי נָעִים וְקַל מַשָּׂאִי.

47 ישמחו במלכותך

THEY WILL REJOICE IN YOUR KINGDOM

A יִשְׂמְחוּ בְמַלְכוּתְךָ
שׁוֹמְרֵי שַׁבָּת וְקוֹרְאֵי עֹנֶג.

B עַם מְקַדְּשֵׁי שְׁבִיעִי
כֻּלָּם יִשְׂבְּעוּ וְיִתְעַנְּגוּ מִטּוּבֶךָ.

C וּבַשְּׁבִיעִי רָצִיתָ בּוֹ וְקִדַּשְׁתּוֹ,
חֶמְדַּת יָמִים אוֹתוֹ קָרָאתָ,
זֵכֶר לְמַעֲשֵׂה בְרֵאשִׁית.

L But my eye has observed my opponents;
my ear can hear when harmful people rise against me.

M The righteous will flourish like a palm tree;
he will grow like a cedar in Lebanon.

N Planted in the House of the LORD,
they will flourish in the courtyards of our God.

O Still yielding fruit in old age,
they will be healthy and youthful,

P Declaring that the LORD is upright;
He is my rock, and there is no wrongdoing in him.

46 Matthew 11:28–30

FROM THE DELITZSCH HEBREW GOSPELS

A Turn to me, all who labor and are burdened,
and I will cause you to rest.

B Accept upon yourself my yoke and learn from me,
for I am humble and lowly in spirit,
and you will find a resting place for your souls.

C For my yoke is pleasant and my burden is light.

47 Yismechu Bemalchutecha

THEY WILL REJOICE IN YOUR KINGDOM

A They will rejoice in your kingdom
who observe the Sabbath and call it a delight.

B The people who sanctify the seventh day
will all be satisfied and delight in your goodness,

C For you favored the seventh day and sanctified it;
you called it the most cherished of days,
A memorial of the work of creation.

48

לכה דודי

O COME, BELOVED

A לְכָה דוֹדִי לִקְרַאת כַּלָּה,
פְּנֵי שַׁבָּת נְקַבְּלָה.

B שָׁמוֹר וְזָכוֹר בְּדִבּוּר אֶחָד,
הִשְׁמִיעָנוּ אֵל הַמְיֻחָד.
יְיָ אֶחָד וּשְׁמוֹ אֶחָד,
לְשֵׁם וּלְתִפְאֶרֶת וְלִתְהִלָּה.

C לִקְרַאת שַׁבָּת לְכוּ וְנֵלְכָה,
כִּי הִיא מְקוֹר הַבְּרָכָה.
מֵרֹאשׁ מִקֶּדֶם נְסוּכָה,
סוֹף מַעֲשֶׂה בְּמַחֲשָׁבָה תְּחִלָּה.

D מִקְדַּשׁ מֶלֶךְ עִיר מְלוּכָה,
קוּמִי צְאִי מִתּוֹךְ הַהֲפֵכָה.
רַב לָךְ שֶׁבֶת בְּעֵמֶק הַבָּכָא,
וְהוּא יַחֲמוֹל עָלַיִךְ חֶמְלָה.

E הִתְנַעֲרִי מֵעָפָר קוּמִי,
לִבְשִׁי בִּגְדֵי תִפְאַרְתֵּךְ עַמִּי.
עַל יַד בֶּן יִשַׁי בֵּית הַלַּחְמִי,
קָרְבָה אֶל נַפְשִׁי גְּאָלָהּ.

F הִתְעוֹרְרִי הִתְעוֹרְרִי,
כִּי בָא אוֹרֵךְ קוּמִי אוֹרִי.
עוּרִי עוּרִי שִׁיר דַּבֵּרִי,
כְּבוֹד יְיָ עָלַיִךְ נִגְלָה.

G לֹא תֵבוֹשִׁי וְלֹא תִכָּלְמִי,
מַה תִּשְׁתּוֹחֲחִי וּמַה תֶּהֱמִי.
בָּךְ יֶחֱסוּ עֲנִיֵּי עַמִּי,
וְנִבְנְתָה עִיר עַל תִּלָּהּ.

48

LECHAH DODI

O COME, BELOVED

A O come, beloved, the bride to greet
The Sabbath Presence let us meet.

B "Observe, remember" in a single word
Which from the Only God we heard.
The LORD is One, and One his name,
For praise, for majesty, and for fame.

C To greet the Sabbath, let us go,
For from this source our blessings flow.
The honored day from times forgot,
The final deed, initial thought.

D Kingly Temple, City royal,
Arise, depart from your turmoil.
Too long your stay in the Vale of Lament;
Now he shall be benevolent.

E Arise, and let your dust be shed;
Majestic garments don instead!
With the son of Jesse from Bethlehem appear;
Redeem, and to my soul draw near.

F Wake up, wake up! For come is your light!
Arise and shine; may it be bright.
Awake, awake; a song to sing!
Revealed is the glory of the King.

G Be not ashamed, be not abased;
Why so downcast, why disgraced?
The poor shall find a place to dwell,
The City built upon the hill.

וְהָיוּ לִמְשִׁסָּה שֹׁאסָיִךְ, H
וְרָחֲקוּ כָּל מְבַלְּעָיִךְ.
יָשִׂישׂ עָלַיִךְ אֱלֹהָיִךְ,
כִּמְשׂוֹשׂ חָתָן עַל כַּלָּה.

יָמִין וּשְׂמֹאל תִּפְרֹוצִי, I
וְאֶת יְיָ תַּעֲרִיצִי.
עַל יַד אִישׁ בֶּן פַּרְצִי,
וְנִשְׂמְחָה וְנָגִילָה.

בּוֹאִי בְשָׁלוֹם עֲטֶרֶת בַּעְלָהּ, J
גַּם בְּשִׂמְחָה וּבְצָהֳלָה.
תּוֹךְ אֱמוּנֵי עַם סְגֻלָּה,
בּוֹאִי כַלָּה, בּוֹאִי כַלָּה.

H Oppressors trampled down at last,
Devourers far away be cast.
As a groom rejoices his bride to see,
So will your God's rejoicing be.

I You will spread to left and right,
The LORD will be great in your sight.
Through the son of Peretz, by his hand,
We shall rejoice and be glad.

J Crown of her husband, come in peace,
Let joy and gladness now increase.
With the treasured people, come, abide
To the faithful ones, come O bride!

ההודיה 49

THE THANKSGIVING

This section from the *Didache* was originally intended as a complete after-meal blessing for Gentile disciples of Yeshua. One who wishes to do so may use the text below as an alternative to the standard *Birkat HaMazon* (Grace after Meals).

נוֹדֶה לְּךָ אָבִינוּ הַקָּדוֹשׁ, עַל שִׁמְךָ הַקָּדוֹשׁ שֶׁהִשְׁכַּנְתָּ A
בְּלִבֵּנוּ, וְעַל הַדַּעַת וְהָאֱמוּנָה וְחַיֵּי עוֹלָם שֶׁהוֹדַעְתָּנוּ עַל
יְדֵי יֵשׁוּעַ עַבְדֶּךָ. לְךָ הַכָּבוֹד לְעוֹלָמִים:

וְאַתָּה יְיָ צְבָאוֹת בָּרָאתָ אֶת הַכֹּל בַּעֲבוּר שִׁמְךָ, מָזוֹן B
וּמִשְׁתֶּה נָתַתָּ לִבְנֵי אָדָם לֵהָנוֹת מֵהֶם, כְּדֵי שֶׁלְּךָ יוֹדוּ.
וְחוֹנַנְתָּנוּ מְזוֹן וּמִשְׁתֵּה הָרוּחַ וְחַיֵּי עוֹלָם עַל יְדֵי עַבְדֶּךָ.
וְעַל הַכֹּל אֲנַחְנוּ מוֹדִים לָךְ כִּי אַתָּה גִּבּוֹר. לְךָ הַכָּבוֹד
לְעוֹלָמִים:

זְכוֹר יְיָ אֶת עֲדָתְךָ לְהַצִּיל אֹתָהּ מִכָּל רָע וּלְהַשְׁלִימָהּ C
בְּאַהֲבָתֶךָ. וְקַבֵּץ אֶת הַמְקֻדֶּשֶׁת מִן אַרְבַּע הָרוּחוֹת
לְמַלְכוּתְךָ שֶׁהֲכִינוֹתָ לָּהּ. כִּי לְךָ הַגְּבוּרָה וְהַכָּבוֹד
לְעוֹלָמִים:

יָבוֹא חֵן וְיַעֲבֹר הָעוֹלָם הַזֶּה. הוֹשַׁע נָא לֵאלֹהֵי דָּוִד. כֹּל D
שֶׁקָּדוֹשׁ, יָבוֹא. כֹּל שֶׁאֵינֶנּוּ, יָשׁוּב. מָרַן אֶתָא, אָמֵן:

49

HaHodayah

THE THANKSGIVING

This section from the *Didache* was originally intended as a complete after-meal blessing for Gentile disciples of Yeshua. One who wishes to do so may use the text below as an alternative to the standard *Birkat HaMazon* (Grace after Meals).

A **We thank you,** our holy Father, for your holy name that you have caused to dwell in our hearts, and for the knowledge, faithfulness, and eternal life that you have made known to us through your servant Yeshua. Yours is the glory forever.

B **You, O LORD of Legions,** created all things for the sake of your name; you gave nourishment and drink for human beings to enjoy, in order that they would give thanks to you. You also bestowed upon us spiritual nourishment and drink and eternal life through your Servant. And for all things, we thank you, because you are powerful. Yours is the glory forever.

C **Remember, O LORD,** your congregation[a] to rescue her from all evil, and to make her complete in your love. Gather the betrothed from the four winds[b] to your kingdom that you have prepared for her.[c] For yours is the power and the glory forever.

D **May grace come,** and may this world pass away. Hoshana to the God of David![d] Everyone who is holy, let him come. Everyone who is not, let him repent. Maran Etha! ("Our Master is coming!") Amen.

a) Psalm 74:2. b) Zechariah 2:10[6]. c) Cf. Matthew 25:34. d) Cf. Matthew 21:9, 15.

ברכת המזון

GRACE AFTER MEALS

This blessing is recited after eating a meal that contains bread.

קריאת מבוא 50

Some begin the *Birkat HaMazon* with one of the psalms below.

תהלים קכו

ON SABBATHS AND HOLIDAYS

שִׁיר הַמַּעֲלוֹת בְּשׁוּב יְיָ אֶת שִׁיבַת צִיּוֹן, הָיִינוּ כְּחֹלְמִים. A
אָז יִמָּלֵא שְׂחוֹק פִּינוּ וּלְשׁוֹנֵנוּ רִנָּה, אָז יֹאמְרוּ בַגּוֹיִם, הִגְדִּיל יְיָ לַעֲשׂוֹת עִם אֵלֶּה. הִגְדִּיל יְיָ לַעֲשׂוֹת עִמָּנוּ, הָיִינוּ שְׂמֵחִים. שׁוּבָה יְיָ אֶת שְׁבִיתֵנוּ, כַּאֲפִיקִים בַּנֶּגֶב. הַזֹּרְעִים בְּדִמְעָה, בְּרִנָּה יִקְצֹרוּ. הָלוֹךְ יֵלֵךְ וּבָכֹה נֹשֵׂא מֶשֶׁךְ הַזָּרַע, בֹּא יָבֹא בְרִנָּה נֹשֵׂא אֲלֻמֹּתָיו:

תהלים קלז

ON WEEKDAYS

עַל נַהֲרוֹת בָּבֶל שָׁם יָשַׁבְנוּ גַּם בָּכִינוּ, בְּזָכְרֵנוּ אֶת צִיּוֹן. B
עַל עֲרָבִים בְּתוֹכָהּ, תָּלִינוּ כִּנֹּרוֹתֵינוּ. כִּי שָׁם שְׁאֵלוּנוּ שׁוֹבֵינוּ דִּבְרֵי שִׁיר וְתוֹלָלֵינוּ שִׂמְחָה, שִׁירוּ לָנוּ מִשִּׁיר צִיּוֹן. אֵיךְ נָשִׁיר אֶת שִׁיר יְיָ, עַל אַדְמַת נֵכָר. אִם אֶשְׁכָּחֵךְ יְרוּשָׁלָיִם, תִּשְׁכַּח יְמִינִי. תִּדְבַּק לְשׁוֹנִי לְחִכִּי אִם לֹא אֶזְכְּרֵכִי, אִם לֹא אַעֲלֶה אֶת יְרוּשָׁלַיִם עַל רֹאשׁ שִׂמְחָתִי. זְכֹר יְיָ לִבְנֵי אֱדוֹם אֵת יוֹם יְרוּשָׁלָיִם, הָאֹמְרִים עָרוּ עָרוּ עַד הַיְסוֹד בָּהּ. בַּת בָּבֶל הַשְּׁדוּדָה, אַשְׁרֵי שֶׁיְשַׁלֶּם לָךְ אֶת גְּמוּלֵךְ שֶׁגָּמַלְתְּ לָנוּ. אַשְׁרֵי שֶׁיֹּאחֵז וְנִפֵּץ אֶת עֹלָלַיִךְ אֶל הַסָּלַע:

BIRKAT HAMAZON

GRACE AFTER MEALS

This blessing is recited after eating a meal that contains bread.

50 INTRODUCTORY READINGS

Some begin the *Birkat HaMazon* with one of the psalms below.

PSALM 126

ON SABBATHS AND HOLIDAYS

A **A SONG OF ASCENTS.** When the LORD returned the exile to Zion, we were like dreamers. Then our mouths were filled with laughter and our tongues with joyful song. Then it was said among the nations, "The LORD has performed great things for them." The LORD has done great things for us! We have rejoiced! O LORD, return our exiles like streams in the desert. Those who sow in tears shall reap in joyful song. Though one weeps as he goes out, bearing the seed to be sown, he will come with joyful song bearing his bundles of grain.

PSALM 137

ON WEEKDAYS

B **BY THE RIVERS OF BABYLON,** there we sat, and there we wept when we remembered Zion. Upon the willows in its midst we hung our harps. For there our captors would ask us for lyrical songs, and our oppressors asked for gladness: "Sing for us one of the songs of Zion." How can we sing the song of the LORD upon foreign soil? If I forget you, O Jerusalem, may my right hand forget its musical skill. May my tongue cling to my palate if I do not remember you—if I do not elevate Jerusalem over my greatest gladness. Remember, O LORD, Jerusalem's day when the children of Edom were saying, "Lay it bare! Lay it bare to its very foundation!" O devastated daughter of Babylon, contentment awaits the one who rewards you with the same payment that you gave to us. Contentment awaits the one who will smash your little children upon the rocks.

זימון

Invitation

At a wedding meal, go to prayer 55, page 110.
At a circumcision meal, go to prayer 57, page 114.

Include this section only if at least three men are present.

C LEADER רַבּוֹתַי נְבָרֵךְ:

D GROUP יְהִי שֵׁם יְיָ מְבֹרָךְ מֵעַתָּה וְעַד עוֹלָם:

E LEADER יְהִי שֵׁם יְיָ מְבֹרָךְ מֵעַתָּה וְעַד עוֹלָם:

If ten or more are present, include words in brackets.

F LEADER בִּרְשׁוּת מָרָנָן וְרַבָּנָן וְרַבּוֹתַי, נְבָרֵךְ {אֱלֹהֵינוּ} שֶׁאָכַלְנוּ מִשֶּׁלּוֹ:

G GROUP בָּרוּךְ {אֱלֹהֵינוּ} שֶׁאָכַלְנוּ מִשֶּׁלּוֹ וּבְטוּבוֹ חָיִינוּ:

H LEADER בָּרוּךְ {אֱלֹהֵינוּ} שֶׁאָכַלְנוּ מִשֶּׁלּוֹ וּבְטוּבוֹ חָיִינוּ.
{בָּרוּךְ הוּא וּבָרוּךְ שְׁמוֹ:}

51 ברכת הזן

FIRST BLESSING: FOR THE FOOD

A **בָּרוּךְ** אַתָּה יְיָ אֱלֹהֵינוּ מֶלֶךְ הָעוֹלָם, הַזָּן אֶת הָעוֹלָם כֻּלּוֹ בְּטוּבוֹ בְּחֵן בְּחֶסֶד וּבְרַחֲמִים, הוּא נוֹתֵן לֶחֶם לְכָל בָּשָׂר כִּי לְעוֹלָם חַסְדּוֹ. וּבְטוּבוֹ הַגָּדוֹל תָּמִיד לֹא חָסַר לָנוּ, וְאַל יֶחְסַר לָנוּ מָזוֹן לְעוֹלָם וָעֶד. בַּעֲבוּר שְׁמוֹ הַגָּדוֹל, כִּי הוּא אֵל זָן וּמְפַרְנֵס לַכֹּל וּמֵטִיב לַכֹּל, וּמֵכִין מָזוֹן לְכָל בְּרִיּוֹתָיו אֲשֶׁר בָּרָא.

B **נוֹדֶה לְּךָ** אָבִינוּ הַקָּדוֹשׁ, עַל שִׁמְךָ הַקָּדוֹשׁ שֶׁהִשְׁכַּנְתָּ בְּלִבֵּנוּ, וְעַל הַדַּעַת וְהָאֱמוּנָה וְחַיֵּי עוֹלָם שֶׁהוֹדַעְתָּנוּ עַל יְדֵי יֵשׁוּעַ עַבְדֶּךָ. לְךָ הַכָּבוֹד לְעוֹלָמִים.

C › **בָּרוּךְ** אַתָּה יְיָ, הַזָּן אֶת הַכֹּל: » אָמֵן.

ZIMMUN

Invitation

At a wedding meal, go to prayer 55, page 111.
At a circumcision meal, go to prayer 57, page 115.

Include this section only if at least three men are present.

C LEADER Gentlemen, let us bless!

D GROUP May the name of the LORD be blessed now and forever.[a]

E LEADER May the name of the LORD be blessed now and forever.

If ten or more are present, include words in brackets.

F LEADER With the permission of my distinguished gentlemen and scholars, let us bless {our God,} the one from whom is our sustenance.

G GROUP Blessed is {our God,} the one from whom is our sustenance, and by whose goodness we live.

H LEADER Blessed is {our God,} the one from whom is our sustenance, and by whose goodness we live. {Blessed is he and blessed is his name.}

51

BIRKAT HAZAN

FIRST BLESSING: FOR THE FOOD

A **BLESSED** are you, O LORD, our God, King of the universe, who nourishes the entire world with goodness, grace, devotion, and compassion. He gives bread to all flesh, for his devotion is eternal.[b] Because of his great goodness we have never lacked, and we shall never lack nourishment forever and ever. For the sake of his great name, for God provides for and nourishes all, who does good to all and prepares nourishment for all of his creatures which he has made.

B **WE THANK YOU,** our holy Father, for your holy name that you have caused to dwell in our hearts, and for the knowledge, faithfulness, and eternal life that you have made known to us through your servant Yeshua. Yours is the glory forever.

C › **BLESSED** are you, O LORD, who nourishes all. » Amen.

a) Psalm 113:2. b) Psalm 136:25.

52

ברכת הארץ

SECOND BLESSING: FOR THE LAND

A **נוֹדֶה לְּךָ** יְיָ אֱלֹהֵינוּ עַל שֶׁהִנְחַלְתָּ לַאֲבוֹתֵינוּ, אֶרֶץ חֶמְדָּה טוֹבָה וּרְחָבָה, וְעַל שֶׁהוֹצֵאתָנוּ יְיָ אֱלֹהֵינוּ מֵאֶרֶץ מִצְרַיִם, וּפְדִיתָנוּ מִבֵּית עֲבָדִים, וְעַל בְּרִיתְךָ שֶׁחָתַמְתָּ בִּבְשָׂרֵנוּ, וְעַל תּוֹרָתְךָ שֶׁלִּמַּדְתָּנוּ, וְעַל חֻקֶּיךָ שֶׁהוֹדַעְתָּנוּ, וְעַל חַיִּים חֵן וָחֶסֶד שֶׁחוֹנַנְתָּנוּ, וְעַל אֲכִילַת מָזוֹן שָׁאַתָּה זָן וּמְפַרְנֵס אוֹתָנוּ תָּמִיד, בְּכָל יוֹם וּבְכָל עֵת וּבְכָל שָׁעָה.

B **וְאַתָּה יְיָ צְבָאוֹת** בָּרָאתָ אֶת הַכֹּל בַּעֲבוּר שִׁמְךָ, מָזוֹן וּמִשְׁתֶּה נָתַתָּ לִבְנֵי אָדָם לֵהָנוֹת מֵהֶם, כְּדֵי שֶׁלְּךָ יוֹדוּ. וְחוֹנַנְתָּנוּ מְזוֹן וּמִשְׁתֵּה הָרוּחַ וְחַיֵּי עוֹלָם עַל יְדֵי עַבְדֶּךָ. וְעַל הַכֹּל אֲנַחְנוּ מוֹדִים לָךְ כִּי אַתָּה גִּבּוֹר. לְךָ הַכָּבוֹד לְעוֹלָמִים:

ON HANUKKAH

C **עַל הַנִּסִּים** וְעַל הַפֻּרְקָן וְעַל הַגְּבוּרוֹת וְעַל הַתְּשׁוּעוֹת וְעַל הַמִּלְחָמוֹת שֶׁעָשִׂיתָ לַאֲבוֹתֵינוּ בַּיָּמִים הָהֵם בַּזְּמַן הַזֶּה:

D **בִּימֵי** מַתִּתְיָהוּ בֶּן יוֹחָנָן כֹּהֵן גָּדוֹל חַשְׁמוֹנַאי וּבָנָיו, כְּשֶׁעָמְדָה מַלְכוּת יָוָן הָרְשָׁעָה עַל עַמְּךָ יִשְׂרָאֵל, לְהַשְׁכִּיחָם תּוֹרָתֶךָ, וּלְהַעֲבִירָם מֵחֻקֵּי רְצוֹנֶךָ. וְאַתָּה בְּרַחֲמֶיךָ הָרַבִּים, עָמַדְתָּ לָהֶם בְּעֵת צָרָתָם, רַבְתָּ אֶת רִיבָם, דַּנְתָּ אֶת דִּינָם, נָקַמְתָּ אֶת נִקְמָתָם. מָסַרְתָּ גִבּוֹרִים בְּיַד חַלָּשִׁים, וְרַבִּים בְּיַד מְעַטִּים, וּטְמֵאִים בְּיַד טְהוֹרִים, וּרְשָׁעִים בְּיַד צַדִּיקִים, וְזֵדִים בְּיַד עוֹסְקֵי תוֹרָתֶךָ, וּלְךָ עָשִׂיתָ שֵׁם גָּדוֹל וְקָדוֹשׁ בְּעוֹלָמֶךָ, וּלְעַמְּךָ יִשְׂרָאֵל עָשִׂיתָ תְּשׁוּעָה גְדוֹלָה וּפֻרְקָן כְּהַיּוֹם הַזֶּה. וְאַחַר כֵּן בָּאוּ בָנֶיךָ לִדְבִיר בֵּיתֶךָ, וּפִנּוּ אֶת הֵיכָלֶךָ, וְטִהֲרוּ אֶת מִקְדָּשֶׁךָ, וְהִדְלִיקוּ נֵרוֹת בְּחַצְרוֹת קָדְשֶׁךָ, וְקָבְעוּ שְׁמוֹנַת יְמֵי חֲנֻכָּה אֵלּוּ, לְהוֹדוֹת וּלְהַלֵּל לְשִׁמְךָ הַגָּדוֹל:

52 ## BIRKAT HAARETZ

SECOND BLESSING: FOR THE LAND

A **WE THANK YOU,** O LORD, our God, for the inheritance you gave to our fathers: a pleasant, good, and spacious land; and because you, O LORD, our God, took us out from Egypt and ransomed us from a house of slavery; and for your covenant that you sealed in our flesh; and for your Torah that you taught to us; and for your statutes that you made known to us; and for the life, grace, and devotion that you have bestowed upon us; and for the nourishing food with which you nourish and provide for us constantly, in every day, at every moment, and in every hour.

B **YOU, O LORD OF LEGIONS,** created all things for the sake of your name; you gave nourishment and drink for human beings to enjoy, in order that they would give thanks to you. You also bestowed upon us spiritual nourishment and drink and eternal life through your Servant. And for all things, we thank you, because you are powerful. Yours is the glory forever.

ON HANUKKAH

C **FOR THE MIRACLES,** and for the deliverance, and for the acts of power, and for the acts of salvation, and for the battles that you performed for our fathers in those days, in this season:

D **IN THE DAYS** of Mattityahu son of Yochanan the Hasmonean high priest and his sons, when the evil Greek empire stood against your people Israel, to cause them to forget your Torah, and to move them away from the statutes of your will. But you, in your abundant compassion, stood for them in the moment of their distress: you took on their struggle, you judged their case, you retaliated on their behalf;[a] you handed over the powerful into the hands of the powerless, the multitude into the hands of the few, the unclean into the hands of the clean, the wicked into the hands of the righteous, and the offenders into the hands of those who occupy themselves with your Torah. And you made a great and holy name for yourself in your world, and you performed an act of great salvation for your people Israel,[b] and a deliverance to this very day. And afterward, your children entered the inner chamber of your House, cleared out your Hall, cleansed your Sanctuary, and kindled lamps in the courtyards of your Holy Place. They appointed these eight days of Hanukkah to give thanks and to praise your great name.

a) Jeremiah 51:36. b) 1 Samuel 19:5.

ON PURIM

E עַל הַנִּסִּים וְעַל הַפֻּרְקָן וְעַל הַגְּבוּרוֹת וְעַל הַתְּשׁוּעוֹת וְעַל הַמִּלְחָמוֹת שֶׁעָשִׂיתָ לַאֲבוֹתֵינוּ בַּיָּמִים הָהֵם בַּזְּמַן הַזֶּה:

F בִּימֵי מָרְדְּכַי וְאֶסְתֵּר בְּשׁוּשַׁן הַבִּירָה, כְּשֶׁעָמַד עֲלֵיהֶם הָמָן הָרָשָׁע, בִּקֵּשׁ לְהַשְׁמִיד לַהֲרֹג וּלְאַבֵּד אֶת כָּל הַיְּהוּדִים, מִנַּעַר וְעַד זָקֵן, טַף וְנָשִׁים בְּיוֹם אֶחָד, בִּשְׁלוֹשָׁה עָשָׂר לְחֹדֶשׁ שְׁנֵים עָשָׂר, הוּא חֹדֶשׁ אֲדָר, וּשְׁלָלָם לָבוֹז. וְאַתָּה בְּרַחֲמֶיךָ הָרַבִּים הֵפַרְתָּ אֶת עֲצָתוֹ, וְקִלְקַלְתָּ אֶת מַחֲשַׁבְתּוֹ, וַהֲשֵׁבְוֹתָ לּוֹ גְּמוּלוֹ בְּרֹאשׁוֹ, וְתָלוּ אוֹתוֹ וְאֶת בָּנָיו עַל הָעֵץ:

G וְעַל הַכֹּל יְיָ אֱלֹהֵינוּ אֲנַחְנוּ מוֹדִים לָךְ, וּמְבָרְכִים אוֹתָךְ, יִתְבָּרַךְ שִׁמְךָ בְּפִי כָּל חַי תָּמִיד לְעוֹלָם וָעֶד. כַּכָּתוּב, וְאָכַלְתָּ וְשָׂבָעְתָּ, וּבֵרַכְתָּ אֶת יְיָ אֱלֹהֶיךָ עַל הָאָרֶץ הַטֹּבָה אֲשֶׁר נָתַן לָךְ.

H › בָּרוּךְ אַתָּה יְיָ, עַל הָאָרֶץ וְעַל הַמָּזוֹן: » אָמֵן.

53

בנין ירושלים

THIRD BLESSING: FOR JERUSALEM

A רַחֵם נָא יְיָ אֱלֹהֵינוּ, עַל יִשְׂרָאֵל עַמֶּךָ, וְעַל יְרוּשָׁלַיִם עִירֶךָ, וְעַל צִיּוֹן מִשְׁכַּן כְּבוֹדֶךָ, וְעַל מַלְכוּת בֵּית דָּוִד מְשִׁיחֶךָ, וְעַל הַבַּיִת הַגָּדוֹל וְהַקָּדוֹשׁ שֶׁנִּקְרָא שִׁמְךָ עָלָיו. אֱלֹהֵינוּ אָבִינוּ רְעֵנוּ זוּנֵנוּ פַּרְנְסֵנוּ וְכַלְכְּלֵנוּ וְהַרְוִיחֵנוּ, וְהַרְוַח לָנוּ יְיָ אֱלֹהֵינוּ מְהֵרָה מִכָּל צָרוֹתֵינוּ. וְנָא אַל תַּצְרִיכֵנוּ יְיָ אֱלֹהֵינוּ, לֹא לִידֵי מַתְּנַת בָּשָׂר וָדָם, וְלֹא לִידֵי הַלְוָאָתָם. כִּי אִם לְיָדְךָ הַמְּלֵאָה הַפְּתוּחָה הַקְּדוֹשָׁה וְהָרְחָבָה, שֶׁלֹּא נֵבוֹשׁ וְלֹא נִכָּלֵם לְעוֹלָם וָעֶד:

ON PURIM

E **FOR THE MIRACLES,** and for the deliverance, and for the acts of power, and for the acts of salvation, and for the battles that you performed for our fathers in those days, in this season:

F **IN THE DAYS** of Mordecai and Esther in Shushan the capital, when the wicked Haman stood against them, he sought to devastate, kill, and destroy all of the Jewish people, including young to old, infants and women, in a single day—on the thirteenth day of the twelfth month, which is the month of Adar—and he sought to plunder their possessions.[a] But in your abundant compassion, you thwarted his plan, spoiled his intentions, and turned his efforts back upon his own head, so they hung him and his sons upon the tree.

G **AND FOR ALL THINGS,** O LORD, our God, we thank you and we bless you. May your name be blessed in the mouths of all living things always, forever and ever. It is written: you shall eat and be satisfied, and you shall bless the LORD your God for the good land that he has given you.[b]

H › **BLESSED** are you, O LORD, for the land and for the nourishment. ›› Amen.

53 ## BINYAN YERUSHALAYIM

THIRD BLESSING: FOR JERUSALEM

A **PLEASE HAVE COMPASSION,** O LORD, our God, upon Israel your people, upon Jerusalem your city, upon Zion, the dwelling place of your glory,[c] upon the kingdom of the house of David your anointed one, and upon the great and holy House that is called by your name.[d] Our God, our Father, our Shepherd, our Nourisher, our Provider, our Maintainer, our Reliever! Relieve us, O LORD, our God, quickly from all our troubles. Do not let us rely, O LORD, our God, upon the gifts of flesh and blood, nor upon their loans, but only upon your hand, which is filled, open, holy, and wide, that we may not be shamed nor humiliated forever and ever.

a) Esther 3:13. b) Deuteronomy 8:10. c) Psalm 26:8. d) Jeremiah 7:10, 11, 14, 30.

ON THE SABBATH

B רְצֵה וְהַחֲלִיצֵנוּ יְיָ אֱלֹהֵינוּ בְּמִצְוֹתֶךָ, וּבְמִצְוַת יוֹם הַשְּׁבִיעִי הַשַּׁבָּת הַגָּדוֹל וְהַקָּדוֹשׁ הַזֶּה. כִּי יוֹם זֶה גָּדוֹל וְקָדוֹשׁ הוּא לְפָנֶיךָ, לִשְׁבָּת בּוֹ וְלָנוּחַ בּוֹ בְּאַהֲבָה כְּמִצְוַת רְצוֹנֶךָ, וּבִרְצוֹנְךָ הָנִיחַ לָנוּ יְיָ אֱלֹהֵינוּ, שֶׁלֹּא תְהֵא צָרָה וְיָגוֹן וַאֲנָחָה בְּיוֹם מְנוּחָתֵנוּ. וְהַרְאֵנוּ יְיָ אֱלֹהֵינוּ בְּנֶחָמַת צִיּוֹן עִירֶךָ, וּבְבִנְיַן יְרוּשָׁלַיִם עִיר קָדְשֶׁךָ, כִּי אַתָּה הוּא בַּעַל הַיְשׁוּעוֹת וּבַעַל הַנֶּחָמוֹת:

ON HOLIDAYS AND ROSH CHODESH

C אֱלֹהֵינוּ וֵאלֹהֵי אֲבוֹתֵינוּ, יַעֲלֶה וְיָבֹא וְיַגִּיעַ וְיֵרָאֶה וְיֵרָצֶה וְיִשָּׁמַע וְיִפָּקֵד וְיִזָּכֵר זִכְרוֹנֵנוּ וּפִקְדוֹנֵנוּ, וְזִכְרוֹן אֲבוֹתֵינוּ, וְזִכְרוֹן מָשִׁיחַ בֶּן דָּוִד עַבְדֶּךָ, וְזִכְרוֹן יְרוּשָׁלַיִם עִיר קָדְשֶׁךָ, וְזִכְרוֹן כָּל עַמְּךָ בֵּית יִשְׂרָאֵל לְפָנֶיךָ, לִפְלֵיטָה לְטוֹבָה לְחֵן וּלְחֶסֶד וּלְרַחֲמִים, לְחַיִּים וּלְשָׁלוֹם בְּיוֹם

ON ROSH CHODESH	רֹאשׁ הַחֹדֶשׁ הַזֶּה.
ON PASSOVER	חַג הַמַּצּוֹת הַזֶּה.
ON SHAVU'OT	חַג הַשָּׁבֻעוֹת הַזֶּה.
ON SUKKOT	חַג הַסֻּכּוֹת הַזֶּה.
ON SHMINI ATZERET AND SIMCHAT TORAH	הַשְּׁמִינִי חַג הָעֲצֶרֶת הַזֶּה.
ON ROSH HASHANAH	הַזִּכָּרוֹן הַזֶּה.

D זָכְרֵנוּ יְיָ אֱלֹהֵינוּ בּוֹ לְטוֹבָה, וּפָקְדֵנוּ בוֹ לִבְרָכָה, וְהוֹשִׁיעֵנוּ בוֹ לְחַיִּים. וּבִדְבַר יְשׁוּעָה וְרַחֲמִים, חוּס וְחָנֵּנוּ, וְרַחֵם עָלֵינוּ וְהוֹשִׁיעֵנוּ, כִּי אֵלֶיךָ עֵינֵינוּ, כִּי אֵל מֶלֶךְ חַנּוּן וְרַחוּם אָתָּה:

On the Sabbath

B **Show favor** and fortify us, O LORD, our God, with your commandments and with the commandment of the seventh day, this great and holy Sabbath. For this day is great and holy before you, to cease on it and to rest on it, with love, according to the commandment of your favor. And in your favor, give us rest, O LORD, our God, that there may not be trouble, sorrow, or groaning on the day of our rest. And show us, O LORD, our God, the consolation of Zion your city, and the building of Jerusalem, the city of your holiness, for you are the Master of salvations and Master of consolations.

On holidays and Rosh Chodesh

C **Our God** and God of our fathers, may there ascend, and come, and arrive, and appear, and be favored, and be heard, and be noticed, and be remembered: the remembrance and notice of us, the remembrance of our fathers, the remembrance of Messiah, son of David, your Servant, the remembrance of Jerusalem, the city of your holiness, the remembrance of your entire people, the house of Israel, before you, for preservation, for goodness, for grace, for devotion, for compassion, for life, and for peace on this day of

On Rosh Chodesh	Rosh Chodesh.
On Passover	the Festival of Matzot.
On Shavu'ot	the Festival of Shavu'ot.
On Sukkot	the Festival of Sukkot.
On Shmini Atzeret and Simchat Torah	the Festival of Shmini Atzeret.
On Rosh HaShanah	Remembrance.

D **Remember** us on it, O LORD, our God, for goodness, and notice us on it for blessing, and save us on it for life. And regarding salvation and compassion, take pity and be gracious to us, have compassion on us and save us, for our eyes are focused on you, because you are God, a gracious and compassionate King.[a]

a) Nehemiah 9:31.

ON ALL DAYS, CONTINUE HERE.

E זְכוֹר יְיָ אֶת עֲדָתְךָ לְהַצִּיל אוֹתָהּ מִכָּל רָע וּלְהַשְׁלִימָהּ בְּאַהֲבָתֶךָ. וְקַבֵּץ אֶת הַמְקֻדֶּשֶׁת מִן אַרְבַּע הָרוּחוֹת לְמַלְכוּתְךָ שֶׁהֲכִינוֹתָ לָהּ. כִּי לְךָ הַגְּבוּרָה וְהַכָּבוֹד לְעוֹלָמִים.

F › וּבְנֵה יְרוּשָׁלַיִם עִיר הַקֹּדֶשׁ בִּמְהֵרָה בְיָמֵינוּ. בָּרוּךְ אַתָּה יְיָ, בּוֹנֵה בְּרַחֲמָיו יְרוּשָׁלָיִם. אָמֵן: » אָמֵן.

54

הטוב והמטיב

FOURTH BLESSING: THE GOOD AND BENEFICENT ONE

A בָּרוּךְ אַתָּה יְיָ אֱלֹהֵינוּ מֶלֶךְ הָעוֹלָם, הָאֵל אָבִינוּ מַלְכֵּנוּ אַדִּירֵנוּ בּוֹרְאֵנוּ גּוֹאֲלֵנוּ יוֹצְרֵנוּ קְדוֹשֵׁנוּ קְדוֹשׁ יַעֲקֹב, רוֹעֵנוּ רוֹעֵה יִשְׂרָאֵל. הַמֶּלֶךְ הַטּוֹב, וְהַמֵּטִיב לַכֹּל, שֶׁבְּכָל יוֹם וָיוֹם הוּא הֵטִיב, הוּא מֵטִיב, הוּא יֵיטִיב לָנוּ. הוּא גְמָלָנוּ, הוּא גוֹמְלֵנוּ, הוּא יִגְמְלֵנוּ לָעַד, לְחֵן וּלְחֶסֶד וּלְרַחֲמִים וּלְרֶוַח הַצָּלָה וְהַצְלָחָה, בְּרָכָה וִישׁוּעָה, נֶחָמָה, פַּרְנָסָה וְכַלְכָּלָה.

B › וְרַחֲמִים וְחַיִּים וְשָׁלוֹם וְכָל טוֹב, וּמִכָּל טוּב לְעוֹלָם אַל יְחַסְּרֵנוּ:

הרחמן

The Compassionate One

C הָרַחֲמָן הוּא יִמְלוֹךְ עָלֵינוּ לְעוֹלָם וָעֶד.

D הָרַחֲמָן הוּא יִתְבָּרַךְ בַּשָּׁמַיִם וּבָאָרֶץ.

E הָרַחֲמָן הוּא יִשְׁתַּבַּח לְדוֹר דּוֹרִים, וְיִתְפָּאַר בָּנוּ לָעַד וּלְנֵצַח נְצָחִים, וְיִתְהַדַּר בָּנוּ לָעַד וּלְעוֹלְמֵי עוֹלָמִים.

F הָרַחֲמָן הוּא יְפַרְנְסֵנוּ בְּכָבוֹד.

G הָרַחֲמָן הוּא יִשְׁבּוֹר עֻלֵּנוּ מֵעַל צַוָּארֵנוּ, וְהוּא יוֹלִיכֵנוּ קוֹמְמִיּוּת לְאַרְצֵנוּ.

H הָרַחֲמָן הוּא יִשְׁלַח לָנוּ בְּרָכָה מְרֻבָּה בַּבַּיִת הַזֶּה, וְעַל שֻׁלְחָן זֶה שֶׁאָכַלְנוּ עָלָיו.

I הָרַחֲמָן הוּא יִשְׁלַח לָנוּ אֶת אֵלִיָּהוּ הַנָּבִיא זָכוּר לַטּוֹב, וִיבַשֶּׂר לָנוּ בְּשׂוֹרוֹת טוֹבוֹת יְשׁוּעוֹת וְנֶחָמוֹת.

ON ALL DAYS, CONTINUE HERE.

E **REMEMBER,** O LORD, your congregation[a] to rescue her from all evil, and to make her complete in your love. Gather the betrothed from the four winds[b] to your kingdom that you have prepared for her.[c] For yours is the power and the glory forever.

F › **REBUILD** Jerusalem, city of holiness, quickly in our days. Blessed are you, O LORD, who builds Jerusalem in his compassion.[d] Amen. » Amen.

54

HATOV VEHAMETIV

FOURTH BLESSING: THE GOOD AND BENEFICENT ONE

A **BLESSED** are you, O LORD, our God, King of the universe, the God who is our Father, our King, our Majestic One, our Creator, our Redeemer, our Molder, our Holy One, the Holy One of Jacob,[e] our Shepherd, the Shepherd of Israel,[f] the Good King, who does good to all, and day after day, he did good, he does good, and he will do good for us. He was generous; he is generous; he will be generous forever, for grace, for devotion, for compassion, for a relieving rescue, success, blessing, and salvation, consolation, provision, and maintenance.

B › May we never lack compassion, and life, and peace, and every good thing and all goodness.

HARACHAMAN

The Compassionate One

C The Compassionate One, may he reign over us forever and ever.

D The Compassionate One, may he be blessed in the heavens and in the earth.

E The Compassionate One, may he be acclaimed in every generation, and always glorified in us from now to everlasting, and honored in us for all time and all eternity.

F The Compassionate One, may he provide for us with dignity.

G The Compassionate One, may he break our yoke from upon our neck,[g] and may he lead us upright[h] to our land.

H The Compassionate One, may he send abundant blessing to us in this house, and upon this table from which we have eaten.

I The Compassionate One, may he send us Elijah the Prophet remembered for good, and may he bring good news: the news of goodness, salvations, and consolations.

---

a) Psalm 74:2. b) Zechariah 2:10[6]. c) Cf. Matthew 25:34. d) Psalm 147:2.
e) Isaiah 29:23. f) Psalm 80:2[1]. g) Jeremiah 30:8. h) Leviticus 26:13.

HOST AND HOSTESS (Include the relevant words in brackets.)

J הָרַחֲמָן הוּא יְבָרֵךְ אוֹתִי {וְאֶת בַּעְלִי/אִשְׁתִּי וְאֶת זַרְעִי} וְאֶת כָּל אֲשֶׁר לִי,

GUESTS (If at one's parents' house, include the words in brackets.)

SOME ADD

K יְהִי רָצוֹן שֶׁלֹּא יֵבוֹשׁ וְלֹא יִכָּלֵם בַּעַל הַבַּיִת הַזֶּה לֹא בָעוֹלָם הַזֶּה וְלֹא בָעוֹלָם הַבָּא, וְיַצְלִיחַ בְּכָל נְכָסָיו, וְיִהְיוּ נְכָסָיו מוּצְלָחִים וּקְרוֹבִים לָעִיר, וְאַל יִשְׁלוֹט שָׂטָן בְּמַעֲשֵׂה יָדָיו, וְאַל יִזְדַּקֵּק לְפָנָיו שׁוּם דְּבַר חֵטְא וְהִרְהוּר עָוֹן, מֵעַתָּה וְעַד עוֹלָם.

L הָרַחֲמָן הוּא יְבָרֵךְ אֶת {אָבִי מוֹרִי} בַּעַל הַבַּיִת הַזֶּה, וְאֶת {אִמִּי מוֹרָתִי} בַּעֲלַת הַבַּיִת הַזֶּה, אוֹתָם וְאֶת בֵּיתָם וְאֶת זַרְעָם וְאֶת כָּל אֲשֶׁר לָהֶם,

M אוֹתָנוּ וְאֶת כָּל אֲשֶׁר לָנוּ, כְּמוֹ שֶׁנִּתְבָּרְכוּ אֲבוֹתֵינוּ, אַבְרָהָם יִצְחָק וְיַעֲקֹב בַּכֹּל מִכֹּל כֹּל. כֵּן יְבָרֵךְ אוֹתָנוּ כֻּלָּנוּ יַחַד, בִּבְרָכָה שְׁלֵמָה, וְנֹאמַר אָמֵן:

N בַּמָּרוֹם יְלַמְּדוּ עֲלֵיהֶם וְעָלֵינוּ זְכוּת, שֶׁתְּהֵא לְמִשְׁמֶרֶת שָׁלוֹם. וְנִשָּׂא בְרָכָה מֵאֵת יְיָ, וּצְדָקָה מֵאֱלֹהֵי יִשְׁעֵנוּ, וְנִמְצָא חֵן וְשֵׂכֶל טוֹב בְּעֵינֵי אֱלֹהִים וְאָדָם:

At a circumcision meal, include *HaRachaman* (The Compassionate One) prayer 58, page 116 , and then continue below.

O ON THE SABBATH הָרַחֲמָן הוּא יַנְחִילֵנוּ יוֹם שֶׁכֻּלּוֹ שַׁבָּת וּמְנוּחָה לְחַיֵּי הָעוֹלָמִים.

ON ROSH CHODESH הָרַחֲמָן הוּא יְחַדֵּשׁ עָלֵינוּ אֶת הַחֹדֶשׁ הַזֶּה לְטוֹבָה וְלִבְרָכָה.

ON A FESTIVAL הָרַחֲמָן הוּא יַנְחִילֵנוּ יוֹם שֶׁכֻּלּוֹ טוֹב.

ON ROSH HASHANAH הָרַחֲמָן הוּא יְחַדֵּשׁ עָלֵינוּ אֶת הַשָּׁנָה הַזֹּאת לְטוֹבָה וְלִבְרָכָה.

ON SUKKOT הָרַחֲמָן הוּא יָקִים לָנוּ אֶת סֻכַּת דָּוִד הַנּוֹפֶלֶת.

Host and Hostess (Include the relevant words in brackets.)

J The Compassionate One, may he bless me, {and my husband/wife, and my offspring,} and all that is mine;.

Guests (If at one's parents' house, include the words in brackets.)

Some add

K Let it be your will that the master of this house not be ashamed or humiliated, neither in this world nor in the world to come. Let him succeed in all his endeavors, and let his endeavors be successful and convenient. Do not let any adversary rule over his efforts, and let no matter of sin or wicked thought attach itself to him, now or forever.

L The Compassionate One, may he bless {my father, my teacher,} the master of this house, and {my mother, my teacher,} the lady of this house, them, and their household, and their offspring, and all that is theirs;

M Us and all that is ours, just as our fathers were blessed—Abraham, Isaac, and Jacob—in everything,[a] from everything,[b] with everything.[c] So may we all be blessed together, with a complete blessing. Let us say: Amen.

N In the heavens above, may their case and ours be heard, that there may be a preservation of peace, and may we bear blessing from the LORD, and righteous acts from our God who saves; may we find grace and be perceived well in the eyes of God and man.[d]

At a circumcision meal, include *HaRachaman* (The Compassionate One), prayer 58, page 117, and then continue below.

O On the Sabbath: The Compassionate One, may he let us inherit the day of complete Sabbath and rest for eternal life.

On Rosh Chodesh: The Compassionate One, may he renew this month for us for goodness and blessing.

On a Festival: The Compassionate One, may he let us inherit the day of complete goodness.

On Rosh HaShanah: The Compassionate One, may he renew this year for us for goodness and blessing.

On Sukkot: The Compassionate One, may he raise up for us the fallen *sukkah* of David.[e]

a) Genesis 24:1. b) Genesis 27:33. c) Genesis 33:11. d) Proverbs 3:4.
e) Amos 9:11, also cf. Acts 15:16–18.

P הָרַחֲמָן הוּא יְזַכֵּנוּ לִימוֹת הַמָּשִׁיחַ וּלְחַיֵּי הָעוֹלָם הַבָּא.

ON A SABBATH OR FESTIVAL מִגְדּוֹל יְשׁוּעוֹת מַלְכּוֹ,

ON A REGULAR WEEKDAY מַגְדִּל יְשׁוּעוֹת מַלְכּוֹ,

Q וְעֹשֶׂה חֶסֶד לִמְשִׁיחוֹ לְדָוִד וּלְזַרְעוֹ עַד עוֹלָם.

R עֹשֶׂה שָׁלוֹם בִּמְרוֹמָיו, הוּא יַעֲשֶׂה שָׁלוֹם עָלֵינוּ וְעַל כָּל יִשְׂרָאֵל, וְאִמְרוּ, אָמֵן:

S יְראוּ אֶת יְיָ קְדוֹשָׁיו, כִּי אֵין מַחְסוֹר לִירֵאָיו. כְּפִירִים רָשׁוּ וְרָעֵבוּ, וְדוֹרְשֵׁי יְיָ לֹא יַחְסְרוּ כָל טוֹב. הוֹדוּ לַייָ כִּי טוֹב, כִּי לְעוֹלָם חַסְדּוֹ. פּוֹתֵחַ אֶת יָדֶךָ, וּמַשְׂבִּיעַ לְכָל חַי רָצוֹן. בָּרוּךְ הַגֶּבֶר אֲשֶׁר יִבְטַח בַּייָ, וְהָיָה יְיָ מִבְטַחוֹ. נַעַר הָיִיתִי גַם זָקַנְתִּי, וְלֹא רָאִיתִי צַדִּיק נֶעֱזָב, וְזַרְעוֹ מְבַקֶּשׁ לָחֶם. יְיָ עֹז לְעַמּוֹ יִתֵּן, יְיָ יְבָרֵךְ אֶת עַמּוֹ בַשָּׁלוֹם.

T יָבוֹא חֵן וְיַעֲבֹר הָעוֹלָם הַזֶּה. הוֹשַׁע נָא לֵאלֹהֵי דָוִד. כֹּל שֶׁקָּדוֹשׁ, יָבוֹא. כֹּל שֶׁאֵינֶנּוּ, יָשׁוּב. מָרַן אֶתָא, אָמֵן:

At a wedding meal, continue with the *Sheva Brachot* (Seven Blessings), prayer 56, page 110.

P The Compassionate One, may he allow us to see the days of the Messiah and the life of the world to come.

ON A SABBATH OR FESTIVAL	A tower of salvations of his King,
ON A REGULAR WEEKDAY	Magnifying the salvations of his King,

Q He shows devotion to his Messiah, to David and to his offspring until eternity.[a]

R May the One who makes peace in his heights[b] make peace for us and for all Israel. And now say, Amen.

S Fear the LORD, his holy ones, for those who fear him have no lack. Young lions may be poor and hungry, but those who seek the LORD do not lack a good thing.[c] Give thanks to the LORD, for he is good, for his devotion is eternal.[d] Opening your hand, you satisfy the desire of every living thing.[e] Blessed is the man who trusts in the LORD, and the LORD will be his assurance.[f] I was a young man, and I grew old, but I have never seen a righteous person forsaken, nor his offspring asking for bread.[g] The LORD will give strength to his people; the LORD will bless his people with peace.[h]

T **MAY GRACE COME,** and may this world pass away. Hoshana to the God of David![i] Everyone who is holy, let him come. Everyone who is not, let him repent. Maran Etha! (Our Master is coming!) Amen.

At a wedding meal, continue with the *Sheva Brachot* (Seven Blessings), prayer 56, page 111.

---

a) Psalm 18:51[50]; 2 Samuel 22:51.
b) Job 25:2.
c) Psalm 34:10–11[9–10].
d) Psalm 106:1, 118:1, 29, 136:1; 1 Chronicles 16:34.
e) Psalm 145:16.
f) Jeremiah 17:7.
g) Psalm 37:25.
h) Psalm 29:11.
i) Cf. Matthew 21:9, 15.

ברכות לסעודת שבע ברכות

55 זימון לשבע ברכות

INVITATION FOR A WEDDING MEAL

A LEADER רַבּוֹתַי נְבָרֵךְ:

B GROUP יְהִי שֵׁם יְיָ מְבֹרָךְ מֵעַתָּה וְעַד עוֹלָם:

C LEADER יְהִי שֵׁם יְיָ מְבֹרָךְ מֵעַתָּה וְעַד עוֹלָם.

דְּוַי הָסֵר וְגַם חָרוֹן,
וְאָז אִלֵּם בְּשִׁיר יָרוֹן,
נְחֵנוּ בְּמַעְגְּלֵי צֶדֶק,
שְׁעֵה בִּרְכַּת בְּנֵי אַהֲרֹן:

D LEADER בִּרְשׁוּת מָרָנָן וְרַבָּנָן וְרַבּוֹתַי,
נְבָרֵךְ אֱלֹהֵינוּ שֶׁהַשִּׂמְחָה בִּמְעוֹנוֹ,
וְשֶׁאָכַלְנוּ מִשֶּׁלוֹ:

E GROUP בָּרוּךְ אֱלֹהֵינוּ שֶׁהַשִּׂמְחָה בִּמְעוֹנוֹ,
וְשֶׁאָכַלְנוּ מִשֶּׁלוֹ וּבְטוּבוֹ חָיִינוּ:

F LEADER בָּרוּךְ אֱלֹהֵינוּ שֶׁהַשִּׂמְחָה בִּמְעוֹנוֹ,
וְשֶׁאָכַלְנוּ מִשֶּׁלוֹ וּבְטוּבוֹ חָיִינוּ.
בָּרוּךְ הוּא וּבָרוּךְ שְׁמוֹ:

Continue with the *Birkat HaZan* (First Blessing: For the Food), prayer 51, page 96.

56 שבע ברכות

SEVEN BLESSINGS

A **בָּרוּךְ** אַתָּה יְיָ אֱלֹהֵינוּ מֶלֶךְ הָעוֹלָם, שֶׁהַכֹּל בָּרָא לִכְבוֹדוֹ:

B **בָּרוּךְ** אַתָּה יְיָ אֱלֹהֵינוּ מֶלֶךְ הָעוֹלָם, יוֹצֵר הָאָדָם:

C **בָּרוּךְ** אַתָּה יְיָ אֱלֹהֵינוּ מֶלֶךְ הָעוֹלָם, אֲשֶׁר יָצַר אֶת הָאָדָם בְּצַלְמוֹ, בְּצֶלֶם דְּמוּת תַּבְנִיתוֹ, וְהִתְקִין לוֹ מִמֶּנּוּ בִּנְיַן עֲדֵי עַד. בָּרוּךְ אַתָּה יְיָ, יוֹצֵר הָאָדָם:

Wedding Meal Blessings

55 Zimmun Lesheva Brachot

INVITATION FOR A WEDDING MEAL

A LEADER Gentlemen, let us bless!

B GROUP May the name of the LORD be blessed now and forever.[a]

C LEADER May the name of the LORD be blessed now and forever.

Remove both pain and wrath,
And then the mute will joyfully sing a song.
Guide us along paths of righteousness;
Pay regard to the blessing of the children of Aaron.

D LEADER With the permission of my distinguished gentlemen and scholars, let us bless our God, in whose dwelling place is gladness, and from whom is our sustenance.

E GROUP Blessed is our God in whose dwelling place is gladness, and from whom is our sustenance, and by whose goodness we live.

F LEADER Blessed is our God in whose dwelling place is gladness, and from whom is our sustenance, and by whose goodness we live. Blessed is he and blessed is his name.

Continue with the *Birkat HaZan* (First Blessing: For the Food), prayer 51, page 97.

56 Sheva Brachot

SEVEN BLESSINGS

A **Blessed** are you, O LORD, our God, King of the universe, for whose glory all things were created.

B **Blessed** are you, O LORD, our God, King of the universe, who created the man.[b]

C **Blessed** are you, O LORD, our God, King of the universe, who created the man in his image,[c] in the image of the likeness of his pattern, and prepared for him from himself a building lasting forever. Blessed are you, O LORD, who created the man.

a) Psalm 113:2. b) Genesis 2:7. c) Genesis 1:26–27.

D **שׂוֹשׂ** תָּשִׂישׂ וְתָגֵל הָעֲקָרָה, בְּקִבּוּץ בָּנֶיהָ לְתוֹכָהּ בְּשִׂמְחָה. בָּרוּךְ אַתָּה יְיָ, מְשַׂמֵּחַ צִיּוֹן בְּבָנֶיהָ:

E **שַׂמֵּחַ** תְּשַׂמַּח רֵעִים הָאֲהוּבִים, כְּשַׂמֵּחֲךָ יְצִירְךָ בְּגַן עֵדֶן מִקֶּדֶם. בָּרוּךְ אַתָּה יְיָ, מְשַׂמֵּחַ חָתָן וְכַלָּה:

F **בָּרוּךְ** אַתָּה יְיָ אֱלֹהֵינוּ מֶלֶךְ הָעוֹלָם, אֲשֶׁר בָּרָא שָׂשׂוֹן וְשִׂמְחָה, חָתָן וְכַלָּה, גִּילָה רִנָּה דִּיצָה וְחֶדְוָה, אַהֲבָה וְאַחֲוָה שָׁלוֹם וְרֵעוּת. מְהֵרָה יְיָ אֱלֹהֵינוּ יִשָּׁמַע בְּעָרֵי יְהוּדָה וּבְחֻצוֹת יְרוּשָׁלָיִם, קוֹל שָׂשׂוֹן וְקוֹל שִׂמְחָה, קוֹל חָתָן וְקוֹל כַּלָּה, קוֹל מִצְהֲלוֹת חֲתָנִים מֵחֻפָּתָם, וּנְעָרִים מִמִּשְׁתֵּה נְגִינָתָם. בָּרוּךְ אַתָּה יְיָ, מְשַׂמֵּחַ חָתָן עִם הַכַּלָּה:

G **בָּרוּךְ** אַתָּה יְיָ אֱלֹהֵינוּ מֶלֶךְ הָעוֹלָם, בּוֹרֵא פְּרִי הַגָּפֶן:

D **REJOICE** greatly and be joyful,[a] O barren one,[b] at the gathering of her children within her with gladness. Blessed are you, O LORD, who gladdens Zion with her children.

E **GLADDEN** greatly the beloved companions, just as you gladdened the one you formed in the Garden of Eden long ago. Blessed are you, O LORD, who gladdens the groom and the bride.

F **BLESSED** are you, O LORD, our God, King of the universe, who created joy and gladness, groom and bride, celebration, joyful singing, festivity and merriment, love and brotherhood, peace and companionship. Quickly, O LORD, our God, let it be heard in the cities of Judah and in the streets of Jerusalem, the sound of joy and the sound of gladness, the sound of the groom and the sound of the bride,[c] the sound of the grooms' cries of joy from their bridal canopies, and young men from their music-filled banquets. Blessed are you, O LORD, who gladdens the groom with the bride.

G **BLESSED** are you, O LORD, our God, King of the universe, who creates the fruit of the vine.

a) Isaiah 61:10.
b) Isaiah 54:1.
c) Jeremiah 33:11.

ברכות לסעודת ברית מילה

57

זמון לסעודת ברית מילה

INVITATION FOR A CIRCUMCISION MEAL

Include this section only if at least three men are present.

A LEADER רַבּוֹתַי נְבָרֵךְ:

B GROUP יְהִי שֵׁם יְיָ מְבֹרָךְ מֵעַתָּה וְעַד עוֹלָם:

C LEADER יְהִי שֵׁם יְיָ מְבֹרָךְ מֵעַתָּה וְעַד עוֹלָם. נוֹדֶה לְשִׁמְךָ בְּתוֹךְ אֱמוּנַי,
בְּרוּכִים אַתֶּם לַייָ:

D GROUP נוֹדֶה לְשִׁמְךָ בְּתוֹךְ אֱמוּנַי, בְּרוּכִים אַתֶּם לַייָ:

E LEADER בִּרְשׁוּת אֵל אָיוֹם וְנוֹרָא, מִשְׂגָּב לְעִתּוֹת בַּצָּרָה, אֵל נֶאְזָר בִּגְבוּרָה,
אַדִּיר בַּמָּרוֹם יְיָ:

F GROUP נוֹדֶה לְשִׁמְךָ בְּתוֹךְ אֱמוּנַי, בְּרוּכִים אַתֶּם לַייָ:

G LEADER בִּרְשׁוּת הַתּוֹרָה הַקְּדוֹשָׁה, טְהוֹרָה הִיא וְגַם פְּרוּשָׁה,
צִוָּה לָנוּ מוֹרָשָׁה, מֹשֶׁה עֶבֶד יְיָ:

H GROUP נוֹדֶה לְשִׁמְךָ בְּתוֹךְ אֱמוּנַי, בְּרוּכִים אַתֶּם לַייָ:

I LEADER בִּרְשׁוּת הַכֹּהֲנִים וְהַלְוִיִּם, אֶקְרָא לֵאלֹהֵי הָעִבְרִיִּים,
אֲהוֹדֶנּוּ בְּכָל אִיִּים, אֲבָרְכָה אֶת יְיָ:

J GROUP נוֹדֶה לְשִׁמְךָ בְּתוֹךְ אֱמוּנַי, בְּרוּכִים אַתֶּם לַייָ:

K LEADER בִּרְשׁוּת מָרָנָן וְרַבָּנָן וְרַבּוֹתַי, אֶפְתְּחָה בְּשִׁיר פִּי וּשְׂפָתַי,
וְתֹאמַרְנָה עַצְמוֹתַי, בָּרוּךְ הַבָּא בְּשֵׁם יְיָ:

L GROUP נוֹדֶה לְשִׁמְךָ בְּתוֹךְ אֱמוּנַי, בְּרוּכִים אַתֶּם לַייָ:

If ten or more are present, include words in brackets.

M LEADER בִּרְשׁוּת מָרָנָן וְרַבָּנָן וְרַבּוֹתַי, נְבָרֵךְ {אֱלֹהֵינוּ} שֶׁאָכַלְנוּ מִשֶּׁלּוֹ:

CIRCUMCISION MEAL BLESSINGS

57 ZIMMUN LISE'UDAT BRIT MILAH

INVITATION FOR A CIRCUMCISION MEAL

Include this section only if at least three men are present.

A LEADER Gentlemen, let us bless!

B GROUP May the name of the LORD be blessed now and forever.[a]

C LEADER May the name of the LORD be blessed now and forever. We give thanks to your name among those faithful to me; you are blessed of the LORD.

D GROUP We give thanks to your name among those faithful to me; you are blessed of the LORD.

E LEADER With the permission of the Fearsome and Awesome One, a stronghold in times of trouble, God girded in power, majestic in the heavens above is the LORD.

F GROUP We give thanks to your name among those faithful to me; you are blessed of the LORD.

G LEADER With the permission of the holy Torah, which is pure as well as explicit, our heritage commanded by Moses,[b] the servant of the LORD.

H GROUP We give thanks to your name among those faithful to me; you are blessed of the LORD.

I LEADER With the permission of the priests and the Levites, I will call to the God of the Hebrews; I will thank him in all the islands; I will bless the LORD.

J GROUP We give thanks to your name among those faithful to me; you are blessed of the LORD.

K LEADER With the permission of my distinguished gentlemen and scholars, I will open my mouth and my lips with singing, and my bones will say, “Blessed is the one who comes in the name of the LORD.”[c]

L GROUP We give thanks to your name among those faithful to me; you are blessed of the LORD.

If ten or more are present, include words in brackets.

M LEADER With the permission of my distinguished gentlemen and scholars, let us bless {our God,} the one from whom is our sustenance.

a) Psalm 113:2. b) Deuteronomy 33:4. c) Psalm 118:26.

N GROUP בָּרוּךְ {אֱלֹהֵינוּ} שֶׁאָכַלְנוּ מִשֶּׁלּוֹ וּבְטוּבוֹ חָיִינוּ:

O LEADER בָּרוּךְ {אֱלֹהֵינוּ} שֶׁאָכַלְנוּ מִשֶּׁלּוֹ וּבְטוּבוֹ חָיִינוּ. בָּרוּךְ הוּא וּבָרוּךְ שְׁמוֹ:

Continue with the *Birkat HaZan* (First Blessing: For the Food), prayer 51, page 96.

58

הרחמן

THE COMPASSIONATE ONE

SOMEONE OTHER THAN THE FATHER

A הָרַחֲמָן הוּא יְבָרֵךְ אֲבִי הַיֶּלֶד וְאִמּוֹ, וְיִזְכּוּ לְגַדְּלוֹ וּלְחַנְּכוֹ וּלְחַכְּמוֹ, מִיּוֹם הַשְּׁמִינִי וָהָלְאָה יֵרָצֶה דָמוֹ, וִיהִי יְיָ אֱלֹהָיו עִמּוֹ: » אָמֵן.

SOMEONE OTHER THAN THE SANDEK

B הָרַחֲמָן הוּא יְבָרֵךְ בַּעַל בְּרִית הַמִּילָה, אֲשֶׁר שָׂשׂ לַעֲשׂוֹת צֶדֶק בְּגִילָה, וִישַׁלֵּם פָּעֳלוֹ וּמַשְׂכֻּרְתּוֹ כְּפוּלָה, וְיִתְּנֵהוּ לְמַעְלָה לְמָעְלָה: » אָמֵן.

C › הָרַחֲמָן הוּא יְבָרֵךְ רַךְ הַנִּמּוֹל לִשְׁמוֹנָה, וְיִהְיוּ יָדָיו וְלִבּוֹ לָאֵל אֱמוּנָה, וְיִזְכֶּה לִרְאוֹת פְּנֵי הַשְּׁכִינָה, שָׁלוֹשׁ פְּעָמִים בַּשָּׁנָה: » אָמֵן.

SOMEONE OTHER THAN THE MOHEL

D הָרַחֲמָן הוּא יְבָרֵךְ הַמָּל בְּשַׂר הָעָרְלָה, וּפָרַע וּמָצַץ דְּמֵי הַמִּילָה, אִישׁ הַיָּרֵא וְרַךְ הַלֵּבָב עֲבוֹדָתוֹ פְּסוּלָה, וְאִם שְׁלָשׁ אֵלֶּה לֹא יַעֲשֶׂה לָהּ: » אָמֵן.

E › הָרַחֲמָן הוּא יִשְׁלַח לָנוּ מְשִׁיחוֹ הוֹלֵךְ תָּמִים, בִּזְכוּת חֲתַן לַמּוּלוֹת דָּמִים, לְבַשֵּׂר בְּשׂוֹרוֹת טוֹבוֹת וְנִחוּמִים, לְעַם אֶחָד מְפֻזָּר וּמְפֹרָד בֵּין הָעַמִּים: » אָמֵן.

F › הָרַחֲמָן הוּא יִשְׁלַח לָנוּ כֹּהֵן צֶדֶק אֲשֶׁר לֻקַּח לְעֵילוֹם, עַד הוּכַן כִּסְאוֹ כַּשֶּׁמֶשׁ וְיָהֲלוֹם, וַיָּלֶט פָּנָיו בְּאַדַּרְתּוֹ וַיִּגְלוֹם, בְּרִיתִי הָיְתָה אִתּוֹ הַחַיִּים וְהַשָּׁלוֹם: » אָמֵן.

Continue with prayer O, page 106.

N GROUP Blessed is {our God,} the one from whom is our sustenance, and by whose goodness we live.

O LEADER Blessed is {our God,} the one from whom is our sustenance, and by whose goodness we live. Blessed is he, and blessed is his name.

Continue with the *Birkat HaZan* (First Blessing: For the Food), prayer 51, page 97.

58

HARACHAMAN

THE COMPASSIONATE ONE

SOMEONE OTHER THAN THE FATHER

A The Compassionate One, may he bless the father of the child and his mother, and may they merit to raise him, to educate him, and to make him wise; from the eighth day onward may his blood find favor, and may the LORD his God be with him. ›› Amen.

SOMEONE OTHER THAN THE SANDEK

B The Compassionate One, may he bless the master of the covenant of circumcision, who has rejoiced to perform this righteous deed with celebration, and may his deed be rewarded and his payment doubled, and may he set him higher and higher. ›› Amen.

C › The Compassionate One, may he bless the delicate circumcised eight-day-old, and may his hands and heart be faithful[a] to God, and may he merit to see the Divine Presence, three times a year. ›› Amen.

SOMEONE OTHER THAN THE MOHEL

D The Compassionate One, may he bless the one who circumcised the flesh of the foreskin, separated it, and drew out the blood of the circumcision; the service of a fearful or delicate-hearted man is invalid if these three things are not done to it. ›› Amen.

E › The Compassionate One, may he send us his Messiah who walks in perfection, in the merit of the groom whose blood was shed for circumcision, to bring good news, the news of goodness and consolations to the one people scattered and separated among the nations. ›› Amen.

F › The Compassionate One, may he send us Elijah, the righteous priest who was taken into concealment, until his throne is established like the sun[b] or a diamond, he wrapped his face in his cloak[c] and was hidden in it. My covenant was with him,[d] life and peace. ›› Amen.

Continue with prayer O, page 107.

a) Exodus 17:12. b) Psalm 89:37[36]. c) 1 Kings 19:13. d) Malachi 2:5.

ברכות אחרונות

ברכה מעין שלוש 59

BLESSING RESEMBLING THREE

This blessing is recited after eating a meal that did not contain bread but did contain (a) grain products other than bread; or (b) wine or grape juice; or (c) fruits with special significance: grapes, olives, figs, pomegranates, or dates.

A בָּרוּךְ אַתָּה יְיָ אֱלֹהֵינוּ מֶלֶךְ הָעוֹלָם,

GRAIN PRODUCTS	WINE OR GRAPE JUICE	FRUITS LISTED ABOVE
עַל הַמִּחְיָה וְעַל הַכַּלְכָּלָה,	עַל הַגֶּפֶן וְעַל פְּרִי הַגֶּפֶן,	עַל הָעֵץ וְעַל פְּרִי הָעֵץ,

B וְעַל תְּנוּבַת הַשָּׂדֶה, וְעַל אֶרֶץ חֶמְדָּה טוֹבָה וּרְחָבָה, שֶׁרָצִיתָ וְהִנְחַלְתָּ לַאֲבוֹתֵינוּ, לֶאֱכוֹל מִפִּרְיָהּ וְלִשְׂבּוֹעַ מִטּוּבָהּ. רַחֵם יְיָ אֱלֹהֵינוּ עַל יִשְׂרָאֵל עַמֶּךָ, וְעַל יְרוּשָׁלַיִם עִירֶךָ, וְעַל צִיּוֹן מִשְׁכַּן כְּבוֹדֶךָ, וְעַל מִזְבְּחֶךָ וְעַל הֵיכָלֶךָ. וּבְנֵה יְרוּשָׁלַיִם עִיר הַקֹּדֶשׁ בִּמְהֵרָה בְיָמֵינוּ, וְהַעֲלֵנוּ לְתוֹכָהּ, וְשַׂמְּחֵנוּ בְּבִנְיָנָהּ, וְנֹאכַל מִפִּרְיָהּ, וְנִשְׂבַּע מִטּוּבָהּ, וּנְבָרֶכְךָ עָלֶיהָ בִּקְדֻשָּׁה וּבְטָהֳרָה.

ON THE SABBATH	וּרְצֵה וְהַחֲלִיצֵנוּ בְּיוֹם הַשַּׁבָּת הַזֶּה.
ON ROSH CHODESH	וְזָכְרֵנוּ לְטוֹבָה בְּיוֹם רֹאשׁ הַחֹדֶשׁ הַזֶּה.
ON PASSOVER	וְשַׂמְּחֵנוּ בְּיוֹם חַג הַמַּצּוֹת הַזֶּה.
ON SHAVU'OT	וְשַׂמְּחֵנוּ בְּיוֹם חַג הַשָּׁבֻעוֹת הַזֶּה.
ON SUKKOT	וְשַׂמְּחֵנוּ בְּיוֹם חַג הַסֻּכּוֹת הַזֶּה.
ON SHMINI ATZERET AND SIMCHAT TORAH	וְשַׂמְּחֵנוּ בְּיוֹם הַשְּׁמִינִי חַג הָעֲצֶרֶת הַזֶּה.
ON ROSH HASHANAH	וְזָכְרֵנוּ לְטוֹבָה בְּיוֹם הַזִּכָּרוֹן הַזֶּה.

BLESSINGS AFTER OTHER FOODS

59 BRACHAH ME'EIN SHALOSH

BLESSING RESEMBLING THREE

This blessing is recited after eating a meal that did not contain bread but did contain (a) grain products other than bread; or (b) wine or grape juice; or (c) fruits with special significance: grapes, olives, figs, pomegranates, or dates.

A **BLESSED** are you, O LORD, our God, King of the universe,

GRAIN PRODUCTS	WINE OR GRAPE JUICE	FRUITS LISTED ABOVE
for the life-giving food and for the sustenance,	for the vine and for the fruit of the vine,	for the tree and for the fruit of the tree,

B and for the produce of the field, and for the pleasant, good, and spacious land that you favored and gave as an inheritance to our fathers, to eat from its fruit and be satisfied from its goodness. Have compassion, O LORD, our God, upon Israel your people, upon Jerusalem your city, upon Zion, the dwelling place of your glory,[a] upon your altar, and upon your Temple. Rebuild Jerusalem, the city of holiness, quickly and in our days; bring us up to its midst, make us glad with its rebuilding. May we eat from its fruit, be satisfied from its goodness, and bless you upon it in holiness and purity.

ON THE SABBATH	And show favor and fortify us on this Sabbath day.
ON ROSH CHODESH	And remember us for goodness on this day of Rosh Chodesh.
ON PASSOVER	And make us glad on this day of the Festival of Matzot.
ON SHAVU'OT	And make us glad on this day of the Festival of Shavu'ot.
ON SUKKOT	And make us glad on this day of the Festival of Sukkot.
ON SHMINI ATZERET AND SIMCHAT TORAH	And make us glad on this day of the Festival of Shmini Atzeret.
ON ROSH HASHANAH	And remember us for goodness on this Day of Remembrance.

a) Psalm 26:8.

C כִּי אַתָּה יְיָ טוֹב וּמֵטִיב לַכֹּל, וְנוֹדֶה לְּךָ עַל הָאָרֶץ

GRAIN PRODUCTS

וְעַל הַמִּחְיָה. בָּרוּךְ אַתָּה יְיָ, עַל הָאָרֶץ וְעַל הַמִּחְיָה:

WINE OR GRAPE JUICE

וְעַל פְּרִי הַגָּפֶן. בָּרוּךְ אַתָּה יְיָ, עַל הָאָרֶץ וְעַל פְּרִי הַגָּפֶן:

FRUITS LISTED ABOVE

וְעַל הַפֵּרוֹת. בָּרוּךְ אַתָּה יְיָ, עַל הָאָרֶץ וְעַל הַפֵּרוֹת:

60 בורא נפשות

WHO CREATES THE SOULS

This blessing is recited after eating foods that do not qualify for the *Birkat HaMazon* (Grace after Meals) or the *Brachah Me'ein Shalosh* (Blessing Resembling Three).

A **בָּרוּךְ** אַתָּה יְיָ אֱלֹהֵינוּ מֶלֶךְ הָעוֹלָם, בּוֹרֵא נְפָשׁוֹת רַבּוֹת וְחֶסְרוֹנָן, עַל כָּל מַה שֶּׁבָּרָאתָ לְהַחֲיוֹת בָּהֶם נֶפֶשׁ כָּל חָי. בָּרוּךְ חֵי הָעוֹלָמִים:

C For you, O LORD, are good and do good to all, and we give thanks to you for the land

GRAIN PRODUCTS	WINE OR GRAPE JUICE	FRUITS LISTED ABOVE
and for the life-giving food. Blessed are You, O LORD, for the land and for the life-giving food.	and for the fruit of the vine. Blessed are You, O LORD, for the land and for the fruit of the vine.	and for the fruit. Blessed are You, O LORD, for the land and for the fruit.

60

Borei Nefashot

WHO CREATES THE SOULS

This blessing is recited after eating foods that do not qualify for the *Birkat HaMazon* (Grace after Meals) or the *Brachah Me'ein Shalosh* (Blessing Resembling Three).

A **Blessed** are you, O LORD, our God, King of the universe, who creates numerous souls with their needs, for all that you have created in order to give life to every living soul. Blessed is the Life of the ages.

Commentary

PRAYERS AND BLESSINGS

ZEMIROT

BIRKAT HAMAZON

EREV SHABBAT / YOM TOV

HOW TO LIGHT SHABBAT CANDLES

To light Shabbat candles, you will need:

- two or more candles
- a match or a lighter
- a non-flammable tray or plate
- a *tzedakah* (charity) box

Traditionally, the woman of the house lights the candles. Use candles that will last about two or three hours. It is traditional to use white candles, but any color will do. Set the candles in a safe and prominent place where they will not need to be moved. They do not need to be on the table, but they should ideally be in the room where the meal will be eaten. You will let the candles burn out on their own; do not blow them out or extinguish them.

Find a source for local candle-lighting times. It is customary to light candles at least eighteen minutes before sunset. The candles should not be lit after sunset.

Before lighting the candles, place a few coins into the *tzedakah* box.

To light the candles according to the Ashkenazi custom (which is common in the United States):

1. Light the candles, then place the match on the tray or plate, allowing it to extinguish itself.
2. Wave both hands in a circular motion over the candles three times, as if you are drawing the light and warmth toward yourself, and then cover your eyes with both hands.
3. Read or sing the blessing.

If you follow the Sephardic custom, first recite the blessing and then light the candles.

After lighting the candles, it is common to pray for one's personal needs and family. One can use the prayer provided (prayer 1F, page 6) or offer a prayer in one's own words.

Once a woman lights the candles, even though the sun has not yet set, she has accepted the sanctity of the Sabbath and its restriction upon herself.

HOW TO CONDUCT THE SHABBAT EVENING MEAL

One should begin the *Erev Shabbat* meal soon after coming home from the Friday evening prayers at the synagogue. For this meal you will need:

- a cup
- wine
- two loaves of challah
- a dish of salt
- a challah cover or napkin
- washing cups and towels (for those who perform ritual hand washing)

The cup is customarily a decorative one called a *Kiddush* cup that is designated only for sacred purposes, but any cup or glass can be used. It should hold at least four ounces of wine or grape juice. It is also good to have a saucer or a small plate under the cup to catch overflowing wine. A pitcher or a decanter may be used to help distribute the wine.

Typically, *Kiddush* is recited while holding the cup of wine. If no wine or grape juice is available, one can recite *Kiddush* over bread. Begin with hand washing (prayer 8, page 22) and then recite *Kiddush*, substituting the blessings for bread (prayer 9, page 22) for the blessings for wine (prayers 6B–C, page 16).

Challah is a traditional type of bread with a braided shape. Two loaves of challah should be present on the table (you do not need to eat them both). Traditional challah recipes tend to have a high egg content, which keeps the bread moist on the Sabbath, when fresh bread cannot be made. Its name comes from the dough offering mentioned in Numbers 15:20–21.

If the traditional braided challah loaves are not available, any bread will do. Ideally, the two loaves should be whole and not sliced before the blessing. Matzah is a convenient option to keep on hand since it does not spoil, and each piece represents a whole "loaf." (Although matzah is mainly used on Passover, it can be eaten all year round.)

Place the salt dish near the challah. Kosher salt, which has large grains, works best for dipping.

The table should be set before sunset. It should be set in a beautiful manner with fine dishes and linens.

Cover the challah (and any other bread or grain items that are present) with a cloth or napkin.

Songs and Blessings

To begin the Shabbat meal, parents first bless their children. The method varies from household to household. In some cases the father recites the blessing; in others both parents recite it. In some homes the children come to receive the blessing; in others the parents go to each child.

Bless each child separately. Place your hands firmly on his or her head, and recite the blessing. There are two versions of the first part of the blessing: one for boys and one for girls. Give each child a few personal words of encouragement and perhaps a hug and a kiss.

When reciting the Friday night songs and blessings, some families have the custom of standing around the table, whereas others remain seated.

The "Father's Prayer" (*Ribbon Kol HaOlamim*) is not frequently recited. If this prayer is particularly meaningful for you and flows well with your evening, include it; otherwise, feel free to go straight from *Shalom Aleichem* to *Eishet Chayil*.

While *Eishet Chayil* is sometimes interpreted as an ode to the mother of the home, it is recited even if no women or only women are present. One can read it, but a more common custom is to sing it to a beautiful melody.

Kiddush

It is customary for the father or the husband of the home to lead *Kiddush*. If a male aged thirteen or older is not present, a woman is to recite *Kiddush*. In some homes, each of the men and boys who are present are allowed to recite *Kiddush* on their own behalf after the host finishes his blessing.

The leader places the cup on the plate. Fill the cup with wine until it overflows a little into the plate. (If it is impractical to overflow the wine, it is not a necessity to do so.)

Hold the cup in your right hand as you recite the blessings through the words "who sanctifies the Sabbath."

In most communities it is customary for everyone to have a sip of wine after the blessing, but there are different ways to accomplish this. The simplest method is to pour a cup for everyone in advance. However, it is ideal for each person to taste the wine from the cup used in the blessing. This was also our Master Yeshua's custom, as demonstrated by his Passover meal:

> And he took a cup, and when he had given thanks he said, "Take this, and divide it among yourselves." (Luke 22:17 ESV)

In our era, though, it is generally considered distasteful and unhygienic to have everyone drink from the same cup. Another way to distribute the cup is as follows:

1. Recite the blessing while holding the cup.
2. Pour a majority of the wine from the cup into an empty pitcher.
3. Refill the remainder of the cup with wine from the wine bottle and drink.
4. Add some wine from the bottle to the pitcher to increase the volume if necessary.
5. Pass around the pitcher, and have each person pour at least some of the wine from the pitcher into their cup.
6. People can then add wine to their cup from a bottle as desired before drinking.

This method follows the idea that when one liquid is added to another, the added liquid assumes the status of the liquid already in the cup. (This concept is derived from the ancient laws of ritual purity.) Thus, if you choose to employ this method of distributing the wine, be sure to begin with the wine that was used in the blessing and add unused wine to it rather than beginning with a cup or pitcher that is full of unused wine and adding the special wine to it.

HAND WASHING AND THE BLESSING FOR BREAD

After the guests have had a chance to take a drink of wine, it is customary to perform a ceremonial hand washing (*netilat yadayim*) before the blessing for bread.

Among disciples opinions vary regarding whether or not to practice ritual hand washing. Allow others to follow their convictions on this matter.

To perform the washing:

1. Remove rings and similar items from your hands. You may wish to set these items at your place setting.
2. Fill the cup with cold water.
3. Lift the cup with your right hand, and pass it to your left hand.
4. Pour water on your right hand two or three times (depending on your custom). Each pour should wet the hand completely up to the wrist.
5. Repeat the pouring on your left hand.

6. Hold your hands upward, and recite the blessing.
7. Dry your hands with the towel.

Avoid conversation from the time you begin the washing until after you eat a bite of bread (which you will do after you recite the blessing for bread as described below).

When everyone is seated, uncover the challah. Using a knife, scratch the surface of the loaf that will be served first in the place where it will be cut.

Lift the two loaves, holding the scratched loaf underneath the other one, and say the blessing. Raise the loaves slightly when saying the name of God. If Matthew 14:19 is any indication, it may have been our Master Yeshua's custom to look up toward heaven when he said the blessing.

Salt and distribute the bread. Common practice varies: Some families slice the bread; others prefer to tear it apart. Some families dip the bread in salt; others sprinkle salt onto the bread. Each person then takes a bite of bread. At this point you may converse freely.

After everyone has taken a bite of bread, the meal is served. There are many customs as to which dishes are served (gefilte fish, a variety of kugels, and roasted chicken make a classic Ashkenazi meal).

During the course of the meal, it is customary to sing *zemirot* (table songs) such as those found in this book (prayers 27–35, pages 48–65).

After the meal, recite the *Birkat HaMazon* (Grace after Meals) (prayer 50, page 94).

1 Candle Lighting

Like many customs and *mitzvot*, lighting candles has a practical function as well as symbolic significance.

In biblical times, oil lamps were the primary way to provide light after nightfall. Clean fuel such as olive oil is not free, so people with limited means may have preferred to eat their nighttime meal in the dark rather than expend the cost of lighting a lamp. However, the Sabbath is a time of honor, enjoyment, and peace; it is not an occasion to be frugal.

The Purpose of Sabbath Candles

As the prophet said, we are to "call the Sabbath 'a delight' and the holy one of HaShem 'honored'" (Isaiah 58:13). Providing light shows honor to the Sabbath. Just as we would gladly provide light for an honored guest in our home, we increase the beauty of the evening by spending the extra cost for a bright Sabbath. Providing light also increases our enjoyment of

1

the Sabbath. In fact, light is associated with joy: "The Jews had light and joy, gladness and honor" (Esther 8:16). Darkness is not conducive to a peaceful atmosphere. Light creates an environment for honor, enjoyment, and peace.

Since the Torah prohibits kindling a fire on the Sabbath, it makes sense to light a lamp shortly before the Sabbath begins so that it lasts as long into the night as possible.

The Torah does not mention Sabbath lights explicitly, but based on this reasoning, it is easy to see how the custom developed and took on an obligatory status. It is fair to assume that even though it may not have been considered a commandment, it would have been common to find homes lit with lamps even at the earliest stages of Sabbath observance.

Gentiles and Candle Lighting

It is appropriate for Gentile disciples of Yeshua to light Sabbath candles, since their beauty and significance are applicable for everyone. They also serve to "remember the Sabbath day," which, according to some opinions, is incumbent upon Gentiles. The *Kli Yakar* writes:

> All nations are obligated to "remember the Sabbath day" in order to affix in their hearts faith in the formation of the world, which gives trustworthy testimony of HaShem regarding his existence. For the prohibition of idolatry is included in the seven commandments of the sons of Noah. Even though the nations are not able to receive the injunction "Do not perform any work," they are nonetheless able to receive upon themselves the commandment of remembering—as they too are obligated in it—so that the formation of the world would be before their eyes as a memorial. (Shlomo Ephraim Luntschitz, *Kli Yakar*, commentary on Exodus 20:8)

However, the relationship of Gentiles to the specific act of lighting Sabbath candles is not one of obligation. Since the sages who formulated the blessing and mandated lighting candles had in mind only the obligation of Jewish people, a Gentile who chooses to partake of the ritual should not recite the traditional blessing. Since it would be a false statement when spoken by a non-Jew, it would be considered a blessing in vain, which should be avoided. Instead, a Gentile should omit (or reword) the blessing.

Eighteen Minutes

The candles are lit eighteen minutes before sunset, which provides a short buffer to prevent Sabbath violation. While it sounds like an arbitrary number, eighteen minutes is a basic unit of time in Jewish law. Prior to

1

more accurate and accessible timekeeping methods, durations were often estimated based on the amount of time it takes to perform simple tasks such as uttering a particular phrase, eating a loaf of bread, or walking a certain distance. Eighteen minutes is the estimated time that it takes to walk the length of a *mil* (about two thirds of a modern mile or about one kilometer).

Two Candles

As the blessing suggests, only one light is needed in order to carry out the ritual, but it is customary to light at least two candles. This practice probably originated for practical reasons: two lights provide more light, and if one goes out prematurely, the other one may stay lit. The two lights are also in keeping with the "double" symbolism in the Sabbath, which is also seen in the two loaves of bread. However, the most common explanation of the symbolism is that the commandment of the Sabbath was given in two ways. In Exodus 20:8, the Torah instructs, "Remember [*zachor*] the Sabbath day to sanctify it," and in Deuteronomy 5:12, the commandment is to "observe [*shamor*] the Sabbath day to sanctify it." The two candles are said to represent these two commandments: *zachor* ("remember") and *shamor* ("observe").

Some households have the custom of lighting an additional candle for each child.

Women Light Candles

Women typically light the Sabbath candles. This is because in a traditional Jewish household, women have the task of managing household affairs, and in a traditional situation, the husband is at the synagogue at the time that the Sabbath begins. However, it is customary for men to set up the candles and get them ready for lighting. When there is no woman of the house present to light the candles, a man is to light them.

The Symbolism of Light

The home is like a miniature sanctuary, and this is even more so the case on the Sabbath. Our table is like an altar, and our festive meals are like the sacred offerings. The loaves of challah stand in for the Bread of the Presence, and the overflowing cup of wine carries the aroma of the drink offerings. We place the priestly blessing on our children, and our sweet songs echo the psalms of the Levites. Even our special linens reflect the Tabernacle's sacred adornments. Along these lines, the glow of the candles evokes the memory of the golden menorah that illuminated the Holy Place.

1

The Sabbath itself is a memorial of creation (Exodus 20:11). From this perspective, the candles remind us of the primordial light created on the first day. The Midrash[a] explains that at sunset on the eve of the first Sabbath, God granted honor to the Sabbath by allowing the light to remain through the night. Light in the midst of the night thus represents the condition of the world before the fall of man, and likewise it illustrates the messianic future when "there will be no more night; there will be no need for the light of a lamp or the light of the sun" (Revelation 22:5). Similarly, the Gemara compares the Sabbath candles to the pillar of fire that guided the Israelites by night.[b]

Just as darkness and night represent exile, light symbolizes redemption and the revelation of God's glory. And as the Torah itself reveals God's glory, it too is light. "A *mitzvah* is a lamp and the Torah is light" (Proverbs 6:23). Likewise, the Messiah who embodies the Torah and is saturated with the Divine Presence is also light. "In him was life, and the life was the light of mankind. The light shines in the darkness, but the darkness could not grasp it" (John 1:4–5). His followers, who carry the revelation of God and his kingdom in the midst of darkness and exile, are called the light of the world (Matthew 5:14).

The Sabbath is called a foretaste of the world to come (*me'ein olam haba*). In the future, every knee will bow to HaShem, and all will acknowledge his kingship. Those of us who submit to his rule even now are like those who light the Sabbath candles before the sunset, willingly taking on the obligations of the Sabbath rather than passively letting them be imposed on us as the sun sets.

A **Commanded us to kindle a lamp** — By the time the Mishnah was compiled (c. 200 CE), the obligation of lighting Sabbath lamps was already assumed and the discussion revolved around what types of fuel and lamp configurations were permitted (m.*Shabbat* 2:1ff). However, even though the Talmud records a blessing to be recited when kindling the Hanukkah lights (b.*Shabbat* 23a), it makes no mention of a blessing for Sabbath lights. According to some opinions, the blessing for Sabbath lights was instituted in the middle ages as a reaction to the Karaite view that no lights or fires whatsoever should remain lit on the Sabbath.[c]

The wording of the blessing, "who has commanded us to kindle a lamp for the Sabbath," naturally makes some people uncomfortable because

a) *Genesis Rabbah* 11:2.
b) b.*Shabbat* 23b.
c) Rabbi Lawrence Hoffman, *My People's Prayer Book: Kabbalat Shabbat* (vol. 8 of *My People's Prayer Book*; Woodstock, VA: Jewish Lights Publishing, 2005), 10–11.

1

there is no explicit commandment in the written Torah to light a lamp. Although the lighting of candles is done in order to accomplish a biblically mandated task (i.e., enjoyment of the Sabbath), the obligation of the practice itself is considered of rabbinic origin.

Nonetheless, if one is concerned that the blessing violates a principle of Yeshua's teaching by elevating a custom to the status of an obligation, he or she may be better off omitting the blessing and simply having in mind the biblical injunctions to bring joy, honor, and holiness to the Sabbath while lighting the candles.

A controversy eventually developed regarding the blessing. Under normal circumstances, blessings are recited prior to carrying out the associated activity. But some held the opinion that by reciting the blessing, a woman formally accepts the Sabbath upon herself and is now legally obligated to its restrictions. If this is the case, she is no longer permitted to light a fire. Thus, in communities that held this opinion, it became customary to light the candles first, but then to block the light so as not to benefit from it until after the blessing is recited.

2 Blessing the Children

God distinguished the Sabbath with blessing and holiness. The Torah states, "God blessed the Sabbath day and sanctified it" (Genesis 2:3). No other day of the week received this distinction. For this reason, the Sabbath is an auspicious time for blessings. In addition to the traditional text, parents may add their own personal blessings and prayers for their children.

A **Ephraim and Manasseh** — The blessing for boys comes directly from Genesis 48. After Joseph was told that his father Jacob was ill, he brought his two sons to his father to be blessed by him. Jacob blessed them by saying, "Israel will bless their children by you, saying, 'May God make you like Ephraim and Manasseh.'"

This has piqued the curiosity of commentators. Why would Israel want their sons to be like Ephraim and Manasseh?

We might point to their personal characteristics. For example, we do not find any indications that these brothers quarreled, even when Jacob placed Ephraim, who was younger, ahead of Manasseh. We can also note that they seem to have retained their devotion to God even though they were raised in the spiritual darkness of Egypt. Yet, these qualities are only implicitly communicated by the Torah. If personal traits such as these are the blessings that Jacob referred to, then why don't we know more about those brothers? Furthermore, why would we desire for our children to be

2

like Ephraim and Manasseh instead of heroes like Abraham, Isaac, Jacob, Moses, David, or Elijah?

The true uniqueness of Ephraim and Manasseh is not in their own greatness so much as in what they were given. Along these lines, while the verb *yesimecha* (יְשִׂימְךָ) can be translated "may he *make* you," it can also have the broader meaning of "may he *emplace* you."

Simply by virtue of the special love that their grandfather Jacob had for Joseph, he adopted them as his own sons, making them peers and co-heirs with Joseph's brothers. Likewise, our desire for our children is for God to bless them "with every spiritual blessing" and grant them the "adoption as sons through Yeshua the Messiah" (Ephesians 1:3, 5).

B **Sarah, Rebekah, Rachel, and Leah** — The blessing given to daughters does not come from a scriptural passage, although it seems to echo the blessing given to Ruth: "May the LORD make the woman who is coming into your home like Rachel and Leah, who both built the house of Israel" (Ruth 4:11).

3 SHALOM ALEICHEM

The Talmud teaches that two angels accompany a person as he returns home from the synagogue on Friday evening. In Rabbinic literature, angels are often portrayed as members of the heavenly court, either as prosecutors or defenders. When the defending angel sees the home prepared for the Sabbath, he declares, "May it be God's will that next Sabbath be like this," and the prosecuting angel is forced to respond, "Amen." But if the prosecuting angel sees that the home is in disarray and not prepared for the Sabbath, he declares, "May it be God's will that next Sabbath be like this," and the defending angel is forced to respond, "Amen."[a]

This explanation is not necessarily meant to be taken on a literal level. Its point is to communicate that each time one carries out a commandment, it strengthens his ability to carry it out in the future. Likewise, neglecting a commandment can lead to a pattern of failure.

Nonetheless, the Scriptures make it clear that God often relates to human beings through angels. Many individuals have spoken with angels, who have brought divine protection, success, and revelation. Jacob even prayed over Ephraim and Manasseh by saying, "May the angel who redeems me from all evil bless the youths" (Genesis 48:16).

a) b.*Shabbat* 119b.

3
The song *Shalom Aleichem* was written in the seventeenth century by mystics who reasoned that if messengers of God are in our presence, it is appropriate to greet them just as one would greet any other messenger.

The song did meet with resistance. The Vilna Gaon criticized the song for being directed toward angels. Rabbi Ya'akov Emden objected to its awkward grammar. But eventually the song became nearly universal and an iconic component of the Friday night ritual.

D **Depart in peace** — Rabbi Ya'akov Emden was among those who objected to this phrase in particular. Why should we ask the angels to leave? Wouldn't it be better for them to stay? Accordingly, some have the custom of omitting this stanza or substituting it with, "When you leave, let it be in peace" (*betzeitchem leshalom,* בְּצֵאתְכֶם לְשָׁלוֹם).

4 A Father's Prayer

This prayer, commonly known by its opening words *Ribbon Kol HaOlamim,* was first published in the seventeenth century. Some communities omit this prayer out of concern for offering supplications on the Sabbath. Others only recite the acrostic introduction of the prayer (concluding with "King who is perfect in his way") since it consists only of praise. Some have the custom of reciting the prayer on Friday prior to *Minchah* (afternoon prayers).

D **I have testified ... then I repeated it. I will yet testify a third time** — This refers to Genesis 2:1–3, which is recited twice in the course of the *Ma'ariv* prayers for the Sabbath and is also included in *Kiddush.*

5 Eshet Chayil

This passage from Proverbs 31 is a poetic and vivid portrayal of a righteous and accomplished woman. It is written in an acrostic form, with each verse beginning with a subsequent letter of the Hebrew alphabet.

Like *Shalom Aleichem, Eshet Chayil* was instituted as part of the Friday evening meal by the mystics of the seventeenth century. They interpreted the *Eshet Chayil* as the *Shechinah* or Divine Presence, specifically the feminine aspect of God.

However, most people today interpret *Eshet Chayil* as an ode to the mother of the home or to righteous women everywhere. Nonetheless, the passage is still recited even if one is not married, or if only men or only women are present.

As for the passage itself, most commentators see it as an allegory. The opening phrase, "Who can find a capable woman," could likewise be understood as if to say, "Who can solve this riddle?"

5

The theme of the book of Proverbs is wisdom and fear of the Lord. Wisdom is equated with the Torah, and it is personified as a woman. The book begins with the equation, "The fear of the LORD is the beginning of knowledge" (Proverbs 1:7). Just as the capable woman's value is "far greater than pearls," the Proverbs also declare that "wisdom is better than pearls" (Proverbs 8:11). "Blessed is the one who finds wisdom ... she is more precious than pearls" (Proverbs 3:13, 15).

Proverbs 31 concludes with the thought, "A woman who fears the LORD should be praised" (Proverbs 31:30), even though there is no mention earlier in the passage about fearing God. The descriptive phrase "who fears the LORD" in Hebrew is exactly the same as the phrase "the fear of the LORD" (*yir'at HaShem*, יִרְאַת יְיָ). This makes it sound as if the woman herself *is* the fear of the LORD—that is to say, the Torah.

This could explain the acrostic form of the passage. The "woman" is composed of the letters of the alphabet, alluding to her identity as the Torah. Rabbi Isaac bar Nehemiah said, "Just as the blessed Holy One gave the Torah to Israel with twenty-two letters, so he praises the upright women with twenty-two letters."[a]

In this view, each of the depictions of the capable woman represents the Torah in some way. For example, when the passage says that the woman purchases a field and plants a vineyard (Proverbs 31:16), this refers to the Torah's promise of the land of Canaan and the establishment of the Jewish people there. The language about her generosity to the poor (Proverbs 31:20) speaks of the commandments to show charity. Her children, the *benei Torah*, are the Jewish people, and her husband who sits among the elders (Proverbs 31:23) corresponds to the scholars and judges who have mastered the Torah.

6 KIDDUSH FOR SHABBAT

Kiddush, along with the *Birkat HaMazon* (Grace after Meals), is the most ancient and important part of the *Erev Shabbat* home liturgy. It appears in the oldest *siddurim*, it is cited by the Gemara, and in the Mishnah, the schools of Hillel and Shammai dispute only about in what order one should recite the blessings.[b]

The purpose of *Kiddush* is to fulfill the commandment, "Remember the Sabbath day, to sanctify it" (Exodus 20:8). By proclaiming the Sabbath's holiness at its onset, it sets the pace for the rest of the day. Furthermore, the ritual of *Kiddush* sets the Sabbath evening meal apart from that of the weekdays. This calls to attention the fact that the meal is eaten in order to honor and celebrate the Sabbath rather than simply to satisfy one's hunger.

---

a) *Yalkut Shim'oni* on Proverbs 31 (Remez 964). b) m.*Brachot* 8:1.

6

Under normal circumstances, *Kiddush* is recited while holding a full cup of wine. Whenever this book mentions wine, non-alcoholic grape juice is also an acceptable option. If no wine or grape juice is available, it is acceptable to pronounce the *Kiddush* over two loaves of bread. In that case, there would be no cover over the bread, and the blessing "who creates the fruit of the vine" would be replaced with "who brings bread out of the earth."

Covering the Bread

It is customary to cover the bread with a napkin or special linen while reciting *Kiddush* over wine.

On an ordinary day, if one were to have both wine and bread at a meal, the traditional order would be to make a blessing over the bread first and then over the wine. But for *Kiddush*, the blessing over the wine is recited first to emphasize the special joy and sanctity of the day. However, in order to maintain the special status of bread, which by all rights should have its blessing first if it is present, we symbolically remove it from the table temporarily by covering it with a cloth.

Gentiles and Kiddush

Like many prayers in Jewish tradition, *Kiddush* contains two parts, one universal and the other specific. The first paragraph is a quotation from the creation narrative, and it describes God as the Creator who rested on the seventh day. The second paragraph focuses on Israel's special relationship with the Sabbath, which God bestowed upon Israel as an inheritance.

Gentiles are certainly welcome to enjoy the Sabbath. In some opinions, Gentiles are even obligated by the commandment to "remember" it. (See the paragraph "Gentiles and Candle Lighting" above, and particularly the quotation from *Kli Yakar*.) The Hebrew word for "remember" is *zachar* (זָכַר), which connotes not only bringing a thought to mind, but actually mentioning it out loud and memorializing it through words. The act of reciting *Kiddush* directly fulfills this command, and thus in a certain way is highly appropriate for Gentiles.

Nonetheless it is important to recognize that the Sabbath was entrusted to the Jewish people in a unique way. Considering this, the traditional second paragraph is not advisable for Gentiles. Here we have provided an alternative from an early Christian document called *Apostolic Constitutions*, which scholars widely acknowledge has a basis in ancient Hellenistic synagogue liturgy. While this text clearly echoes with the traditional liturgy, it retains its universal scope and is therefore particularly appropriate for a Gentile reader.

6

A **He ceased from all his work** — The word "work" is a translation of the Hebrew term *melachah* (מְלָאכָה). Unfortunately, the English language is at a loss to convey the meaning precisely. *Melachah* speaks of creative activities—acts by which one exerts his or her influence on the world, changing things from one state or identity to another.

There are two primary passages in the Torah in which the term *melachah* is used extensively. One is this passage from the creation narrative in Genesis along with the commandments to refrain from *melachah* on the Sabbath; the other is the account of the construction of the Tabernacle, its implements, and the priestly garments in Exodus. Numerous literary parallels can be seen between the account of the creation of the world and the construction of the Tabernacle. Also, the instructions about the *melachah* of the Tabernacle and its furnishings are interrupted at two points (Exodus 31:14–15, 35:2) to say "do not do *melachah* on the Sabbath."

The sages who established Jewish law noted this, so they based their legal definition of prohibited *melachah* on the types of activities involved in building the Tabernacle. These activities involve things like spinning thread, dyeing fabric, cutting things to specific measurements, and harvesting. In total, they enumerated thirty-nine general categories of prohibited labor.

B **We thank you, our Father** — This passage comes from the *Didache*, a text from the community of followers of Yeshua in the late first or early second century CE. While the grapevine is symbolic of many things in Scripture, in this case the cup of wine is understood to represent the Davidic dynasty to which the office of Messiah belongs.

Recommended for Messianic Gentiles

The basis for this prayer is found in an ancient Christian document called *Apostolic Constitutions*. This text contains what several scholars have identified as ancient Hellenistic Jewish synagogue liturgy, including traces of the *Amidah* and other prayers. These ancient Jewish prayers were modified to suit Christian needs over the ensuing centuries. In many cases, it is possible to reconstruct likely older readings.

E **O Lord of Legions** — This appears to have been an ancient liturgical formula. See Prayer of Manasseh 1:1 (Odes 12:1); Baruch 3:1. The Greek term *pantokrator* (παντοκράτωρ) literally means "all-mighty," but it corresponds in the LXX to the Hebrew term *tzeva'ot* (צְבָאוֹת), which means "legions" or "armies."

6

E **God of Israel** — This is not in the original prayer in *Apostolic Constitutions.* We added this phrase in keeping with wording that is common in many ancient prayers. For example, see 2 Samuel 7:27; 1 Chronicles 17:24; Baruch 3:1, 4. It parallels the phrase in the traditional *Kiddush* which says, "our God."

The teachings in *Apostolic Constitutions* relating to the Sabbath tend to focus on the creation narrative rather than the Exodus from Egypt or the giving of the Torah. This may reflect the idea that although the regulations regarding prohibited labors were given at Mount Sinai to the Jewish people as a unique covenantal sign, the creation narrative describes Sabbath's relationship to all humanity. Thus the focus on creation may stem from apostolic teaching to Gentiles.

Yet in the process of universalizing the prayers it had inherited from Judaism, ancient Christian literature had a tendency to lose sight of the centrality of Israel and its role as a connecting point between God and the nations. Phrases like this were likely edited out of Christian literature as the centuries progressed; thus we felt it necessary to include this phrase here.

By your word — In *Apostolic Constitutions,* this reads, "through Christ." However, scholars have argued that "by your word" is probably the original reading. This concept is in keeping with the strains of thought inherent in Philo, the Targums, and the prologue to the Gospel of John.

As a memorial — As the traditional *Kiddush* states, the Sabbath is "a memorial of the work of creation." In the Ten Commandments, Israel is instructed to remember the Sabbath, "for in six days the LORD made heaven and earth, the sea, and all that is in them, and rested on the seventh day" (Exodus 20:11 ESV). By resting on the seventh day, we imitate God's pattern of creation, thereby proclaiming him as the sole Creator.

For on it you ceased — This phrase borrows its wording directly from Genesis 2:3.

To meditate on the words of your Torah — Literally from Greek, "on your own laws." This is an unlikely concept to be found in a Christian prayer, but it strongly reflects Jewish thought.

The sages in the Talmud (b.*Avodah Zarah* 3b) and in the midrashic work *Tanna Devei Eliyahu Rabba* (13:1), described God's daily schedule, explaining that he studies Torah for the first part of every day. *Tanna Devei Eliyahu Rabba* 18:2 states that "If any scholar sits reading, reciting, and studying the Torah, the blessed Holy One sits across from him and reads and recites with him." This is based midrashically on the verse "Pour

6

out your heart like water before the presence of the Lord!" (Lamentations 2:19 ESV).

Anthropomorphism of this sort is not to be taken literally. In *Tanna Devei Eliyahu Rabba*, the intention is to inspire students to follow God's example and spend time in study. The Talmud's description serves to describe metaphorically how God interacts with the world.

In Jewish thought, the Torah is the blueprint of creation. The creation narrative itself teaches that the world came into existence when God spoke his words. But existence itself does not cease to depend upon the Creator; rather, God continues every moment to uphold creation. God upholds creation in the same manner that he first created it: through his word. Thus, "studying" or "engaging in the words of the Torah" are terms that describe God maintaining the universe.

While God created for six days, on the seventh day he ceased and began to maintain his creation—that is, "to meditate on the words of [his] Torah."

E **An expression of praise to God** — The traditional prayers for the Sabbath express the idea that the Sabbath itself praises God. The introduction to Psalm 92 reads, "A psalm. A song for the Sabbath day. It is good to give thanks to the LORD..." In the prayer *Le'El Asher Shavat* (recited each Sabbath morning before the *Shema*), this verse is interpreted to mean that the Sabbath actually sings, "It is good to give thanks to the LORD."

The Midrash on Psalm 92 explains this in more detail:

> When Adam saw the power of the Sabbath [to protect against judgment], he intended to sing a hymn to the Sabbath: "A psalm, a song for [i.e., to] the Sabbath day." The Sabbath said to him, "You would sing a hymn to me? Let you and I together sing a hymn to the blessed Holy One together: It is good to give thanks to the LORD."

What he has given to mankind — This phrase may allude to Yeshua's statement that "The Sabbath was made for man" (Mark 2:27 ESV).

7 KIDDUSH FOR FESTIVALS

RECOMMENDED FOR MESSIANIC GENTILES

The first half of the festival *Kiddush* recommended for Gentiles is based on the same prayer as the Sabbath *Kiddush*, found in *Apostolic Constitutions*. The second half is constructed from relevant verses and patterned after the traditional festival *Kiddush* prayer.

7

E **The wisdom that you created** — This reflects the concept common in ancient Jewish writings that God created by means of a personified "wisdom." This is first found in Proverbs, in phrases like "The LORD by wisdom founded the earth" (Proverbs 3:19). It is later developed in the Targums, which interpolated into Genesis 1:1 that God created "by wisdom." In early Christianity, the personified wisdom was readily identified with the Messiah.

Wisdom, being the instrument of creation, logically must have been the first created thing. This is stated in Proverbs:

> The LORD possessed me at the beginning of his work, the first of his acts of old. Ages ago I was set up, at the first, before the beginning of the earth. When there were no depths I was brought forth, when there were no springs abounding with water. Before the mountains had been shaped, before the hills, I was brought forth." (Proverbs 8:22–25 ESV)

The idea is expressed in later Jewish literature as well:

> Then the Creator of all things gave me a command, and my Creator chose the place for my tent. He said, "Make your dwelling in Jacob, and in Israel receive your inheritance." Before the ages, in the beginning, he created me, and for all the ages I shall not cease to be. (Sirach 24:8–9 NRSV)

Yet it is surprising to find the statement that God created wisdom (personified as the Messiah) in *Apostolic Constitutions*, since it defies the Orthodox Christian tenet that the Son is co-eternal and not created. Nonetheless, the presence of the concept here reflects the antiquity of the prayer and its origins in Jewish sources.

A shadow of things to come — The festivals are a small foretaste of the Messianic Era. See the commentary on the last verse of *Chafetzah Nafshi* (prayer 27E).

8 HAND WASHING

The practice of washing hands ritually before eating bread is subject to controversy in Messianic Judaism, since the Gospels record two occasions on which Yeshua or his disciples were criticized for not washing.[a] Some argue from these texts that Yeshua specifically objected to ritual hand washing; others suggest that the point of his teaching in these instances was about kindness

a) Luke 11:38; Mark 7:2.

8

to others, not whether or not someone should wash his hands. Furthermore, there are important contextual differences between the type of hand washing performed in the Gospels and that which is observed today.

Both perspectives have a solid basis for their decision. It is important to show humility by allowing others to follow their own convictions on this matter.

Some individuals do not object to the practice of washing itself, but to the blessing. Why would we thank God for giving a commandment to wash hands before eating bread, when there is no such command in the Bible?

In Judaism, there is a clear distinction between commandments that are derived directly from the Torah (these are called *mi-de'oraita*) and commandments that are enjoined by the sages (these are called *mi-derabbanan*). By and large, there is no blessing recited for rabbinic commandments. However, traditional Judaism places seven rabbinic commandments into a special category. While these seven are recognized as rabbinic in origin, they are treated as biblical commandments, thus meriting a blessing before performing them. These are the seven:

- Reciting a blessing before eating (and some other enjoyable activities)
- Ritual washing of hands before eating bread
- Lighting a lamp before the Sabbath
- Constructing a boundary that will allow carrying on the Sabbath
- Reciting *Hallel* on certain special occasions
- Celebrating Hanukkah with the lighting of a *chanukkiyah*
- Celebrating Purim with the reading of the Scroll of Esther

The philosophy in traditional Judaism is that God intended for these commandments to be revealed through the sages at a later time. The scriptural justification offered is typically Deuteronomy 17:11 and 32:7.

When it comes to hand washing it might be helpful to note that

- the wording of the blessing does not literally say "who commanded us to wash hands before eating bread." It only says that he commanded us "about" hand washing in general. This is at the very least a true statement, since there are commandments about washing hands for priests (Exodus 30:19–21, 40:31), for general people in matters of ritual purity (Leviticus 15:11), and for city elders (Deuteronomy 21:6). Furthermore, there are other passages that speak of the cleansing of hands in a spiritual manner as well (Psalm 24:4; James 4:8; cf. also Isaiah 1:16, Hebrews 10:22).

8

- the wording of the commandment does not technically say "washing of hands." Although the phrase *netilat yadayim* is a technical term referring to ritual hand washing, the words literally mean "taking up the hands," as one might take up a tool or a weapon. This speaks to the dedicatory nature of the observance and the message that we should be intentional with the use of our hands for godly purposes, even when doing something as mundane as eating.

The Purpose of Hand Washing

Washing hands before eating bread is not unique to the Sabbath. In traditional Jewish households it is done any time one eats bread.

During Temple times, people washed hands in order to attain a ritually pure status, which was necessary for those who ate from a sacrifice or from sanctified produce such as tithes. Today, hand washing before eating common bread is performed merely in order to "establish a routine" for those who would eat the priestly contributions (b.*Chullin* 106a). It does not actually accomplish ritual purity, nor is it necessary to become ritually pure in today's circumstances.

Gentiles and Hand Washing

There is nothing to prevent a Gentile from washing hands. However, the blessing is intended to reflect the obligatory nature of the rabbinic ordinance of hand washing. The sages who instituted hand washing did not in any way intend to obligate Gentiles to do so. Thus, it is not advisable to recite the traditional blessing in this case.

Some would argue that it would be completely pointless for Gentiles to wash ritually at all. Rambam writes that on a biblical level, Gentiles[a] are not susceptible to impurity at all and would thus have no need of ritual washing. On a rabbinic level, he writes that the sages deemed Gentiles permanently impure, in which case ritual washing would not have any effect (Rambam, *Mishneh Torah*, Tum'at Met 1:13–14).

This, however, cannot be considered the end of the issue for Gentiles in Messianic Jewish communities. We must take into account Peter's revelation not to call any person "common or unclean" (Acts 10:28). Furthermore, the Apostolic community considered it important to ritually immerse Gentiles who turned to God and followed Yeshua. The significance of this immersion is manifold, but one primary purpose of

a) Technically, the Rambam does not say "Gentiles" (*goyim*, גוֹיִם) but rather "idolaters" (*akkum*, עכו"ם) or, more literally, "worshipers of stars and constellations." Nonetheless, the Rambam's words are typically interpreted to refer to any non-Jew.

8

immersion is to express repentance and to dedicate one's life to the service of the true God.

Hand washing likewise can be seen as an act of dedication, and at least in this symbolic sense there is benefit for anyone, Jewish or Gentile.

9 Blessing for Bread

The Talmud (b.*Brachot* 35a) explains that it is forbidden to derive pleasure from this world without first saying a blessing. On the one hand, "the earth and its fullness belong to HaShem" (Psalm 24:1); on the other hand, "heaven belongs to HaShem, but the earth he has given to mankind" (Psalm 115:16). This is not an inconsistency, the sages explain. Before saying a blessing, everything belongs to HaShem, but afterward, he gives it to mankind. To say a blessing is thus to gain permission from God to benefit from the creation which is rightly his. In this way, eating without first saying a blessing is akin to the sin of stealing sanctified property.

Yeshua and Breaking Bread

The Gospels make it clear that Yeshua spoke blessings before eating. When he fed the multitudes, he lifted his eyes to heaven and blessed God. At his last meal, he compared the bread to his body after making the blessing. The two on the road to Emmaus finally recognized their master after they saw him make a blessing on the bread. According to the *Fragment from the Gospel of the Hebrews* found in St. Jerome's *Lives of Illustrious Men* 2, Yeshua also made a blessing and broke bread at his first post-resurrection appearance to James.

A **We thank you, our Father, for the life** — This blessing comes from the *Didache* with the instructions "and concerning the piece of bread" and was evidently recited by believers before eating bread. Although bread is not directly mentioned in this blessing, the term "life" is probably meant to compare the physical sustenance of food with the spiritual life found in Yeshua.

Yours is the glory forever — While this line, a doxology, is reminiscent of modern Christian worship, it seems to have been a common feature of Jewish liturgy in ancient times. One example of a doxology appears in 1 Chronicles 29:11–12, which is included in the traditional Jewish daily morning prayers. Another example of a doxology in Jewish liturgy is the prayer *Yishtabach* at the end of the praise section (*Pesukei Dezimrah*) of the daily morning prayers. The doxology "Yours is the glory forever" is also found in the early apocryphal text *Prayer of Manasseh*, which is understood by most scholars to be Jewish in origin.

9

B **Scattered over the mountains** — In the form of grain. This is a metaphor for the Diaspora and the exile.

Your assembly — From the Greek *ekklesia.* Although this term is often translated "church," it appears numerous times in the Septuagint to refer to the assembly of Israel.

Into your kingdom — Although this blessing does not make specific reference to the land of Israel, the ingathering from exile is certainly in view. The request to gather us together "into your kingdom" anticipates the coming of the Messiah and the great ingathering that initiates the Messianic Era.

C **Who brings bread out of the earth** — The Hebrew term used here for bread, *lechem,* is also a general term for food, as we find Yeshua used the term in Matthew 6:11. Bread is considered the main part of any meal. When bread is present, the blessing for the bread is the only one needed since the term *lechem* encompasses the other foods.

Bread is unique in that it can only be prepared by humans and not animals; it represents a token of God's special relationship with mankind. The wording of the blessing comes from Psalm 104:14–15, which illustrates this distinction: "He makes the grass to grow for the livestock and plants for man to labor, to bring bread out of the earth; wine which gladdens the heart of man, making his face shine with oil, and bread which sustains man's heart."

YOM SHABBAT / YOM TOV

10 KIDDUSHA RABBA

Kiddusha Rabba is not considered a biblically mandated practice, since *Kiddush* on Friday evening just after the Sabbath begins fulfills the biblical requirement (b.*Pesachim* 105a). *Kiddusha Rabba* means "the great *Kiddush*," but this is an example of antiphrasis, using a term in a way opposite its literal meaning. *Kiddusha Rabba* practice probably originated sometime in the fourth century CE, and initially consisted simply of the blessing, "who creates the fruit of the vine." Even today, some have the custom of beginning only with the line, "Therefore, the LORD blessed the Sabbath day and sanctified it."

The purpose of *Kiddusha Rabba* is to remind people once again about the sanctity of the Sabbath. The meal that we are eating is not just to satisfy ourselves but to glorify our Creator by celebrating the Sabbath. By making a bless-

10

ing on wine before the meal, it sets it apart as different from a normal weekday lunch.

The Gemara (b.*Pesachim* 106a) relates an amusing story. The famous fourth-century sage Rav Ashi visited a city, and the people there asked him to recite *Kiddusha Rabba*. Having never heard of this before, he was not sure what to do. He figured that it probably started like any other *Kiddush*, so he began with "who creates the fruit of the vine," and then briefly paused. When he saw an old man start bending down to drink his wine, he knew that it was all they wanted him to say.

A **Therefore, a Sabbath rest still remains** — In this passage, the author of Hebrews encourages his readers to look forward to the age to come, which is likened to the Sabbath. The Mishnah calls it "the day that is entirely restful Sabbath for eternal life" (m.*Tamid* 7:4).

Ceased from his work — Just as on the weekly Sabbath we cease from labor in imitation of God, we also cease from our life of work in the age to come.

Let us be careful to enter that rest — On weekdays, we make all of our preparations so that we are ready to enjoy the Sabbath when it comes. Likewise, we must make preparations in this age so that we can enjoy rest in the age to come. According to the author of Hebrews, the labor of preparation for the future world is the act of *emunah*, which means "faith" or "faithfulness."

B **If you hold back your feet** — Some commentators see Isaiah 58:13–14 as relating to the commandment in Exodus 16:29: "Let everyone remain settled. No one shall go out from his place on the seventh day." This speaks of the *techum*, which is a limit as to how far a person may travel outside a city on the Sabbath. It is referred to in the book of Acts as a "Sabbath day's journey" (Acts 1:12).

Whatever you please on my holy day — Even though we abstain from work on the Sabbath, it is not simply a day for recreation. It is a day to seek God's desires rather than to focus on our own needs and desires.

Call the Sabbath a delight — The Sabbath is to be celebrated, not merely observed. The Hebrew word for "delight" is *oneg* (עֹנֶג), and people often refer to joyful activities on the Sabbath as *oneg shabbat*. In recent times, *oneg shabbat* (or simply *oneg* for short) has come to describe a festive gathering on Friday night or Saturday where there are refreshments, songs, and Torah study.

10

Although festive meals happen on holidays and other times, the term *oneg* is normally only used for this kind of event on the Sabbath itself. An *oneg shabbat* does not have to include a full meal; most synagogues just offer a few snacks when they host an *oneg shabbat,* since people normally eat their Sabbath meals at home.

B **The holy one of the LORD honored** — In this verse, "holy one of the LORD" refers to the Sabbath. We treat the day with honor by being selective about what activities we engage in.

Speaking inappropriately — Even the way we speak should be different on the Sabbath. Although it is not forbidden to talk about what a person does for a living, one should not make business deals. It is also against the spirit of the day to plan activities on the Sabbath that will involve prohibited work, even if the activity will occur on another day.

I will let you ride upon the heights of the earth — There are physical and spiritual benefits to honoring and celebrating the Sabbath. The sages say that if Israel were to keep one Sabbath properly, the Messiah would come immediately (y.*Ta'anit* 1:1).

C **The children of Israel shall observe the Sabbath** — This instruction is given in the context of the building of the Tabernacle. This shows that even holy tasks are subject to the laws of the Sabbath. It also teaches that the types of labor involved in constructing the Tabernacle are the activities that are prohibited on the Sabbath.

The LORD created heaven and earth — When God finished creating every domain in the universe and filled them all with life, matter, and energy, he rested, because the work was complete. Thus, keeping the Sabbath testifies to the basic truth of monotheism: God is the sole Creator of the universe.

D **Remember the Sabbath day** — The term "remember" (*zachor,* זָכוֹר) implies commemoration through verbal expression. This includes activities such as *Kiddush,* which serve to declare the day's holiness.

To sanctify it — On one hand, the Torah teaches that God already sanctified the Sabbath (Genesis 2:3), and thus the Sabbath has inherent holiness regardless of our behavior. On the other hand, we are commanded to sanctify the Sabbath—that is, to treat it in accordance with its holiness.

Se'udah Shlishit

In ancient Israel, it was normal to eat two meals per day: an early lunch in the morning and supper at night. On the Sabbath it is considered a *mitzvah* to have a third meal during the mid afternoon. This meal is neither lunch nor supper; it is an otherwise non-existent meal between them.

The name *Se'udah Shlishit* means "third meal." Another typical name for this meal is *Shalosh Se'udot* (or *Sholosh Se'udos*), which literally means "three meals." In Ashkenazi culture the term is typically slurred as "sholleh-shudess."

The Talmudic sages found scriptural support for this practice in Exodus 16. When Moses commanded the Israelites to eat the manna on the Sabbath, he used the word "today" (*ha-yom*, הַיּוֹם), literally "the day," three times (b.*Sanhedrin* 117b). At any rate, by adding a third meal to the two customary meals eaten every day, it sets the Sabbath apart and adds joy and delight to the day.

Since *Se'udah Shlishit* is not eaten at a normal mealtime, people are not often very hungry. Thus, the meal is often light, consisting of items like fruit or cake. Although it is not an absolute requirement, it is considered ideal to have two loaves of challah present at the meal and to drink a glass of wine.

Messianic Aspects

Because of its uniqueness, *Se'udah Shlishit* has strong messianic connotations.

The Talmudic sages teach that in the merit of eating three meals on the Sabbath, one will be rescued from three ordeals in the future (b.*Shabbat* 118a). They base this on a midrashic exegesis. First, as noted above, the practice of eating three meals is based on Exodus 16, which uses the term *ha-yom* ("today" or "the day") three times. In turn, the word "day" is associated with future calamities in the Scriptures:

The "birth pangs" of the Messiah:

> Behold, I am sending you Elijah the prophet before the great and awesome **day** of HaShem comes. (Malachi 3:23[4:5])

The judgment of *Geihinnom*:

> That **day** is a day of fury, a day of trouble and distress, a day of devastation and desolation, a day of darkness and gloom, a day of dense, dark clouds. (Zephaniah 1:15)

The war of Gog and Magog:

> It will be on that day, on the **day** when Gog comes against the land of Israel—the utterance of HaShem—my raging anger will arise. (Ezekiel 38:18)

Furthermore, the verse will be fulfilled that promises, "And I will feed you with the inheritance of your father Jacob" (Isaiah 58:14), which is a reference to the Messianic Era.

13 Eat It Today

This reading does not appear in most *siddurim*; it is included in some that follow *Nusach Sefarad*. It is appropriate for *Se'udah Shlishit* because this meal is connected with Exodus 16:25, which uses the phrase "today" three times in reference to the Sabbath.

15 Blessing for Bread

At *Se'udah Shlishit*, the blessing over the bread is recited before the blessing over the wine in most communities. This is different from the Friday night *Kiddush* and the Saturday morning *Kiddusha Rabba*, when the blessing for wine is first.

Se'udah Shlishit follows the normal weekday order. Any other day of the week, if bread and wine are present at the meal, it is customary to recite the blessing over the bread first, because it is considered the main staple of all foods.

At *Kiddush*, the blessing over the wine is recited first to emphasize the special joy and sanctity of the day. Since the evening and morning meals are normal meals that people eat every day, they require special sanctification to help remind us that we are eating in honor of God and the Sabbath.

This difference is not necessary for *Se'udah Shlishit* because the entire meal is special. There is no need to change *Se'udah Shlishit*, because this is a meal that only exists on the Sabbath, and as such, it has inherent holiness. The mere fact that we are eating in the middle of the afternoon makes it unique enough.

17 Psalm 23

While Psalm 23 does not mention the Sabbath at all, it is appropriate to the themes of the Sabbath meals for a number of reasons. It speaks of rest, comfort, and restoring the soul. It speaks of trust and assurance in God that he will provide for our needs.

This psalm is also significant because of its messianic connotations. It was written by David, progenitor of the Messiah. He refers to his head being

17

"moistened" with oil, which alludes to his anointing as king. He uses the unusual term "moistened" rather than "anointed" to indicate that his royal status is made evident to his detractors.

Finally, the psalm is apropos because it speaks of God's provision in terms of food and drink. David says that God sets a table opposite his tormentors, meaning that even those who oppose him can see that God has blessed him.

In biblical symbolism, a cup represents one's allotment or ultimate outcome from God. The overflowing cup symbolizes the abundant generosity of God's blessing. Accordingly, it is customary to overflow the cup of wine used for *Kiddush* and *Havdalah*.

HAVDALAH

HOW TO PERFORM THE HAVDALAH CEREMONY

To perform the *Havdalah* ceremony, you will need several objects:

- a cup
- a saucer or plate
- wine
- a container of spices
- a multi-wicked candle

It is also helpful to have a napkin nearby for wiping hands or for cleaning up any incidental mess.

Grape juice is an acceptable alternative to wine. If neither wine nor grape juice is available, one can use another beverage such as beer, coffee, milk, or fruit juice.

Havdalah is usually performed using a special candle made from several intertwining or twisted wicks. If you do not have a candle of this sort, hold two or more regular candles together so that their flames join together to produce one bright light.

The *Havdalah* spice container comes in many forms. One common style is a silver tower-shaped cup that has a flag atop its cover. Some use a small wooden box or a bag made of sheer material. If a large group of people is present, consider using many containers of spices in order to save time.

The spices for the ceremony vary. One common tradition is to use dried bay leaves and cloves, but any natural nice-smelling spice is acceptable, ideally in its whole form rather than ground. In some communities it is common to use fresh herbs.

To begin the ceremony, the leader places the cup on the plate. Fill the cup with wine until it overflows a little into the plate. (If it is impractical to overflow the wine, it is not a necessity to do so.)

Light the multi-wicked candle. Someone other than the leader can hold the candle, or the candle may be placed in a holder. It is common to dim or turn off the lights during the ceremony so that the candle produces a strong effect.

One person recites all the blessings on behalf of all who are present. Customs vary as to whether to stand or sit when reciting *Havdalah.*

Hold the cup in the right hand, and recite the first paragraph, which begins with "Behold, God is my salvation." It is common in some communities for everyone to join in with the words "For the Jews there was light and gladness, joy and honor. So may it be for us!" Continue all the way through the blessing through the words "who creates the fruit of the vine."[a] Then, without drinking the wine, set down the cup.

Lift the container of spices with the right hand, and recite the blessing for spices. Then pass around the spices, and give everyone present a chance to smell them.

Next, recite the blessing for the firelight. During this blessing it is customary for everyone to extend a hand toward the flame and curl their fingers, examining the reflection of the light in their fingernails and noting the distinction between light and darkness. After reciting the blessing for the firelight, gaze into the light of the candle momentarily.

Finally, lift the cup once more with the right hand, and recite the concluding blessing.

When finished, it is customary to extinguish the flame either in the wine that overflowed onto the plate or in any leftover wine in the cup.

Some have a custom of dipping their little fingers into the wine and dabbing the wine on their eyelids; this reflects the idea that the commandments enlighten the eyes (Psalm 19:9[8]). Some dab it on their eyes and ears to express hope that they only see and hear good things. Some dab it in their pockets as an expression of hope for their livelihoods. Some dab it on the back of their necks, the place where the *luz,* the bone from which one is resurrected

a) One who uses a beverage other than grape juice or wine should not recite "who creates the fruit of the vine." Instead, he would say, "Blessed are you, O LORD, our God, King of the universe, by whose word all things came to be." / בָּרוּךְ אַתָּה יְיָ אֱלֹהֵינוּ מֶלֶךְ הָעוֹלָם, שֶׁהַכֹּל נִהְיָה בִּדְבָרוֹ.

from the dead, is believed to be located (see commentary on *Melaveh Malkah*, page 156).

Havdalah means "distinction," "separation," or "division." Distinction is the essence of holiness. To make the Sabbath holy, one must give it definition and distinguish it from other days of the week. This distinction is accomplished in two ways: by modifying our behavior throughout the day, and by drawing bold and clear dividing lines between holy time and common time.

As the Sabbath concludes and the work week begins, we do not just let the holiness fade away unnoticed. Just as candle lighting prior to the Sabbath ushers in the time of holiness with ceremony, we end the Sabbath with ceremony and intention through this beautiful and symbolic ritual.

Additionally, through *Havdalah* we express our hope that the peace and blessing of the Sabbath would continue with us throughout the week.

According to the Talmud,[a] *Havdalah* originated along with *Kiddush* with the men of the Great Assembly. If this is true, then the practice dates back possibly as early as the fourth century BCE. The Talmud explains that it originally took the form of a brief blessing inserted into *Ma'ariv* (evening prayers) on Saturday. Later, when the Jewish community became more affluent, the ritual was moved to the home where it was recited over a cup of wine. But when the Jewish community faced difficult times once again, it became customary to recite it during *Ma'ariv*, and then once again at home with a cup of wine if one could afford it.

The First Day of the Week

Havdalah on Saturday night marks the first day of the week. This period of time holds special significance for disciples of Yeshua. It was on the first day of the week—possibly Saturday night—that our Master was resurrected from the dead. While it was common for all of the Jewish community in the first century to celebrate *Havdalah*, for the early disciples it was a weekly reminder of the Messiah's victory over death.

In ancient times, there were special representatives in each town who would take turns making pilgrimages to the Temple. Those who were not scheduled to make the pilgrimage would remain in their towns, fasting and praying. But they only fasted on four days of the week: Monday, Tuesday, Wednesday, and Thursday. After explaining that they avoided fasting on Friday and Saturday because of the Sabbath, the Talmud questions why they did not fast on the first day of the week. One explanation

a) b.*Brachot* 33a.

was "on account of the *Notzrim*."[a] *Notzrim* means "Nazarenes," and refers to the followers of Yeshua. This suggests that the followers of Yeshua would have considered the first day of the week to be a time of rejoicing and an inappropriate time for fasting.

But why would followers of Yeshua have any effect on Jewish practice as a whole? Rashi simply says that it was because "they had made it their holiday." A common interpretation is that Jews at the time avoided fasting on that day because they did not want to arouse the wrath of Christianity, but this is anachronistic because while the Temple was still standing, the followers of Yeshua constituted a small sect within Judaism and were generally well regarded. Even had they been antagonistic, the sect would have been too small and powerless at the time to pose a threat to the Jewish community. This suggests that the practice of avoiding fasts on the first day of the week might have been in deference to the followers of Yeshua among the representatives rather than out of fear or opposition to them.

18 Got Fun Avrohom

This prayer was composed sometime during or before the eighteenth century in Eastern Europe. It is traditionally recited by women prior to *Havdalah*, although Rabbi Levi Yitzchok of Berditchev instructed that every man, woman, and child should recite it three times. It was composed in Yiddish, the common language of Jews in Eastern Europe, because women from that era were not often fluent in Hebrew.

19 Anna Eloheinu

This beautiful prayer for peace is found only in the Yemenite *Nusach Baladi*.

This prayer contains a reference to the "Prince of Peace." The phrase *sar shalom* ("Prince of Peace") appears only once in the Tanach, in Isaiah 9:5[6]. This prayer's use of "Prince of Peace" as a name of the Messiah is rare in Jewish literature. Christianity's emphasis on the passage as a messianic prophecy has caused the Jewish community to focus instead on Hezekiah as the historical fulfillment of the passage. It may be that the relative isolation of the Yemenite community from Christian missionaries has allowed them to remain open to its messianic interpretation.

Nonetheless, there are other Jewish interpretations of "Prince of Peace" as a messianic title. Targum Jonathan renders the passage, "His name is called from beforehand: Wonderful, Counselor, the Mighty God who endures forever, the Messiah, whose peace shall be great upon us in his days." The minor

a) b.*Ta'anit* 27b.

19
tractate *Perek HaShalom* says, "And [other reading: Rabbi Jose the Galilean said:] also the name of the Messiah is called 'Peace', for it is said: '(And his name shall be called ...) Father of Eternity, Prince of Peace.'"[a]

20 Hinneh El Yeshu'ati

This prayer expresses hope and confidence in God's provision and protection. As we embark on a new week with its challenges, we trust that God will save and help us.

This prayer is woven together from numerous passages in Scripture. A common thread in most of these verses is the mention of "salvation," which in Hebrew is *yeshu'ah* (יְשׁוּעָה). This sounds similar to the name of our Master Yeshua because his name is a contraction of Yehoshua (יְהוֹשֻׁעַ), which means "HaShem saves" or "HaShem is salvation."

When the Hebrew Scriptures speak of salvation, they are not typically referring to a personal salvation from hell or from sin. Rather, "salvation" from a Jewish perspective is a national or even global event. It is the repair of everything that is wrong with the world. While *yeshu'ah* can mean anything from "victory" to "recovery," it is often synonymous with *ge'ullah*, which means "redemption."

As the Sabbath departs, we are reminded of our hope and need for the ultimate redemption to occur. This prayer affirms our trust and expectation that God will send *yeshu'ah* soon.

Wine at Havdalah

Just as with each of the Sabbath meals, the overflowing cup of wine at *Havdalah* is symbolic of God's abundant blessings. The *Havdalah* prayer connects the wine with salvation by quoting the passage, "I will lift the cup of salvations" (Psalm 116:13).[b] This is also the case with the Passover, as each of the four cups of wine that we drink at the *seder* relates to another aspect of God's redemption of the Israelites from Egypt.

The Talmud (b.*Pesachim* 119b) connects the "cup of salvations" with the cup over the Grace after Meals that will be recited in the great messianic banquet. After Abraham, Isaac, Jacob, and Moses decline the offer to lead the Grace after Meals, David arises and says, "I will make the blessing. It is appropriate for me to make the blessing, as it is said, 'I will lift up the cup of salvations, and I will call on the name of HaShem'" (Psalm 116:13).

a) Marcus van Loopik, *The Ways of the Sages and the Way of the World* (Tubingen, Germany: J. C. B. Mohr, 1991), 345.

b) Many translators render the phrase as "cup of salvation," but the Hebrew word *yeshu'ot* ("salvations," יְשׁוּעוֹת) is actually plural.

20

As we drink wine in connection with salvation, it is appropriate to reflect on our Master, who compared his spilled blood to the wine of Passover—the cup of salvations. Yeshua said of this cup, "I will not drink from this fruit of the vine from now until that day when I drink it with you and it is new in the kingdom of my Father" (Matthew 26:29).

Smelling the Spices

During the *Havdalah* ceremony it is customary to smell spices. A common Ashkenazi custom is to use a mixture of bay leaves and cloves. Other common choices include cinnamon, nutmeg, allspice, or myrtle leaves (such as those from the four species waved during *Sukkot*). It is customary not to use artificial scents.

The Sabbath is full of sweetness, and the sweet spices also symbolize our hope that the sweetness of the Sabbath carries into the week. We want the holiness and blessing and the new things we learned not to stay "bottled up" on the Sabbath, but to infuse the rest of the week with holiness. Similarly, the Midrash compares Abraham to a vial of myrrh with a tightly fitting cap. When HaShem said, "Go," it was as if his scent was released as he brought knowledge of the true God into the world.[a]

Paul uses similar terminology when he rejoices that "through us [God] spreads knowledge of him everywhere, for we are the fragrant aroma of the Messiah to God among those who are being saved and those who are being lost" (2 Corinthians 2:14–15).

The Talmud explains that on the Sabbath, God gives to man an extra measure of "soul," so to speak. When the Sabbath ceases, that soul departs. This is based on a midrashic interpretation of Exodus 31:17. The phrase *shavat vayinnafash* (שָׁבַת וַיִּנָּפַשׁ) which means, "he ceased and was refreshed," is creatively re-read as *shavat—oy, nefesh!* This would mean, "[The Sabbath] ended, woe to the soul!"[b] One explanation for smelling spices at *Havdalah* is to help us recover from this loss of soul and to prevent our weekday soul from departing with it. Loss of one's soul is death; the spices revive us.

While this explanation is figurative and should not be taken literally, it is remarkable that the dawning of the first day of the week is associated with resurrection. It was the first day of the week when Yeshua rose from the dead, and when the women brought spices to his tomb. *Havdalah* is a perfect time to commemorate our Master's resurrection each week with the smelling of spices and rekindling of the flame.

a) *Genesis Rabbah* 39:2.
b) b.*Beitzah* 16a; b.*Ta'anit* 27b.

20

E **The firelight** — Since it is forbidden to kindle a fire on the Sabbath,[a] by kindling lights before and after, we clearly mark its boundaries. In ancient times, it would be necessary to rekindle the lamps after the sun had set in order to have light in a house.

A multi-wicked candle is used because of the emphasis of *Havdalah* on distinction. Distinction can best be made when the light is bright, and the light of a many-wicked candle (which legally qualifies as a torch) makes a much brighter light than individual lamps do.

It is customary to reach one's hands toward the *Havdalah* candle and look at the reflected firelight in one's fingernails. This is done in order to use the fire for a practical purpose and to perceive the separation between light and darkness.

Just as our first weekday activity is the kindling of a flame, the creation of light was the first act of creation recorded in the book of Genesis.[b] The *Midrash Rabbah* explains that the fire of *Havdalah* commemorates this: "Why do we make the blessing, 'who creates the light of the fire' over the light at the conclusion of the Sabbath? Because this was the beginning of its creation."[c]

But the midrash goes on to say that this is spiritual light, not natural light. Along the same lines, the midrash *Yalkut Shim'oni* explains:

> What is meant by, "By your light we see light" (Psalm 36:10[9])? This is the light of Messiah, as it is said, "God saw the light, that it was good" (Genesis 1:4). This teaches that before the world was created, the blessed Holy One looked forward to the generation of Messiah and its deeds. He hid [the primordial light] for Messiah and his generation beneath his throne of glory.

This light is reflected in Jerusalem, the Temple, the menorah, and teachers of the Torah—anything that reveals the glory of God—and it is referred to as the "light of the world,"[d] a term that Yeshua used for himself[e] and his followers.[f]

---

a) Exodus 35:3.
b) Genesis 1:3.
c) *Genesis Rabbah* 12:6.
d) *Genesis Rabbah* 59; b. *Bava Bathra* 4a.
e) John 8:12.
f) Matthew 5:14–16.

MELAVEH MALKAH

After the Sabbath is over, it is customary to have another special meal. This practice is mentioned in the Talmud, which means that it dates back at least to Talmudic times.[a]

Melaveh Malkah literally means "escorting the queen." The Sabbath is likened to an honored guest. Just as one would not hastily dismiss a distinguished visitor, we figuratively escort the departing Sabbath with a farewell party.

At a *Melaveh Malkah* meal, it is considered ideal to set the table just as for each of the three Sabbath meals, complete with meat, wine, and two loaves of bread. However, since most people are not hungry after a full day of eating, it is considered acceptable just to have a little snack like cake or fruit.

Stories about the righteous feature prominently at this meal. In Chasidic communities it is customary to tell stories about the Ba'al Shem Tov or other great rebbes. For followers of Yeshua, it would be appropriate to tell stories about our Master and his disciples as well as other great heroes and luminaries in our movement.

Melaveh Malkah has strong messianic connections as well as a close link to resurrection.

The Midrash speaks of an indestructible part of the body called the *luz* (also called the *niskoy*) from which one is resurrected from the dead.[b] This body part only receives its nourishment from *Melaveh Malkah*.[c]

The traditional songs for *Melaveh Malkah* make frequent mention of Elijah the Prophet, who is the forerunner of the Messiah. Elijah and Messiah would not come on the Sabbath, since they have a lot of work to do. Thus, when the Sabbath ends, we renew our hope that they will arrive soon.

MELAVEH MALKAH IN THE NEW TESTAMENT

Surprisingly, there is an indication that the early followers of Yeshua observed something similar to *Melaveh Malkah*:

> On the first day of the week, when we were gathered together to break bread, Paul talked with them, intending to depart on the next day, and he prolonged his speech until midnight. There were many lamps in the upper room where we were gathered. (Acts 20:7–8 ESV)

a) b.*Shabbat* 119b.
b) *Genesis Rabbah* 28:3.
c) *Mishnah Brurah* 300.

Rather than Sunday as is commonly assumed, this event could have happened on Saturday night. The "first day of the week" begins at nightfall on Saturday. Paul intended to depart the next day—Sunday—because travel is forbidden on the Sabbath. Since this gathering began in the evening, it makes perfect sense that Paul's speech would extend until midnight. This also explains the many lamps that were burning.

When it says that they "gathered together to break bread," it does not mean that they observed a Eucharist ceremony. "To break bread" is just a Hebrew idiom that means "to share a meal." Thus it appears that the disciples joined together to share a meal on Saturday night.

The story of resurrection that follows makes the connection with *Melaveh Malkah* even stronger:

> And a young man named Eutychus, sitting at the window, sank into a deep sleep as Paul talked still longer. And being overcome by sleep, he fell down from the third story and was taken up dead. But Paul went down and bent over him, and taking him in his arms, said, "Do not be alarmed, for his life is in him." And when Paul had gone up and had broken bread and eaten, he conversed with them a long while, until daybreak, and so departed. (Acts 20:9–11 ESV)

21 RIBBON HAOLAMIM

Some have the custom of reciting this prayer prior to *Havdalah*; others do it afterward. The prayer borrows much of its wording from the Jerusalem Talmud.[a] It may have originated as a home-based version of the brief blessing inserted into *Ma'ariv* on Saturday evening.

This prayer asks for blessing and protection in the coming week. It concludes by asking God to fulfill his scriptural promises to send the Messiah.

22 THE MEAL OF DAVID

Melaveh Malkah is called "the meal of David the anointed king." King David wrote the words, "O LORD, let me know my end, and what are the measure of my days; I shall know how frail I am" (Psalm 39:5[4]).

The Talmud comments on this verse that David asked God when he would die. HaShem would not tell him the exact date, but only that he would die on the Sabbath. From then on, David would spend every moment of the Sabbath engrossed in Torah study in order to stave off the Angel of Death.[b] Legend

a) y.*Brachot* 5:2.
b) b.*Shabbat* 30a–b.

holds that after the conclusion of every Sabbath, King David would host a feast of celebration and thanks for having made it through another week. This is how the after-Sabbath meal became known as "the meal of David the anointed king."

For followers of Yeshua, this should strike a chord—gathering together as the new week begins to celebrate that our anointed King is alive.

WHAT ARE ZEMIROT?

Zemirot (the singular is *zemer*) are songs that are sung at the Sabbath table during the meal, often between courses. They serve to transform the Sabbath meal into a spiritually uplifting experience. *Zemirot* are written to channel the pleasure and joy of eating satisfying and delicious foods into feelings and expressions of gratitude, joy, awe, love, and yearning for God.

Our Master Yeshua taught us that "the Sabbath was made for man" (Mark 2:27 ESV). This teaches us that the Sabbath is a gift. When we receive a gift from a person we love dearly, we cherish that gift and revel in it. When we express our enjoyment and delight in what we received, we are in actuality expressing our affection for the giver. In the same way, many *zemirot* overflow with expressions of love for the Sabbath. These are expressions of love for God, who gave the Sabbath to us.

Zemirot are an extremely important tool for passing on love for the Sabbath and Jewish identity to the next generation. Music has a way of reaching the heart, creating memories, and helping us bond with others through a shared experience.

Although there is some flexibility, most *zemirot* have a certain customary time when they are recited. Some are typically sung at the Friday night meal; some during the Saturday morning meal (*Kiddusha Rabba*); some at the afternoon meal (*Se'udah Shlishit*), and some are reserved for *Havdalah* or the meal on Saturday night (*Melaveh Malkah*).

Unlike the blessings and prayers, the *zemirot* are not set in stone. People select two or three (or more as desired) to sing at any given meal. Don't feel limited by the songs in this book; sing any songs you like that are fitting for the Sabbath table.

If the *zemirot* in this book seem too long and complicated, don't worry. It is perfectly fine to just sing the chorus, or maybe one verse. Many short Sabbath table songs are just a couple of lines excerpted from one of these songs.

EREV SHABBAT

27 CHAFETZAH NAFSHI

Chafetzah Nafshi was written by Aaron Eby. The phrase *chai Yeshua* (Yeshua lives) is encoded in its verses.

A **My soul ... my flesh** — Both the physical and spiritual aspects of a person can take delight in the Sabbath.

Enter his rest — This language is borrowed from Psalm 95 and Hebrews 4:11.

B **From Sabbath to Sabbath** — This line comes from Isaiah 66:23.

Ariel — A term for Jerusalem used in Isaiah 29.

Cling to the sign of his covenant — This alludes to Isaiah 56:4–7.

C **They ceased ... according to the commandment** — This alludes to Luke 23:56.

Permitted ... to do good — This refers to Yeshua's statement in Matthew 12:12.

It is holy to you — This comes from Exodus 31:14.

You are not committed to its hand — This sentiment is taken directly from the Talmud (b.*Yoma* 85b). It bears remarkable similarity to Yeshua's statement that "the Sabbath was made for man, not man for the Sabbath" (Mark 2:27 ESV).

D **They shall keep the Sabbath** — This comes from Exodus 31:16.

We were slaves — The Sabbath is a remembrance of the exodus from Egypt. See Deuteronomy 5:15.

E **There still remains a Sabbath** — This comes from Hebrews 4:9. It refers to the common belief in Judaism that the millennia of human history parallel the days of the week. The Messianic Era, a time of peace, blessing, and rest, corresponds with the weekly Sabbath.

A day that is entirely Sabbath — This phrase is taken from a line that is included in the *Birkat HaMazon* (Grace after Meals) on the Sabbath.

A taste of the world to come — This line is a quotation of the song *Mah Yedidut Menuchatech*. The joy, peace, blessing, and holiness experienced on the Sabbath is a tiny fraction of what is in store in the future.

27

E **A shadow of things that are yet coming** — This refers to Colossians 2:17, which states that the Sabbath, festivals, and New Moon celebrations are shadows, and the Messiah is the reality. Far from being a disparaging remark, this passage combats asceticism and self-deprivation by showing that by delighting ourselves on the Sabbath, we are experiencing the messianic future here and now.

28 HADAR LEVUSHAH

Hadar Levushah was written by Aaron Eby. The name *Aharon* is encoded in its verses. This song combines the mystical idea of the Sabbath as a bride with our Master Yeshua's statement that the Sabbath was made for man.

A **Blessed from the beginning of creation** — See Genesis 2:3; Exodus 20:11.

Sanctified (betrothed) with joy — The Hebrew word for "betrothed" (*mekuddeshet,* מְקֻדֶּשֶׁת) also means "sanctified." The sages of the Midrash noticed this:

> Why did God bless the Sabbath? ... Because it has no partner. The first day has the second day, the third day has the fourth day, and the fifth day has the sixth day. But the Sabbath has no partner! ... The Sabbath said to the blessed Holy One, "Master of the universe, everyone else has a partner, but I do not!" The blessed Holy One said to her, "The assembly of Israel is your partner." And so it was that when Israel stood before Mount Sinai, the blessed Holy One said to them, "Remember the promise that I made to the Sabbath: 'The assembly of Israel is your partner.' As it is said, 'Remember the Sabbath day to sanctify (that is, betroth) it'" (Exodus 20:8).

By the mouth of her groom — This alludes to *Kiddush*, which is pronounced over a cup of wine, just as betrothal is performed with a cup of wine.

Clothed in beauty — This language is borrowed from Proverbs 31:25, in the chapter that speaks of the "capable woman." Seventeenth-century Jewish mystics interpreted this passage as referring to the Divine Presence which enters the home on the evening of the Sabbath.

B **Prepared for her husband** — This borrows language from Revelation 21:2, which speaks of the New Jerusalem descending to earth.

The Sabbath is given to man — This refers to our Master Yeshua's saying in Mark 2:27, "The Sabbath was made for man, not man for the Sabbath" (ESV).

28

C **Your treasure** — This is Israel (see Exodus 19:5; Psalm 135:4).

The faithful of the house — This is Moses (see Numbers 12:7).

Sapphires — Tradition holds that the tablets of the Ten Commandments were carved from sapphire (*Midrash Tanchuma*, Ki Tisa 29; *Leviticus Rabbah* 32:2).

You, your son, and your daughter — This refers to Exodus 20:10 and Deuteronomy 5:14.

D **Our healer ascended to the scroll of the prophets** — This refers to our Master Yeshua's reading from Isaiah in the synagogue at Nazareth, described in Luke 4:16–30. This event occurred on the Sabbath, as it says, "As was his custom, he went to the synagogue on the Sabbath day" (ESV). He is referred to as "healer" here in reference to his Sabbath healing miracles and in allusion to the proverb he quotes regarding himself: "Physician [that is, healer], heal yourself" (Luke 4:23).

The LORD has anointed me to bring good news to the poor — This is the passage our Master Yeshua read, beginning with Isaiah 61:1.

Today these words are fulfilled — This refers to Luke 4:21. The word "today" (*ha-yom*, הַיּוֹם) is a title of the Sabbath, based on Exodus 16:25.

E **Satisfied from his goodness** — This borrows its language from the blessing recited after eating a snack (the Blessing Resembling Three). This in turn comes from Jeremiah 31:14, which speaks of the abundance of the Messianic Era.

The table in the kingdom — This refers to the future messianic banquet. See Luke 22:30.

29 MAH YEDIDUT MENUCHATECH

Mah Yedidut Menuchatech was written by an unknown person named Menachem, whose name is encoded in its verses. It first appeared in the sixteenth century. This song is customarily sung at the Friday evening meal.

A **You Sabbath Queen** — The personification of the Sabbath as a bride and a queen is very ancient. Reference to this concept is found in the Talmud:

> Rabbi Chanina would wrap himself in a garment and stood in the evening at the onset of the Sabbath, saying, "Come, and let us go out to greet the Sabbath Queen!" Rabbi Yannai would put on his robes at the onset of the Sabbath and say, "Come, O Bride! Come, O Bride!" (b.*Shabbat* 119a)

29

Rabbi Chanina was born in the second century CE. But he may not have been the first to personify the Sabbath in such a way. Ignatius of Antioch was one of the early church fathers who played a significant role in transitioning the body of Yeshua's followers away from Judaism. At that time, the believers both observed the Sabbath and treated the first day of the week with special honor. Ignatius made efforts to downplay Sabbath observance and to transfer its solemnity to the first day of the week. He wrote:

> And after the observance of the Sabbath, let every friend of Christ keep the Lord's Day as a festival, the resurrection-day, the queen and chief of all the days of the week. (Ignatius, *Letter to the Magnesians* 9:4)

It seems likely that Ignatius borrowed the term "queen" from contemporary references to the Sabbath. If he did, the idea of the Sabbath as a queen may date back as early as the first century CE.

A **We will run to greet you** — The mystics of Safed in the seventeenth century, inspired by Rabbi Chanina and Rabbi Yannai in the Talmudic passage above, developed a custom of welcoming the Sabbath by singing several psalms.

You shall not do any work — This phrase alludes to Leviticus 23:3 and Jeremiah 17:22.

B **To take pleasure** — This Hebrew word *lehit'aneg* (לְהִתְעַנֵּג) is a verb form of the term *oneg* ("delight," עֹנֶג), and thus alludes to Isaiah 58:13.

C **Aromatic wines** — Wines scented or flavored with spices were common in the ancient world.

Three times — This refers to the three meals that are enjoyed on the Sabbath: Friday evening, Saturday morning, and Saturday afternoon.

D **Possess Jacob's inheritance** — This refers to Isaiah 58:14: "I will feed you with the inheritance of your father Jacob."

Without limits — The Talmud (b.*Shabbat* 118a) notes that whereas Abraham and Isaac were promised a land with specific borders, God's promise to Jacob was unbounded: "You shall spread abroad to the west and to the east and to the north and to the south" (Genesis 28:14 ESV).

They will merit redemption — The sages (b.*Shabbat* 118b) teach based on Isaiah 56:4, 7 that if Israel were to keep just two Sabbaths correctly, the complete redemption would come immediately.

29

D **You will be my treasure** — This comes from Exodus 19:5.

For six days, you may labor — This alludes to Exodus 34:21.

E **Personal desires are forbidden** — This stanza is based on the sages' interpretation of Isaiah 58:13.

F **Restore the soul** — This alludes to Psalm 19:8[7].

My soul thirsts — This alludes to Psalm 42:2[1].

Fenced in like a flower garden — The Sabbath is protected by fence laws—additional stringencies that help to avoid profaning the Sabbath on a biblical level. These stringencies are observed out of love for the beauty and holiness of the Sabbath.

Sons and daughters — This alludes to the Sabbath commandment: "You, your son, your daughter ..." (Exodus 20:10; Deuteronomy 5:14).

G **A foretaste of the world to come** — The Talmud (b.*Brachot* 57b) teaches that the Sabbath is one-sixtieth of the world to come. One-sixtieth has significance in Jewish law in that it is considered barely beyond the threshold of perception. By calling the Sabbath "one-sixtieth part of the age to come," it expresses that it represents a barely discernible hint of what the future world will be like.

The birth pangs of Messiah — Judaism teaches that before the Messiah arrives, the Jewish community will have to endure suffering and persecution that can be likened to a woman's pain during childbirth (b.*Sanhedrin* 98b). This imagery comes from Jeremiah 30:6 and Micah 5:2[3]. Yeshua taught that "nation will rise against nation, and kingdom against kingdom, and there will be famines and earthquakes in various places. All these are but the beginning of the birth pains" (Matthew 24:7–8 ESV; see also Mark 13:8).

The Talmud (b.*Shabbat* 118a) asserts that one who keeps the Sabbath will be spared from the suffering of the birth pangs of Messiah.

Sorrow and grief will flee — This alludes to Isaiah 35:10; 51:11.

30 Menuchah Vesimchah

Menuchah Vesimchah may have been written by Mosheh ben Kalonymos of Mayence (Mainz), Germany, in the eleventh century, although it first appears in print in the sixteenth century. The name *Mosheh* is encoded in its verses. This song is normally sung at the Friday evening meal.

30

A **Light for the Jews** — This alludes to Esther 8:16. Light is associated with the evening of the Sabbath. (See "The Symbolism of Light" on page 130 in the commentary on the lighting of the Sabbath candles.)

Keep it and remember it — This refers to the two expressions of the Sabbath commandment in Exodus 20:8 and Deuteronomy 5:12.

B **The highest heavens** — This list of created things is arranged in the order in which they were created.

The Lord is the Creator of all — This comes from Isaiah 26:4. The point of this verse is to continue the thought from the previous verse: Those who keep the Sabbath testify that the Lord is the Creator of all, including the highest heavens, etc.

In Isaiah 26:4, the phrase *tzur olamim* (צוּר עוֹלָמִים) means "everlasting rock." However, the author of this song interpreted it creatively as "Creator of all" (literally, "former of worlds") based on later developments in Hebrew.

C **For God rested on it from all his creative activity** — This alludes to Genesis 2:3.

D **God will fortify you** — This alludes to the *Birkat HaMazon* (Grace after Meals), which states, "Show favor and fortify us ... with the commandment of the seventh day."

The breath of all living — This refers to the prayer *Nishmat Kol Chai*, which is included in the Sabbath morning prayers and in the Passover Haggadah. There are some traditions in Judaism dating back at least to the middle ages that attest that Shim'on Keifa (Simon Peter) wrote this prayer.

We will esteem you — This refers to a special version of the *Kedushah* (Holiness) section of the *Amidah* that is recited during the *Musaf* (additional) service on the Sabbath.

Eat joyfully, for he has already shown favor — This alludes to Ecclesiastes 9:7. The sense is that we eat our meal with the assurance that God has accepted our special Sabbath prayers.

E **With the double loaves** — This refers to the custom of having two loaves at each of the three meals of the Sabbath.

Great Kiddush — This is *Kiddusha Rabba*, the blessing that is recited prior to the meal after the Sabbath morning prayers.

The one who delights in it — This alludes to Isaiah 58:13–14.

30

E **When the redeemer comes** — This refers to the Messiah. When he comes, Sabbath keepers will receive their reward.

31 YAH ECHSOF

Yah Echsof was written by Aharon ben Ya'akov of Karlin, who lived in Lithuania in the eighteenth century. The Tetragrammaton (the four-letter name of God), *Aharon,* and *Neshamah* ("soul") are encoded in the first three words of each verse. This song is normally sung at the Friday evening meal. This song is deeply mystical, and it is not possible to elucidate its full meaning here.

A **Resembles and unifies** — Just as Israel is set apart from all the nations of the world (Leviticus 20:24, 26), the Sabbath is separate from the other days by virtue of its holiness. In this way, Israel and the Sabbath are like twins. Furthermore, Israel and the Sabbath have a partnering relationship, as the sages have noted. (See commentary on *Hadar Levushah* on page 161)

Your treasure — This is Israel (see Exodus 19:5; Psalm 135:4).

Unifies with your Torah — The sages considered the Sabbath to be equivalent to all of the commandments:

> Just as we find that the [Messiah] Son of David will come [in reward] for [keeping] all of the commandments, the [Messiah] Son of David will come [in reward] for [keeping] the commandment of just one day of the Sabbath, since the Sabbath is equivalent in weight to all of the commandments. (*Exodus Rabbah* 25:12)

Unlock for them sweetness and willingness — Grant them these attributes, so that they may in turn find God's favor.

C **He Who Was and Is** — According to mystical teaching, God's name (Y-H-V-H) is composed from the letters that form the Hebrew terms "was," "is," and "will be": *hayah* (היה), *hoveh* (הוה), and *yiyheh* (יהיה). This alludes to Moses' conversation with God at the burning bush in Exodus 3, where God says, "I will be who I will be" (Exodus 3:14). This name of God signifies his unchanging nature. Although the terms *hayah* and *hoveh* appear together in other Jewish literature in reference to God (such as in the song *Adon Olam*), in the Bible this title is only found in Revelation 1:4, 1:8, and 4:8.

Protect those who protect — As the song *Ki Eshmerah Shabbat* states, "If I keep the Sabbath, God will keep me."

31

C **Anticipate your holy Sabbath** — The commandment to "remember the Sabbath day" (Exodus 20:8) can be observed every day of the week as one prepares for the coming Sabbath.

As a deer longs for streams of water — This alludes to Psalm 42:2[1].

Unifies with your holy name — In Chasidic teaching, *Shabbat* (Sabbath) is one of the names of God.

Delay parting from the Sabbath — It is a Chasidic custom to extend the Sabbath as long as possible on Saturday night.

Closed off from them — That is to say, may the holiness of the Sabbath permeate the rest of the week.

And purify their heart with truth — This alludes to the *Kedushat HaYom* (Holiness of the Day) section of the Sabbath *Amidah* prayer.

D **From the river that comes forth from Eden** — This alludes to Genesis 2:10 and Psalm 36:9[8] and the mystical teachings associated with those passages. This river is also mentioned in Revelation 22:1.

To crown Israel with majesty — This alludes to one of the morning blessings mentioned in the Talmud (b.*Brachot* 60b).

Glorify you through your holy Sabbath — Observing the Sabbath is an act of worship that declares that God is King.

The inheritance of Jacob — This alludes to Isaiah 58:14.

Your chosen one — This alludes to Isaiah 45:4.

E **Lovesick for you** — This borrows language from the song *Yedid Nefesh,* which in turn alludes to Song of Songs 5:8.

Take refuge in the shadow of your wings — This is a quotation from Psalm 36:8–9[7–8].

32 Yah Ribbon Alam

Yah Ribbon Alam was written by Yisra'el ben Mosheh Najara, who lived in Israel in the sixteenth century. This song is written in Aramaic, and the name *Yisra'el* is encoded in its verses. This song is normally sung at the Friday evening meal. This song is unusual in that it only hints at the Sabbath, focusing more explicitly on pure praise of God.

A **Every world** — This could also be translated "every age."

32

C **Who created all life** — The Sabbath is a memorial of the completion of creation, and it testifies that God created all things.

D **Your works are very great and mighty** — This bears similarity to Revelation 15:3.

You humble the proud — This is a common sentiment throughout the Scriptures.

Straighten the bent — This alludes to Psalm 146:8.

E **Rescue your flock from the mouth of lions** — This alludes to Psalm 22:22[21]. The lions' mouths represent persecution during exile.

F **The city of beauty** — This may allude to Lamentations 2:15.

33 Tzur Mishelo Achalnu

The composer of *Tzur Mishelo Achalnu* (The Creator Whose Food We Have Eaten) is not known, although some scholars believe it was written in France no later than the fourteenth century. This song is unusual in that there are no names or phrases encoded in its verses.

This song is widely sung as an introduction to the *Birkat HaMazon* (Grace after Meals) at any of the Sabbath meals. The stanzas of this song are parallel to the blessings of the *Birkat HaMazon*.

A **The Creator** — The Hebrew word here is *tzur* (צוּר), which in Biblical Hebrew means "rock," so it connotes God's stability and steadfastness. However, later Jewish writers also associated it with the term *yotzer* (יוֹצֵר), which means "maker, creator."

We have eaten ... We are satisfied — This alludes to Deuteronomy 8:10, which instructs that when one has eaten and is satisfied, he must bless God.

Extra, according to the LORD's word — This borrows wording from 2 Kings 4:44, which speaks of the miracle of Elisha feeding his one hundred disciples with twenty loaves of bread. This story has clear and direct parallels to the multiplication miracles recorded in the Gospels.

Those of us who live in a time and place of abundance should recognize that while we may not have experienced an overt miracle, the end result is the same as for those whom Elisha and Yeshua fed. We should be just as grateful.

33

This line may also allude to the blessings promised in the Torah: "The LORD your God will make you abundantly prosperous [literally, have extra] in all the work of your hand" (Deuteronomy 30:9).

B **Nourishes his world** — This is quoted from the first blessing of the *Birkat HaMazon.*

Our shepherd, our Father — These titles are used in the third blessing of the *Birkat HaMazon.*

His bread ... his wine — King David said, "The earth is the LORD's and the fullness thereof" (Psalm 24:1 ESV). By reciting blessings for foods, we are granted legal permission to eat them. If one does not recite a blessing, it is similar to the sin of making personal use of things consecrated to the Temple (b.*Brachot* 35a).

C **With our mouths** — Just as we use our mouths to eat, so we should use them to say thanks.

There is none as holy as the LORD — This is a quotation from 1 Samuel 2:2.

D **For the pleasant, good, and spacious land** — This is quoted from the second blessing of the *Birkat HaMazon.*

E **He has asserted his devotion toward us** — This alludes to Psalm 117:2.

F **Have compassion ... on your people** — This alludes to the third blessing of the *Birkat HaMazon.*

On Zion, the dwelling place of your glory — This is quoted from the third blessing of the *Birkat HaMazon.*

G **May the Son of David, your servant** — This refers to the Messiah. It is important to pray for the Messianic Kingdom to be established, because only then will Israel have true sovereignty over the land and be able to bless God for it.

Come and redeem us — Redemption here does not refer to personal forgiveness of sins, but the process of restoring the people of Israel and the entire world into a state of blessing, goodness, peace, and divine revelation.

The breath of our nostrils, the Messiah of the LORD — This is a quotation from Lamentations 4:20, which speaks of the capture of King Josiah. With the coming of the Messiah as King, the "breath of our nostrils" will be restored.

33

H **Fill the city of Zion** — May it be populated with residents and people attending the pilgrimage festivals.

There we will sing a new song — The Passover Haggadah tells us that when the redemption comes, "we will give thanks to [God], singing a new song about our redemption and the ransom of our souls." The prayer of Zechariah in Luke 1:68–79 is just such a "new song."

Ascend — Visiting Israel, Jerusalem, or the Temple is always referred to as "ascending."

I **Compassionate One** — This alludes to the final section of the *Birkat HaMazon.*

In accordance with the LORD's blessing — Just as we are full to overflowing with God's blessings, so we fill our cup of blessing.

34 YOM ZEH LEYISRA'EL

Yom Zeh Leyisra'el was written by Yitzchak ben Shlomoh Luria Ashkenazi, who lived in Israel in the sixteenth century. The phrase *Yitzchak L. Ch.* is encoded in its verses.

Some versions of the song contain several more verses that spell out the full phrase *Yitzchak Luria Chazak* (Yitzchak Luria, be strengthened). These verses do not appear in early siddurim. They were most likely added by Sabbateans, a group that believed that Shabbetai Zevi was the messiah.

This song is normally sung at the Friday evening meal.

A **Light and gladness** — This alludes to Esther 8:16. Light is associated with the evening of the Sabbath. (See "The Symbolism of Light" on page 130 in the commentary on the lighting of the Sabbath candles.)

C **An additional soul** — As explained in the commentary regarding smelling the *Havdalah* spices, the Talmud (b.*Ta'anit* 27b, b.*Beitzah* 16a) states that on the Sabbath, God gives to man an extra measure of "soul," so to speak. This does not mean that two beings are possessing one body, as it might sound. Rather, Rashi explains that on the Sabbath, a person is given a greater spiritual capacity to benefit from and appreciate the physical delights of the Sabbath (Rashi on b.*Ta'anit* 27b, b.*Beitzah* 16a).

D **Sanctified and blessed** — These two words are used to describe what God did to the Sabbath in Genesis 2:3 and Exodus 20:11.

In six days you finished the creation of the world — This alludes to Genesis 2:2.

34

E **Creative activity** — Normally translated as "work" or "labor," the word *melachah* (מְלָאכָה) describes activity that is prohibited on the Sabbath. As explained in the commentary on the Friday night *Kiddush* ("he ceased from his work") on page 137, *melachah* speaks of creative activities—acts by which one exerts his or her influence on the world, changing things from one state or identity to another.

I will merit royal beauty — This refers to the messianic redemption. The sages say that if Israel were to keep one Sabbath properly, the Messiah would come immediately (y.*Ta'anit* 1:1).

Tribute to the Fearsome One — This alludes to Psalm 76:12[11].

F **The destroyed one** — This refers to Jerusalem.

The grieved one — This refers to the Jewish people.

Spends the Sabbath singing and praising — The song highlights the irony that the Jewish people have dedicated themselves to the commandments to rest, rejoice, and delight on the Sabbath, all while the Temple and Jerusalem lay in ruins and the nation is scattered in exile.

The joyful and dutiful observance of the Sabbath in the midst of pain and difficulty is reminiscent of a note in the Gospel of Luke. After Yeshua had been executed and buried, on the Sabbath his followers "rested according to the commandment" (Luke 23:56 ESV). See the song *Uvashabbat* for an elaboration on this theme (prayer 40, page 75).

35 Lechem Bemalchut Shamayim

Lechem Bemalchut Shamayim was written by Aaron Eby in collaboration with Troy Mitchell. The name *Aharon* is encoded in its verses. The chorus was written first, and the verses were added several years later.

A **Blessed is he** — This line comes from Luke 14:15, where it was expressed by a person who was listening to Yeshua's parables. The word translated "blessed" is *ashrei* (אַשְׁרֵי), which expresses a sense of ultimate contentment and reward.

Kingdom of Heaven — Even though the Greek text in Luke 14:15 literally says "kingdom of God" (*basileia tou theou*, βασιλείᾳ τοῦ θεοῦ), this is how Luke represented the Hebrew idiom "kingdom of Heaven" (*malchut shamayim*, מַלְכוּת שָׁמַיִם).

B **I have baked what I will bake** — This comes from Exodus 16:23, where Moses instructs the people regarding the manna, "The rest day of the holy

35

Sabbath for the LORD is tomorrow. Bake what you will bake, and boil what you will boil, and leave what is extra to save it for the morning."

B **The hidden manna** — This comes from Revelation 2:17, where Yeshua declares, "To one who overcomes, I will give some of the hidden manna."

C **New in my Father's kingdom** — This refers to Matthew 26:29.

D **Inviting many guests** — This alludes to the parable in Luke 14:16.

Highways and byways — This alludes to Luke 14:23.

To the east and to the west — This refers to Matthew 8:11.

E **Sit with Torah to learn** — This refers to the practice of discussing Torah at the Sabbath table.

Hearts that burn — This alludes to the Emmaus Road experience (Luke 24:32), where the Messiah expounded and explained the Torah.

In the breaking of the bread — This refers to Luke 24:35.

Yom Shabbat

36 Baruch El Elyon

Baruch El Elyon was written by Baruch ben Shmuel, who lived in Germany in the thirteenth century. The phrase *Baruch Chazak* (Baruch, be strengthened) is encoded in its verses. This song is normally sung at the Saturday morning meal.

A **Who gave rest** — Who gave the Sabbath for rest.

Ransom for our souls — The Sabbath provides reprieve and relief during a period of exile. Furthermore, the Talmud teaches that in the merit of the three meals of the Sabbath, a person escapes three future ordeals: the "birth pangs" of Messiah, punishment in the afterlife, and the war of Gog and Magog. (See commentary on *Se'udah Shlishit*: "Messianic Aspects" on page 147.)

The outcast city — This borrows language from Jeremiah 30:17. Zion (that is, Jerusalem) appears to be outcast or rejected because no one cares for her. Jeremiah promises that Jerusalem will be restored as a part of the messianic redemption.

36

B **Grain offering in a pan** — Leviticus 2:5 describes a grain offering fried in a shallow pan, which results in a firm, flat cake. Grain offerings are modest, but they reflect the humility and pure motives of someone with little to offer.

C **Rides upon the heavens** — This phrase is borrowed from Psalm 68:5[4]. The word here for "heavens," *aravot* (עֲרָבוֹת), is often translated "deserts." However, Jewish mystical literature typically interprets this as a name for the topmost layer of heaven.

A family's offering — This term comes from 1 Samuel 20:29, describing a celebratory event.

D **The double payment** — This reflects the belief that God treats us according to the principle of "measure for measure." The Sabbath is a financial challenge, since it requires us to take time away from work and to spend extra money in preparation for the day. Nonetheless, we are confident that God will repay us both in this age and in the age to come.

The one for whom the sun shone — This is an allusion to Genesis 32:31, where it literally says of Jacob, "The sun shone for him as he passed Penuel." Thus, one who keeps the Sabbath will receive an inheritance like Jacob, as stated in Isaiah 58:13–14.

E **Qualified for an affinity to holiness** — Observing the Sabbath makes one more receptive to a higher degree of holiness.

It is an offering to God — Observance of the Sabbath in all its details is an act of worship, just like the offerings in the Temple.

F **His Spirit will rest upon them** — This phrase can also be translated, "He will be content with them."

G **Remember the Sabbath day, to sanctify it** — This comes from Exodus 20:8.

His honor will be bestowed — Literally, "His horn will be raised." In Hebrew, "horn" (like the horn of an animal) is an idiom for power or honor.

H **The Sabbath queen is holy for you** — This comes from Exodus 31:14. The sages noted that the Sabbath is "for you," that is, for human benefit and enjoyment (b.*Yoma* 85b).

37 KI ESHMERAH SHABBAT

Ki Eshmerah Shabbat was written by Avraham Ibn Ezra, who is famous for his Torah commentary as well as his poetry. He lived in Spain in the twelfth century. The name *Avraham* is encoded in the song's verses. This song is normally sung at the Saturday morning meal.

A **God will keep me** — "Keep" in the sense of "protect, preserve." A similar idea is expressed in the Midrash regarding the Torah in general. *Exodus Rabbah* 36:4 notes that "the commandment is a lamp" (Proverbs 6:23 ESV) and "the spirit of man is the lamp of the LORD" (Proverbs 20:27 ESV). God asks us to take care of his "lamp" (the commandments), and he will take care of our "lamp" (the soul).

By observing the Sabbath properly, we reap its blessings and benefits. This is in accordance with the promise in Isaiah 58:13–14. Jeremiah 17:24–25 goes so far as to promise that if the people sanctify the Sabbath by abstaining from prohibited activity, then Jerusalem will be ruled by Davidic kings and will be "inhabited forever"—a clear reference to the Messianic Era.

The author Ahad Ha'am noted the important role the Sabbath has played in preserving the Jewish people when he quipped, "More than the Jews have kept the Sabbath, the Sabbath has kept the Jews." His words were probably inspired by this song.

It is a sign forever — This is taken from Exodus 31:17.

B **It is forbidden to do as you please** — These prohibitions are mentioned in Isaiah 58:13.

I will ponder God's Torah — *Apostolic Constitutions*, an early Christian document which some scholars believe contains ancient Hellenistic synagogue liturgy, states that God's reason for resting on the Sabbath was to "meditate on his own laws."

C **Find comfort for my soul** — This may be an allusion to Jeremiah 6:16. The word for "comfort" used in this song is *nofesh* (נֹפֶשׁ), which is related to the word *vayinnafash* ("and was refreshed," וַיִּנָּפַשׁ) in Exodus 31:17.

By giving them double bread — Twice the regular amount of manna fell on the sixth day (Exodus 16:5).

D **Deputies** — This refers to the priests, the descendants of Aaron.

To arrange the Bread of the Presence — According to Leviticus 24:8–9, the Bread of the Presence is arranged on the Sabbath day and also eaten

37

by the priests. The priests would place the new bread on the table each Sabbath and eat the bread prepared on the previous week.

D **Therefore, fasting on the Sabbath ... is forbidden** — Because of the commandment to eat the Bread of the Presence on the Sabbath, it is forbidden to hold a public or private fast on the Sabbath. This excludes Yom Kippur (the Day of Atonement) if it falls on the Sabbath, because fasting on that day is biblically commanded.

E **Honored day, a day of delights** — This again alludes to Isaiah 58:13.

F **Leads to excision** — This refers to the punishment described in Exodus 31:14.

38 YOM SHABBATON

Yom Shabbaton (Day of Ceasing) was written by Yehudah HaLevi, who lived in Spain in the twelfth century. The name *Yehudah* is encoded in its verses. This song is normally sung at the Saturday morning meal.

A **Its remembrance** — This alludes to the commandment to "remember the Sabbath" (Exodus 20:8). The term "remembrance" (*zecher*, זֵכֶר) connotes "making mention."

A pleasing aroma — This phrase alludes to the sacrifices, which are called a "pleasing aroma" to God. This suggests that our observance of the Sabbath is satisfying to God much as is the offering of sacrifices.

On it a dove found comfort — This alludes to Genesis 8:9, which speaks of the dove that Noah sent out to find dry land. Allegorically, the dove in this song represents Israel.

And it is where those who are weary will rest — This is a quotation of Job 3:17. The reference here is mysterious, since in context the verse is referring to death. It may be that the author was simply using biblical language to describe how the Sabbath is a time of rest, without meaning to imply the literal context. Alternatively, he may have intended to compare the Sabbath to the afterlife.

C **This day is honored** — This alludes to Isaiah 58:13.

By the faithful — This phrase may also be interpreted "by the sons of the faithful [patriarchs]."

Fathers and sons are careful to observe it — This may allude to the wording of the commandment, "Observe the Sabbath day ... you or your son or your daughter" (Deuteronomy 5:12, 14).

38

C **The two stone tablets** — Sabbath observance is one of the Ten Commandments given at Mount Sinai.

Great in Power and Firm in Strength — These names of God come from Isaiah 40:26.

D **We will do, and we will heed** — This comes from Exodus 24:7.

The LORD is one — This is a quote from the *Shema*, the passage beginning with Deuteronomy 6:4, which observant Jews recite at least twice daily during the prayers. Yeshua referred to this passage as the most important commandment.

The Midrash states that the Israelites unanimously cried, "The LORD is our God; the LORD is one!" in response to the words, "Hear O Israel ... I am the LORD your God" (Deuteronomy 5:1, 6).

Gives strength to the weary — This comes from Isaiah 40:29. This alludes to the teaching in b.*Shabbat* 88b that when God spoke each of the Ten Commandments, the souls of the Israelites departed due to the shock of hearing God's voice. He revived them with the dew of resurrection.

Several commentators explain that this verse from Isaiah speaks of the weariness of exile that Israel experiences while waiting for the Messiah to arrive. Radak comments, "When he desires, he gives strength and vigor to Israel, who are in exile and weary and exhausted, lacking strength" (Radak, commentary on Isaiah 40:29).

Yeshua spoke of the redemption in terms of rest (Matthew 11:28–30), citing Jeremiah 6:16: "And find rest for your souls."

E **Mount of Myrrh** — This name is taken from Song of Songs 4:6. This name is usually applied to Mount Moriah, where the Temple stood and the fragrant incense was burned. In this case, it refers to Mount Sinai. The word for "myrrh" (*mor*, מֹר), is similar to the word for "teacher" (*moreh*, מוֹרֶה).

Furthermore, the sages said (b.*Shabbat* 88b) that when each of the Ten Commandments was uttered, the world was filled with a sweet fragrance. This is derived from an allegorical reading of Song of Songs 5:13, which states, "His cheeks are like beds of spices, mounds of sweet-smelling herbs. His lips are lilies, dripping liquid myrrh" (ESV).

When Yeshua was buried, his disciples bound him with seventy-five pounds of myrrh and aloes. While it was common in those days to use spices in burial, this was a highly atypical, extremely large amount. This

38

may have reflected their love for him as teacher and for the sweetness of his words.

E **Remember and keep** — This refers to the two expressions of the Sabbath commandment in Exodus 20:8 and Deuteronomy 5:12.

Brace yourself, and gather your strength — This is a quotation from Nahum 2:2[1].

F **Traveled like a wandering flock** — This refers to the exile and dispersion of the Jewish people.

Swore at the waters of Noah — This refers to Isaiah 54:9, where HaShem compares his promise not to flood the earth again with his promise to restore the Jewish people from exile.

Yeshua also compared the destruction of Jerusalem and the onset of exile to the destruction brought on by the flood in the time of Noah (Matthew 24:37–39; Luke 17:26–27).

39 Yom Zeh Mechubbad

A **This day is honored** — This alludes to Isaiah 58:13.

Rested on it — This alludes to Genesis 2:3.

B **You may do your work for six days** — This verse borrows wording from Exodus 35:2, Leviticus 23:3, and Deuteronomy 5:13–14.

C **It is first of the holy assemblies** — In the list of festivals and holy days in Leviticus 23, the weekly Sabbath is mentioned first.

Sanctify with wine — Recite the *Kiddush* blessing.

Break two complete loaves of bread — It is preferable to have two whole loaves of bread at each Sabbath meal.

When the phrase "break bread" occurs in the New Testament, some people mistakenly interpret it as referring to a Eucharist ceremony. This line is an example that shows that "breaking bread" is a Hebrew idiom meaning "to share a meal" and does not refer to the Eucharist.

D **Eat rich foods, drink sweet drinks** — Do not be afraid to spend extra for the sake of the Sabbath. According to the Talmud (b.*Beitzah* 16a), the income a person is decreed to receive each year excludes any expenditures for the sake of the Sabbath.

39

D **Clothing to wear, their daily bread** — This strongly echoes Yeshua's assurances that God will provide for those who seek first the kingdom of God (Matthew 6:25–34).

E **You will lack nothing, but you will eat and be satisfied and bless** — These lines allude to Deuteronomy 8:9–10, which in context refer to the land of Israel as a reward for keeping the commandments.

Blessed you more than all other peoples — This alludes to Deuteronomy 7:14, which refers to the blessings that come in reward for obedience.

F **The heavens declare his glory** — This is a quotation from Psalm 19:2[1].

And the earth is also filled with his devotion — This alludes to Psalm 33:5 and Psalm 119:64.

See that his hand has made all these — This alludes to Isaiah 66:2. Each of the verses in this stanza are cited to affirm that God is willing and able to bless those who are faithful to him.

For he is the Maker, whose deeds are perfect — This alludes to Deuteronomy 32:4.

40 UVASHABBAT

Uvashabbat was written by Aaron Eby. The name *Aharon* is encoded in its verses.

A **They ate the manna for forty years** — This is taken from Exodus 16:35.

The grain of heaven — This refers to Psalm 78:24.

A double measure — See Exodus 16:5.

And on the Sabbath they ceased according to the commandment — This line comes from Luke 23:56, where it described the women who prepared spices for Yeshua's burial.

B **He took them from Egypt** — The Sabbath is a remembrance of the exodus (Deuteronomy 5:15).

Make me a Sanctuary — This line comes from Exodus 25:8.

They strengthened their arms — This borrows wording from Proverbs 31:17.

Pleased with the labor — The account of the building of the Tabernacle is one of the main passages in which the term for labor that is prohibited on the Sabbath (*melachah*, מְלָאכָה) appears. The sages determined what

40

types of activities are prohibited on the Sabbath based on the types of work involved in building the Tabernacle.

C **The shepherd of the flock was struck** — This alludes to Zechariah 13:7, which is quoted in Matthew 26:31 and Mark 14:27. It is a reference to Yeshua's execution.

The day of their preparation — The sixth day of the week is referred to as the "day of preparation" because it is the day to prepare for the Sabbath (Matthew 27:62; Mark 15:42; Luke 23:54; John 19:14, 31, 42). This is the day when Yeshua was killed.

He rested — Yeshua spent the Sabbath in the state of death, which is truly a complete rest. Death is often compared in Scripture to sleep.

The heart of the earth — This alludes to Matthew 12:40.

The sealed chamber — This refers to Yeshua's tomb. Isaiah refers to the tombs of the dead as closed chambers in Isaiah 26:20, where he speaks of the future resurrection.

Although the valley of death's shadow — This alludes to Psalm 23:4. The phrase "death's shadow" is used in several places in Scripture to refer to a place of death, a state of mourning, and the exile.

Would flow tears for them — This line borrows wording from Jeremiah 9:17[18] in reference to the exile. Even on the darkest and saddest day in their lives, Yeshua's followers remained faithful to the Torah's command to keep the Sabbath.

D **When Shiloh comes** — This is a reference to Genesis 49:10. Shiloh is a name for the Messiah.

His resting place will be glorious — This refers to Isaiah 11:10.

All flesh will come — This alludes to Isaiah 66:23, which states that "from Sabbath to Sabbath, all flesh will come to worship before me."

The resting place — This is a name for the Temple in Isaiah 66:1.

SE'UDAH SHLISHIT

41 YEDID NEFESH

Yedid Nefesh was written by El'azar ben Mosheh Askari, who lived in Israel in the sixteenth century. He described this hymn as "a prayer for union and the desire of love." A close look reveals a desperate prayer for the coming of the Messiah and the ultimate redemption.

The Tetragrammaton (the four-letter name of God) is encoded in its verses. This song is normally sung at the Saturday afternoon meal (*Se'udah Shlishit*). This song is often also recited in the synagogue on Friday afternoon prior to the *Kabbalat Shabbat* prayers and on certain holidays.

A **Beloved of the soul** — God uses this term for Israel in Jeremiah 12:7.

Draw your servant ... Your servant will run — This alludes to Song of Songs 1:4: "Draw me after you; let us run" (ESV).

Sweeter than the honey from a honeycomb — This alludes to Psalm 19:11[10].

B **Beautiful** — This term, *hadur* (הָדוּר), which is sometimes translated "splendid," may allude to Isaiah 63:1: "Who is this coming from Edom, in crimsoned garments from Bozrah, he who is splendid [*hadur*] in apparel ...?"

Brightness of the universe — This could also be translated "light of the world."

My soul is lovesick for you — This alludes to Song of Songs 5:8.

Please God, please heal my soul — This borrows its wording from Numbers 12:13. The Hebrew word for "soul" is *nefesh* (נֶפֶשׁ), which is a feminine noun. All references to the soul in this song are therefore feminine. In this case, the text literally reads, "Please heal *her*."

Showing it your pleasant brightness — Brightness here refers to the revelation of God's glory and the period of the messianic redemption.

Have eternal gladness — Some manuscripts have the word *shifchat* ("maidservant," שִׁפְחַת) rather than *simchat* ("gladness," שִׂמְחַת), which would cause the line to read "become your eternal maidservant."

C **Your beloved son** — This refers to Israel.

41

C **My heart has cherished these things** — Some manuscripts read this line as *anna eli, machmad libbi* (אָנָּא אֵלִי, מַחְמַד לִבִּי), which means "Please, my God, O desire of my heart."

Have pity — Some manuscripts have the word *chushah* ("rush" or "hasten," חוּשָׁה) rather than *chusah* ("have pity," חוּסָה).

Do not remain concealed — During exile, God's kingship is not readily apparent. This is a prayer that God would be revealed in the world through the messianic redemption.

D **Spread your shelter of peace** — This is a reference to the prayer *Hashkivenu* recited during *Ma'ariv*.

May the earth be illuminated by your glory — This is an allusion to Ezekiel 43:2, which refers to the return of the Divine Presence to the Temple.

Let us rejoice and be glad — This is a quotation of Song of Songs 1:4.

For the appointed time has come — This is a quotation from Psalm 102:14[13], where it is a prayer for the arrival of the messianic redemption.

MOTZA'EI SHABBAT

42 ELIYAHU HANAVI

The author of this song is unknown. The lines form an alphabetic acrostic pattern: each line begins with a successive letter of the Hebrew alphabet.

This song is customarily sung at *Havdalah* or during *Melaveh Malkah*. We sing about Elijah the prophet at this time because it is his duty to herald the coming of the Messiah (Malachi 3:23[4:5]). The Gospels identify Elijah with John the Immerser (Matthew 11:14, 17:10–13; Mark 9:11–13; Luke 1:17, 7:27). Revelation 11:3–6 anticipates an Elijah-like herald prior to Yeshua's future coming.

According to the Talmud, the Messiah will not come on the Sabbath or on a festival day (b.*Eruvin* 43b). Now that the new week has begun, we reaffirm our hope that Elijah will soon come to announce the Messiah's arrival.

A **Elijah the Tishbite ... the Gileadite** — This comes from 1 Kings 17:1. Tishbite means "inhabitant of Toshab."

42

B **Zealous for the sake of God** — This is a reference to the identification of Elijah with Phinehas, the priest mentioned in Numbers 25. The identification of Elijah with Phinehas is widespread in ancient Jewish literature. (For example, see Targum Pseudo-Jonathan on Exodus 6:8 and Numbers 25:12.)

Yekutiel — This is Moses. *Yalkut Shimoni* (Vayikra 1:428) identifies Moses with Yekutiel (Jekuthiel) mentioned in 1 Chronicles 4:18.

C **Twelve generations** — This follows the belief that Elijah was Phinehas the priest. Phinehas was the grandson of Aaron, who married the sister of Nahshon son of Amminadab (Exodus 6:23). Nahshon was an ancestor of King David. When Elijah was taken to heaven, David's descendant Jehoram had just taken the throne (2 Kings 1:17). From Nahshon to Jehoram there are twelve generations.

Hairy ... leather belt — This is based on 2 Kings 1:8. John the Immerser is also referred to by this description in Matthew 3:4 and Mark 1:6.

D **Furious about sun worship** — This refers to his rebuke against the people for following the prophets of Baal (1 Kings 18:21).

Swore against seasonal rain — This refers to 1 Kings 17:1.

Three years — See 1 Kings 18:1.

E **Departed** — This refers to Elijah's flight from Jezebel in 1 Kings 19:3.

Ravens fed — See 1 Kings 17:4.

Pitchers and jars were blessed — This refers to 1 Kings 17:16.

F **Heeded** — See 1 Kings 18:39.

Answered with fire — See 1 Kings 18:38.

G **Sent from the uppermost heavens** — This alludes to Elijah's mission to be sent to herald the coming of the Messiah (Malachi 3:23[4:5]).

Return the hearts of children to fathers — This refers to Malachi 3:24[4:6].

H **I am fiercely zealous** — This refers to 1 Kings 19:10.

Rode upon horses of fire — This refers to the story of Elijah's departure in 2 Kings 2:11.

Did not taste the flavor of death — Elijah was supernaturally taken to heaven.

42

I **Called "Tishbite" by name** — Although "Tishbite" refers to where he was from, it has become part of his name. Scripture refers to him as "Elijah the Tishbite" in several places.

Grant us success in the Torah — It is a common belief that all of the unresolved mysteries in the Torah will be answered by Elijah when he returns.

Good news — The Hebrew term for good news, *besorah* (בְּשׂוֹרָה), corresponds with the Greek term that is often translated "gospel" (evangelion, εὐαγγέλιον). This concept refers to the good news of the messianic redemption.

From gloom to light — "Gloom" is a term for exile, and "light" refers to redemption.

J **From the lions' mouths** — This refers to persecution during exile.

L **Sees his face in a dream** — There are many tales of people who have encountered Elijah or seen a vision of him.

Bless his people with peace — This is from Psalm 29:11.

43 HaMavdil

The name Yitzchak HaKatan (Isaac the Lesser) is encoded in the verses of this song. It may have been authored by Yitzchak ben Yehudah ibn Gayyat, who lived in Spain in the eleventh century.

This song is usually recited immediately after *Havdalah*. However, other than the reference to separating "between holy and common," there is no mention of the Sabbath in the song. Some commentators assert that it was originally written as a prayer for the *Ne'ilah* service at the close of Yom Kippur. This explains its numerous petitions for forgiveness and redemption.

Each verse of this song ends with a quotation from Scripture that concludes with the word "night."

B **I ask that God fulfill for me** — This borrows wording from Psalm 57:3[2].

Morning has come as well as night — This refers to Isaiah 21:12. In Rashi's interpretation of this verse, "morning" refers to the salvation of Israel, whereas "night" is the punishment of Israel's enemies.

C **Righteousness is like Mount Tabor** — This alludes to Psalm 36:7[6].

43

C **Yesterday has passed** — This comes from Psalm 90:4.

D **I swim in sorrows each night** — This comes from Psalm 6:7[6].

E **My curls with the dampness of the night** — This comes from Song of Songs 5:2. Wet hair is an indication that a person has slept outside, an expression of mourning and desperation.

F **In the blackness of the night** — This comes from Proverbs 7:9.

G **The path of life** — This comes from Psalm 16:11.

Lift me out of my poverty — This comes from Isaiah 38:12. The word *dillah* ("loom," דִּלָּה) is reinterpreted as *dallut* ("poverty," דַּלּוּת).

H **Who makes you sing at night?** — This comes from Job 35:10.

I **Day speaks forth to day** — This comes from Psalm 19:3[2].

44 LaNer Velivsamim

LaNer Velivsamim was written by Sa'adya ben Amram, who lived in the seventeenth century in Yemen. The word *le-Sa'adya* (of Sa'adya) is encoded in its verses.

This song is customarily recited after *Havdalah* in Yemenite Jewish communities.

A **My soul waits** — Having just "descended" from the spiritual elevation that comes with the Sabbath, the soul is weak. The spices help to resuscitate the soul, and the fire brings light into the darkness of the mundane weekdays.

B **Build me a road** — That is to say, "Prepare the proper way to for me to go." During the Sabbath, life is simple, and our tasks are straightforward. But we need God's guidance as we enter the week and have to begin making life decisions again.

BIRKAT HAMAZON

49 HAHODAYAH

A **Your holy name that you have caused to dwell in our hearts** — The term "name" is used here as a reference for the Dwelling Presence or Holy Spirit of God, known in rabbinic writings as the *Shechinah*. This is based on passages in the Bible that refer to Jerusalem as the place where God would choose to cause his name to dwell (Deuteronomy 12:11, 14:23, 16:2, 6, 26:2). Similarly, the Talmud records a blessing that the watchmen in the Temple would say to one another on the Sabbath: "May he who caused his name to dwell in this house cause love, brotherhood, peace and friendship to dwell among you" (b.*Brachot* 12a).

B **You gave nourishment and drink for human beings to enjoy** — A similar statement can be found in 1 Timothy 4:3–4. This is a very Jewish sentiment that opposes the practice of asceticism, which was common among many first-century sects. The Jerusalem Talmud even contains the opinion that "in the future each man will have to give an account for every [permissible pleasure] that his eyes saw but he did not eat" (y.*Kiddushin* 4:12). This is not an excuse for hedonism, but for giving thanks to God, who created the world "for the sake of [his] name," i.e., so that people would enjoy it and glorify God in thanks.

Spiritual nourishment and drink — Torah teaching is often compared with food and drink. This may be a direct reference to 1 Corinthians 10:3–4, which indicates that the children of Israel in the wilderness also received spiritual food and drink from the Messiah.

C **Gather the betrothed** — The Hebrew term for "betrothed" (*mekuddeshet*, מְקֻדֶּשֶׁת) literally means "sanctified." The term is used in the traditional betrothal formula, "Behold, you are sanctified to me by means of this ring."

50 INTRODUCTORY READINGS

A **Psalm 126: When the LORD returned the exile to Zion** — The Sabbath is considered a foretaste of the world to come, which is why this psalm is often included on Sabbath and festival days. Psalm 126 may be understood to refer to the return from the Babylonian exile, but in a prophetic sense, it speaks of the redemption in the Messianic Era. Its recitation on Sabbaths allows us a glimpse of the joy of Messiah's return.

50

B **Psalm 137: By the rivers of Babylon** — It is traditional to recite this Psalm during the week to help us remember that we remain in a state of exile and look longingly for the future redemption and the return of the Messiah.

C **Zimmun: Gentlemen, let us bless** — The purpose of the *Zimmun* ("Invitation") is to join together officially for communal prayer (similar to the function of the *Barechu* prayer offered during the synagogue service). The praise of a group in unity is more glorifying to God than the same individuals each making a blessing alone. This principle is derived from passages such as "Magnify the LORD with me, and let us lift up his name together" (Psalm 34:4[3]) and "When I call on the name of the LORD, [you–plural] ascribe greatness to our God" (Deuteronomy 32:3). When the *Zimmun* is recited, one is designated as the leader throughout the entire blessing, and the others respond with "Amen" when appropriate (cf. 1 Corinthians 14:16).

51 Birkat HaZan

A **Who nourishes the entire world** — The first blessing is universal in scope, using terms such as "the entire world," "all flesh" and "all of his creatures." The goal, first and foremost, is to recognize God as the source of all nourishment and sustenance to everyone and everything: to humans of all backgrounds as well as other creatures. Our Master Yeshua noted God's universal goodness, causing the sun to shine and the rain to fall on the righteous as well as the unrighteous. He taught us to imitate God by showing kindness even to our enemies (Matthew 5:43–47).

He gives bread to all flesh — The word used here for "bread" is *lechem* (לֶחֶם), which is often used idiomatically for all types of food. Our Master Yeshua used the term this way when he prayed, "Give us our portion of bread today" (Matthew 6:11).

God provides for and nourishes all — Likewise, Paul explained to the pagans in Lystra that although God permitted the nations to go their own way, he provided nourishment from the earth as a witness to his existence and goodness (Acts 14:17).

52 Birkat HaAretz

A **A pleasant, good, and spacious land** — It is important to note that the commandment in the Torah to bless after eating instructs that we are to give thanks "for the good land" (Deuteronomy 8:10). This is the origin

52

of the second blessing (see b.*Brachot* 48b–49a). In fact, a literal reading of the passage does not even mention the food itself; nonetheless, the Talmudic sages reasoned that we are to give thanks for the land because of the food that it produced. The traditional practice of elaborating on the land's goodness is derived from this verse as well, interpreting that not only are we to give thanks for the land, but for the fact that it is "good."

A **Took us out from Egypt** — The Torah commands us that we are to eat unleavened bread on Passover so that we remember the day of the exodus from Egypt all the days of our lives (Deuteronomy 16:3). Mentioning the exodus whenever we eat throughout the year helps us fulfill that commandment.

For your covenant that you sealed in our flesh — An alternative non-traditional form of this blessing reads, "And for the covenant that you made with our father Abraham (וְעַל בְּרִיתְךָ שֶׁכָּרַתָּ אֶת אַבְרָהָם אָבִינוּ)," a version that is true of Jewish people and Gentile believers as well.

And for your Torah that you taught to us — The Torah and the covenant with Abraham are mentioned because they are intrinsically connected with the land of Israel. The land of Israel belongs to the Jewish people because of the promise God made to Abraham (Genesis 15:18–21). The ability of the Jewish people to be blessed in the land is contingent upon their observance of the Torah (Deuteronomy 8:1, 30:5–6). Thus, it is appropriate to give thanks for the covenant and the Torah along with the land. Paul tells us that before Messiah, Gentiles were "excluded from the commonwealth of Israel, and strangers to the covenants of promise" (Ephesians 2:12) but now are called "sons of Abraham" (Galatians 3:7). In Yeshua "the blessing of Abraham" has come to them (Galatians 3:14). Therefore, Gentiles also can pray this prayer with a sense of connection to the land and the Torah of Israel.

C **For the miracles** — Just as God has kept his people alive by providing food and other basic human needs, he has also sustained us by means of miracles and military victory.

G **You shall eat and be satisfied, and you shall bless the LORD** — This is the primary verse from which the commandment to bless after eating is derived (Deuteronomy 8:10). Its purpose is to prevent us from forgetting God's past and continued provision, which may lead to breach of his covenant (Deuteronomy 8:11–19).

53 Binyan Yerushalayim

A **Please have compassion** — This appears to be more of a petition than a blessing. Like several prayers in Judaism, this part of the *Birkat HaMazon* may have begun as a blessing and later been modified to a petition after Jerusalem was destroyed.

Upon Jerusalem your city — A blessing for the restoration of Jerusalem is necessary because the status of Jerusalem, the throne of David, and the Holy Temple represent the difference between exile and redemption. The promise of the land (for which we are commanded to give thanks) anticipates fulfillment in the rebuilding of Jerusalem and the Temple and in the establishment of the Davidic monarchy. Even though Jewish people have long resided within the boundaries of the promised land, the land has been under the authority of foreign and secular governments. This is a direct and earnest plea for the messianic redemption.

Upon the kingdom of the house of David your anointed one — Merely inhabiting the land of Israel is not enough, since the commandment states that "you shall bless the LORD your God for the good land that he has given *to you*" (Deuteronomy 8:10). Thus, this commandment looks forward to ultimate fulfillment when the land is again under Israel's sovereignty. The prophets promise that this sovereignty will take the form of the restored Davidic dynasty—meaning that the Messiah, the Son of David, will take his place as King.

Upon the great and holy House that is called by your name — The Torah prescribes many offerings in the form of agricultural produce, which thank God for his provision. However, these offerings cannot be presented anywhere except at the Temple in Jerusalem. Therefore, it becomes necessary to pray for the Temple's restoration so that we may give thanks in the way that the Torah commands.

B **Show favor and fortify us** — Not only does God provide sustenance with food, he also restores us with rest on the Sabbath. The Sabbath is also a foretaste of the world to come, in which all trouble and sorrow will cease.

C **May there ascend** — This prayer is offered at several points in the liturgy during appointed times. It expresses the desire that God would respond by showing mercy and bringing redemption due to the special nature of the day.

F **Amen** — Usually, one does not say "amen" to one's own blessing. However, the word is included here to draw a distinction between the first three

53
blessings and the fourth. The first three blessings are understood to be biblically mandated; the fourth was added later in response to a historical event (see below).

54 HATOV VEHAMETIV

A **He did good, he does good, and he will do good for us** — The most common explanation for the fourth blessing is that it was added in 135 CE when Jews slain in the city of Bethar during the Bar Kokhba revolt were finally afforded burial (b.*Ta'anit* 31a). Other sources, however, may support an earlier date for its appearance in the *Birkat HaMazon* (Grace after Meals).

The fourth blessing is an elaboration on a simple blessing recited upon hearing good news: "Blessed are you, O LORD, our God, who is good and does good." This blessing is also recited when one is drinking wine and is given a second glass of wine that is superior in quality to the first (b.*Brachot* 59b). It seems likely that the blessing was recited by many at the wedding in Cana (John 2:1–11).

HARACHAMAN

C **May he reign over us forever and ever** — This echoes the declaration of the Israelites immediately following the crossing of the Sea of Reeds, who proclaimed, "The LORD will reign forever and ever" (Exodus 15:18). Like that generation who witnessed their redemption, we willingly accept God's kingship over us.

D **May he be blessed in the heavens and in the earth** — This resonates with the words of our Master Yeshua, who prayed, "As your will is done in heaven, so may it also be on earth" (Matthew 6:10), a common sentiment expressed by Judaism.

E **May he be acclaimed in every generation** — Before bringing the petitions to God which follow, we accept his kingship and express the desire above all that he be glorified.

G **May he break our yoke** — When Israel's redemption is complete, the people will live in the promised land as a sovereign, independent nation, under the authority of God alone, with the Messiah as King.

I **May he send us Elijah the Prophet** — Based on Malachi 3:23[4:5], Jewish tradition interprets that Elijah the Prophet will come to announce the Messiah's arrival. At Yeshua's first coming, the Gospels identify Elijah

54

with John the Immerser (Matthew 11:14, 17:10–13; Mark 9:11–13; Luke 1:17, 7:27). Revelation 11:3–6 anticipates an Elijah-like herald prior to the return of the Messiah.

I **May he bring good news** — The Hebrew term "bring good news" is equivalent to the Greek term often translated "preach the gospel."

M **In everything, from everything, with everything** — This reflects a passage in the Talmud (b.*Bava Batra* 16b–17a) that ties three verses together that connect the blessing of the patriarchs with the word *kol* (כֹּל), which means "everything" or "all." Genesis 24:1 states, "The LORD blessed Abraham in everything." In Genesis 27:33 Isaac says that he has eaten "from it all," referring to the food that he had eaten before blessing Jacob. Jacob himself stated in Genesis 33:11, "For I have everything." The passage in the Talmud explains that God gave them a foretaste of the world to come. Perhaps this has bearing on our Master Yeshua's words, "Your father Abraham rejoiced to see my day; he saw it and was glad" (John 8:56).

So may we all be blessed together, with a complete blessing — We do indeed receive a complete blessing by means of our Master Yeshua. According to Paul, God also has blessed us "with every spiritual blessing" (Ephesians 1:3) and grants us "sufficiency in everything" (2 Corinthians 9:8). As he provides seed to the sower and bread for food, he also increases the harvest of righteousness, enriching us "in everything," leading us to give thanks to God (2 Corinthians 9:10–11).

N **In the heavens above, may their case and ours be heard** — The apostles teach us that "we have an Advocate with the Father: Yeshua the Messiah, the righteous one" (1 John 2:1), "who was raised, who is at the right hand of God, who pleads on our behalf" (Romans 8:34).

O **The day of complete Sabbath and rest for eternal life** — The Sabbath offers a foretaste of the world to come, the time of future reward when redemption is complete (cf. Mark 10:30; Luke 18:30) and God restores the world to perfection. Similarly, one can liken the world to come to a time of eternal Sabbath rest (cf. Hebrews 4).

The fallen *sukkah* of David — David's *sukkah* ("booth") is a metaphor for the Davidic dynasty, the royal family of David. James, the brother of Yeshua, cited Amos 9:11–12 in reference to the Messiah's coming (Acts 15:16–18). He used this passage to show that the prophets taught that the coming of the Messiah would bring Gentiles to God. The verse states, "I will rebuild the fallen *sukkah* of David," meaning that God would place the Messiah, the son of David, upon the throne.

54

P **A tower of salvations of his King** — The Midrash *Shocher Tov* explains:

> What is meant by "a tower"? King Messiah will become like a tower for them, as it is said, "A tower of salvations is his king," and it is written, "The name of the LORD is a strong tower; one who is righteous runs into it and is protected" (Proverbs 18:10).

Magnifying the salvations of his King — Salvation does not come in an instant, but it is "magnified" and grows little by little. The Midrash *Shocher Tov* compares it to sunrise. If the sun were to spring up suddenly out of darkness, the world would be blinded by its light. Instead, the light of dawn first brightens the sky before the sun itself emerges. The redemption will come in the same way. The prophet Isaiah describes it in this way: "Then your light will burst forth like the dawn" (Isaiah 58:8). Proverbs teaches, "The path of the righteous is like the light of dawn, progressively brightening until the day is fully come" (Proverbs 4:18).

S **For those who fear him have no lack** — The final paragraph of the *Birkat HaMazon* (Grace after Meals) expresses confidence based on a long string of passages from the Bible that God will meet our needs. Such faith is commended and taught by our Master Yeshua, who taught us not to worry about what we will eat, drink, or wear, but to seek God's kingdom and righteousness (Matthew 6:31–33).

WEDDING MEAL BLESSINGS

55 ZIMMUN LESHEVA BRACHOT

In ancient times, the wedding celebration lasted for a full week, and even today in many communities there are special traditions for that entire period of time. This special *Zimmun* ("Invitation") is recited not only during the wedding reception, but any time a meal is eaten in the presence of a newlywed couple within the first seven days of their marriage, if any new guests and a *minyan* are present.

D **In whose dwelling place is gladness** — When joy is present among those called by God's name, the Divine Presence is understood to dwell there in an even fuller measure. This can be compared to the Temple, where celebration and joy abounded and some mourning rituals were forbidden among the priests.

Circumcision Meal Blessings

57 Zimmun Lise'udat Brit Milah

When a child receives ritual circumcision, it is customary to celebrate with a festive meal.

C **Those faithful to me** — This is a poetic way to refer to close friends and family.

I **In all the islands** — This is poetic language symbolizing the distant reaches of the earth (cf. Psalm 97:1).

58 HaRachaman

The *sandek* is the man given the special honor of handing the child to the *mohel*, or of holding the child as the circumcision takes place. A *mohel* is a specialist, often a doctor, rabbi, or both, who performs the ritual circumcision procedure.

A **May his blood find favor** — "Blood" is intended as a reference to circumcision (cf. Exodus 4:24–25), which in turn is representative of the child's inclusion in God's covenant. Thus, it is desired that God would be with the child on account of his covenant participation.

Specific mention of the blood drawn by circumcision is an allusion to sacrifice. Blood, normally in the form of animal sacrifice, is an important part of covenant ceremony in the Scriptures. The blood of the Passover sacrifice is also intrinsically connected to circumcision.

The new covenant, to which we gain access through Yeshua the Messiah, was also initiated through literal blood at the time of his suffering and death. Our Master explained the symbolism of the cup of wine at his Passover meal: "This is my blood of the covenant" (Matthew 26:28; Mark 14:24).

While circumcision is an important *mitzvah* ("commandment") that God commanded and desires, our hope for our children is that they will grow to become faithful disciples of Yeshua, that his blood would find favor, and that God will circumcise their hearts (Deuteronomy 30:6; Romans 2:29), in fulfillment of the new covenant promise.

E **In the merit of the groom whose blood was shed** — The term "groom" (*chatan*, חָתָן) can refer to any honored person; in this case, the honor is

58

given to the circumcised child. This title also looks forward to our hope that he will grow and be married.

Yeshua compared himself to a bridegroom (e.g., Matthew 9:15), and he came as "a servant to the circumcision" (Romans 15:8).

F **May he send us Elijah** — See commentary on *HaRachaman*, page 189.

The righteous priest — The predominant opinion, both in Jewish tradition and with the church fathers, is that Elijah was of priestly descent.

Taken into concealment — This is a reference to Elijah's ascent to heaven described in 2 Kings 2:10–11.

Until his throne is established like the sun — "His" may refer to the Messiah, or this may refer to the glory of Elijah's arrival to announce the Messiah. At Yeshua's transfiguration, Elijah appeared "in glory" (Luke 9:31).

He wrapped his face in his cloak — Elijah wrapped his face in his mantle after hearing the "sound of a gentle blowing" (1 Kings 19:12–13).

My covenant was with him — This is the covenant of priesthood that God bestowed upon the descendants of Aaron. Ancient Jewish texts identify Elijah with Pinchas, the great-grandson of Aaron, to whom God gave his "covenant of peace" (e.g., *Yalkut Shimoni*).

Blessings after Other Foods

59 Brachah Me'ein Shalosh

This blessing is called the "Blessing Resembling Three" because it contains a distillation of the three main blessings in the full *Birkat HaMazon*.

This blessing is to be recited after eating one or more of the seven species, a special set of foods for which the Torah praises the land of Israel. Deuteronomy 8:8 describes the promised land as "a land of wheat and barley, of vines and fig trees and pomegranates, a land of olive oil and honey." The term "vines" is representative of grapes. The honey mentioned here is customarily interpreted as date honey.

These seven species reflect the unique nature of Israel's climate. They are all types of produce that depend on the land receiving just the proper amount of rain. Since rain in the land of Israel specifically hinges on covenant faithful-

59

ness (Deuteronomy 11:13–18), these products are especially symbolic of that covenant.

Other than wheat and barley, the fruits included in the seven species all grow high in trees. One has to look up in order to see and harvest them. In contrast, the species for which the land of Egypt is known—"the cucumbers and the melons and the leeks and the onions and the garlic" (Numbers 11:5)—grow on the ground. This reminds us to keep ourselves focused on the one who gives us life and sustains us: our Father who is in heaven.

A **Life-giving food** — This term (*michyah*, מִחְיָה) literally means "that which gives or preserves life." It is the same term used by Joseph when he explained to his brothers that they should not be angry with themselves because God had sent him before them "to preserve life" (Genesis 45:5). This term for food, particularly foods derived from grains, might be reflected in the *Didache*'s blessing prior to eating bread: "We thank you, our Father, for the life ..."

C **For the land and for the fruit** — One who eats fruit that grew in the land of Israel should say, "For the land and for its fruit" (עַל הָאָרֶץ וְעַל פֵּרוֹתֶיהָ).

60 Borei Nefashot

A **In order to give life to every living soul** — This blessing expresses the idea that God intentionally created the world with needs in order to satisfy us, showing us that it is his nature to give.

Life of the ages — "Ages" is plural, meaning that God provides life in this age as well as in the age to come.

Song Index